THE GARDENING WHICH? GUIDE TO
GROWING YOUR OWN
VEGETABLES

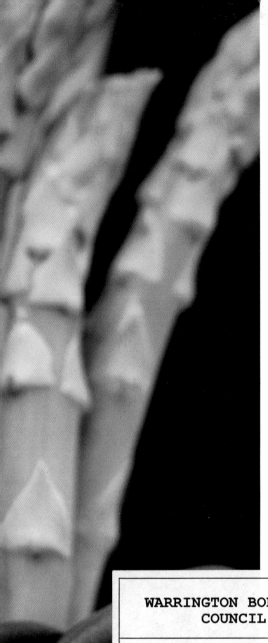

THE GARDENING WHICH? GUIDE TO
GROWING YOUR OWN
VEGETABLES

LIZ DOBBS

Consultant **Steve Mercer**

WHICH?
BOOKS

CONSUMERS'
ASSOCIATION

C O N T

E N T S

INTRODUCTION

Just as we say on the cover, this book is, pure and simple, about growing vegetables – both traditional and exotic varieties. Our advice is distilled from 18 years of research by *Gardening Which?*. If you follow it, you should be able to avoid the disappointment of lavishing care and attention on plants that never produce a crop.

For each vegetable or herb, a calendar leads you through the year from sowing and planting to harvesting and storing, while throughout the book our tried-and-tested tips will help you avoid problems such as pests and diseases.

Symbols highlight the easiest vegetables for beginners to grow and the most high-yielding vegetables, as well as those that will thrive in containers or ornamental borders.

You will also find recommendations for the best-tasting varieties to grow. Over the course of a year, *Gardening Which?* carried out taste tests on a wide variety of commonly grown vegetables. The results were extraordinary, and demonstrated that there is a world of flavour out there to which consumers rarely have access, limited as they are to the few varieties chosen by the major growers. Even the humble runner bean can be described as anything from 'biscuity' to 'like marzipan', while tomatoes with their fascinating range of hues and shapes, are just as diverse in flavour. With more and more varieties becoming available as seed, gardeners have the opportunity that many people don't, to expand their taste horizons.

Where to grow

It is still true that if you want to grow a serious amount of produce, a vegetable plot is your best option. But if space in your garden is tight,

do not despair. Grow vegetables and herbs in pots on the patio, tucked into flower borders or up fences and trellis. Make a tiny raised bed for a constant supply of fresh salads or a mini-vegetable bed, to grow lots of baby vegetables. It is surprising how much can be fitted into even the smallest garden.

How to grow

Vegetable-growing has an image problem – lots of digging, giant leeks and hours of toil and effort. The 'Dig for Victory' approach may have served Britain well during the Second World War (when, incidentally, the British ate more healthily than before or since) but things have changed. As long as you understand the basics – and our step-by-step guide will help you with this – you can adapt vegetable-growing to fit into your lifestyle rather than *vice versa*.

One major reason for growing your own is to have vegetables that are free from chemicals. You can be absolutely sure how they have been grown and what has been sprayed on them. *Gardening Which?* takes the view that organic methods are preferable wherever possible, while accepting that some gardeners will want to use some pesticides or fertilisers at least in the short term. Go as far down the organic route as you feel comfortable with.

What to grow

Deciding which of the 50-plus vegetables and 20 or so culinary herbs to grow can be daunting. We have resisted the temptation to give plans for 'typical' vegetable plots or recipes for patio vegetable collections.

A much better approach is to think about the vegetables you buy each week and those you enjoy eating in restaurants. Include seasonal

treats, such as asparagus and new potatoes, and concentrate on produce that is best eaten really fresh, such as salads. Opting for the costlier items could make significant savings on the weekly food bill. Then turn to the A–Z section to find out how to grow them.

Think small

Short of space? Then forget giant cabbages and parsnips. Think instead of the kind of vegetables you buy. Nowadays it is more likely to be a bag of mixed salad leaves, rather than a whole lettuce. Consider baby carrots and needle beans that need no preparation, or baby cauliflowers and cabbages just right for a meal for two.

Be adventurous

Monotonous rows of green should be a thing of the past. Try rainbow chard, Tuscan cabbages, red kale, yellow courgettes or red sprouts to brighten up your garden and your plate – or whatever takes your fancy.

The variety of vegetables available to gardeners is increasing all the time. At the last count this included over 450 varieties of tomato – from tiny cherry tomatoes to huge beefsteaks for slicing. If you enjoy cooking, why not grow your own garlic, peppers, winter squash, borlotti beans or pak choi?

Get growing

Harvesting a crop of super-fresh vegetables you have grown yourself gives you a great sense of achievement. And if it's a toss-up between stepping into the garden to assemble a superb tasty salad, rather than going to the supermarket, or swapping some of your ornamental plants for ones that are attractive, fun to grow *and* edible, growing your own food plants surely has to be the winner.

IN CONTAINERS

Anyone who can grow bedding plants in pots, window boxes or hanging baskets can do equally well with herbs and vegetables in containers. You do not even need a garden, just a reasonably sunny place on a windowsill or on your patio. So if your garden has more concrete than soil, you can still grow fresh vegetables.

Some edible plants are attractive in their own right and can hold their own alongside flowering plants. For intense colour, try chard with its brightly coloured stems, red, frilly, loose-leaved lettuce, blue-green kales, the purple-leaved varieties of basil or sage, or bright-yellow varieties of lemon balm, marjoram or pot marigold. For added height, mangetout peas and runner beans will give a good display, as well as a worthwhile crop, in a pot, with some support.

Mediterranean herbs are a natural choice for containers, and most will tolerate the hottest spot on the patio, even if the compost dries out now and again. Position them where you can appreciate the scent as you brush past the leaves. A group of your favourite herbs in a window box near the kitchen will not only look attractive, but prompt you to pick and use them regularly. If you do not have a greenhouse, tomatoes, especially the dwarf types, are easy in pots or baskets. You could even consider exotic vegetables, such as aubergines or peppers, on a sunny patio.

Some vegetables, while not ornamental in appearance, can be grown in large pots to provide useful crops or a tasty treat for a special occasion. Impress your family or dinner guests by serving up delicious new potatoes grown in a large tub or a converted dustbin. Add to that a regular supply of salad leaves and spring onions, the occasional courgette or cucumber throughout the summer. Instead of buying baby vegetables, in plastic bags, try growing a potful of beetroots, carrots, leeks or turnips – an ordinary 30-cm pot will equal several supermarket punnets.

Opposite Red kale in a galvanised planter at the Chelsea Flower Show, 1999

Top left Herbs are excellent subjects for pots

Middle A mixture of lettuces in a large terracotta container

Far left A group of vegetables, herbs and ornamentals fills the corner of a patio

Left Oriental greens and dwarf beans

HOW TO GROW EDIBLE PLANTS IN CONTAINERS

Planting one type of vegetable per container seems to work best. Mixed plantings of different vegetables, or vegetables and flowers in the same container, soon lose their visual impact once you start harvesting. Herbs are an exception; they work well as mixed plantings as only small amounts of leaf are taken. But the vigour of the plants needs to be matched – for example, you should keep invasive plants such as mint separate from slower-growing plants such as tarragon.

Containers with a different type of plant in each can be combined to create eye-catching displays. However, to keep the interest going, it is well worth having some pots of plants in reserve to replace harvested crops. Late-flowering plants such as fuchsias, impatiens and marguerites all work well.

What type of container?

You can use almost any container, providing it is a reasonable size and has drainage holes in the bottom.

Where cost is a consideration, use plastic or recycled containers as they are the cheapest. Terracotta looks attractive and is timeless but larger sizes are expensive. The sides of terracotta pots are porous so compost tends to dry out. This is not a problem for most herbs, but it can limit cropping of vegetables. Line the inside of the pot with polythene to keep the compost moist.

What size container?

The bigger the container the better, unless you are prepared to water the plants twice a day in summer. As a guide, use at least a 2-litre (15-cm) pot for single smaller vegetables – a lettuce, say. Better still, use 10-litre containers

Fill with compost or soil

Give plants room to grow

(about the size of a domestic bucket) for a single larger vegetable or a group of three or five lettuces. Thirsty crops such as beans, cucumbers and tomatoes will benefit from a 15-litre container (the size of a builder's bucket).

Avoid shallow containers, i.e. under 15cm deep, as these do not give the roots enough depth and, as a result, the compost tends either to become waterlogged, or dries out very quickly.

Which compost?

Multipurpose compost is convenient, and all vegetables will crop well when grown in it, but large quantities can be expensive. Consider using the compost out of growing bags, which should be cheaper; a typical growing bag should contain at least 30 litres of compost. Tip the contents of the growing bag into deeper containers to make watering easier. Another way to eke out the compost is to add up

to half by volume of garden topsoil. If you do this, be prepared for some weeds; otherwise top up the pot with a layer of pure compost to act as a mulch to suppress weed seeds.

Planting up

Cover the base of the container with a layer of crocks (broken terracotta pots), stones and/or gravel – broken-up expanded polystyrene packaging material is a modern substitute. Any additions to the compost, such as topsoil or grit (a couple of handfuls are sometimes added in to improve drainage for Mediterranean-type herbs, such as rosemary and thyme), should be mixed in well before filling the pots. Add the compost, then plant the young plants, firming down gently as you go. Alternatively sow seed beetroot (see page 72), carrot and salad crops into the container as you would if you were sowing directly into the soil. Cover with

'Tumbler' tomatoes bred for containers and hanging baskets

1cm of compost. Leave a 2–3cm gap between the top of the compost and the rim of the pot to make watering easier.

Aftercare

Early in the summer, try not to overwater young plants, otherwise the compost will get waterlogged. Once the plants are growing and the weather is warmer, you need to water frequently so the compost never completely dries out.

Some plants, lettuces in particular, start to suffer if left in full sun during the hottest part of the summer. It will be easier to keep them watered if they are in a shaded or semi-shaded part of the patio.

The compost should have sufficient nutrients for even the greediest of crops for at least four weeks after planting. After that you will need to supply extra plant food. Vigorous leafy crops, such as cabbages or lettuces, will need a balanced liquid fertiliser, i.e. one with equal proportions of nitrogen, phosphate and potash. For fruiting crops such as cucumbers, peppers and tomatoes, use a liquid tomato feed; this will provide more potash. Follow the application rates for each product.

Watch out for pests and diseases, and follow the advice given for each vegetable if necessary. Slugs and snails can be prevented by fixing a barrier of copper tape around the container.

Hanging baskets

If you use hanging baskets, crops will not be large but they can be hung at a convenient height for picking and should not be bothered by slugs. Herbs such as mint, parsley, chives, small sage plants and basil work well, as do edible flowers such as nasturtium and pot marigolds. If you can cope with the extra watering, consider growing the dwarf tomato 'Tumbler'. Dwarf peas and dwarf French beans will tumble from a basket, too.

Vegetables for pots and tubs

The following vegetables will grow well in pots. You could try others, too, though celery and cauliflowers are likely to bolt. A dwarf red sprout or smaller types of cabbage could be worth trying, but large cabbages and Brussels sprouts will struggle.

Aubergine
Beetroot
Broad beans
Cabbage, spring
Cabbage, summer
Carrots
Chard
Chicory
Courgettes
Cucumber, outdoor
French beans
  (dwarf varieties)
Garlic
Kale
Leeks, baby
Lettuce
Onions
Onions, salad
Oriental greens
Peas, garden
Peas, mangetout
Peppers and chillies
Potatoes
Radishes, summer types
Runner beans
Salad leaves
Spinach
Tomatoes
Turnips

VEGETABLES
IN THE BORDER

It is possible to combine vegetables, herbs and flowers imaginatively in the same border to make an attractive feature for your garden.

Visually, some vegetables can more than hold their own among flowers. Take the spectacular globe artichoke, feathery asparagus or a pyramid covered in bright-red runner bean flowers, for example.

Most gardens have an ornamental border planted with shrubs and perennials. They are usually in a favourable site with reasonable soil and often have gaps that need filling at various times during the year.

The conventional approach is to use bedding plants to fill the gaps with summer flowers, but why not try some annual vegetables instead? They can look very attractive before harvesting.

Choose vegetable plants with colourful or interesting foliage to set off flowering plants nearby. Most of the vegetables and herbs recommended for containers would be perfect in the border. A patch of early carrots or a group of lettuces, say, will fit in perfectly. Use frilly lettuce, bright-red beetroot or chives as an edible edging.

To brighten up a dull border after the summer flowers have died down, use winter vegetables. Try the blue-green, strap-shaped leaves of leeks, huge, crinkled Savoy cabbages, variegated chicory or forms of kale with red or blue-grey leaves.

Further back in the border, find room for the larger perennial vegetables, such as globe artichokes or cardoons. Rhubarb is a long-lived plant for the middle or end of a border.

Although vegetables that run to seed may be a disaster in the vegetable plot, they are not out of place in a border. Bolted lettuces, for example, take on a strange vertical form, and chicory produces a lovely pale-blue flower that attracts insects. Leeks and kale will add winter interest to a border and it is worth leaving a few to flower in the spring.

Opposite Cabbages, courgettes and kale look good in an ornamental border
Top left Ornamental and edible cabbages mingle with edible nasturtium flowers
Middle Herbs are colourful in flower
Left Asparagus is ornamental as well as delicious
Right Coloured lettuces make excellent early border fillers

HOW TO GROW VEGETABLES IN YOUR BORDER

Work in a little organic matter

Scatter some balanced fertiliser

Plant vegetables with a trowel

Vegetable plants can benefit from the extra shelter provided by a mature, established shrub border early in the season and from the partial shade in high summer. The downside is that they will have to compete for moisture and nutrients with established border plants and may not get enough sunlight.

You will have to abandon the convention for planting vegetables in neat rows. Patches of smaller vegetables or single plants of larger ones will look more natural in a border. Follow the cottage garden approach of just filling any available space with whatever vegetable or herb takes your fancy.

Long-term plants

Perennial vegetables are worth growing in a border as they can be tricky to accommodate in a small vegetable plot where annual crop rotation is practised. Globe artichokes and cardoons both look spectacular in leaf and flower. They are large plants, so put them towards the back of the border. Give them plenty of room and generous amounts of organic matter.

The feathery foliage of asparagus provides a backdrop for large border flowers. Rhubarb may not be an obvious choice for a border but its red stems and huge leaves are actually quite attractive and it is an effective groundcover; few weeds will thrive beneath it. Give it plenty of room to spread, adding a terracotta forcing pot for structural interest in winter and early spring.

Many of the shrubby herbs will thrive in a sunny border where the soil is well-drained. Rosemary and sweet bay have evergreen foliage and will contribute year-round interest. Both can be clipped into formal shapes.

Perennial herbs such as chives or low shrubby herbs such as sage or thyme can be planted at the front of a border as a colourful but neat edging.

Annual fillers

Treat summer vegetables just as you would bedding plants. Start the tender types off in small pots somewhere warm and stand them in a sheltered spot until you are ready

to plant them out. Plant them with a trowel, using the spacings given in the A–Z section as a guide.

An easy alternative to sowing seed if you need only a few plants is to buy small plants from the garden centre (see pages 56–7).

Hardy vegetables such as lettuces, carrots, radishes and spring onions can be sown directly into the soil. If weeds are likely to be a problem, scratch a pattern of shallow lines into the soil and sow the vegetable seed into these. Cover them with soil and keep the area well watered. The vegetable seeds should come up in a pattern and be easy to distinguish from the weeds. Hand-weed a couple of times until the vegetable plants are well established.

Winter fillers

Borders that are planted with tender summer bedding have gaps over the dormant season – from late autumn to late spring. Winter or early summer vegetables such as kale or broad beans can be sown late in the autumn and will occupy the space before the herbaceous plants have emerged and before the summer bedding is planted.

If you can find the space in mid- to late summer, add a few hardy winter vegetables such as leeks, Savoy cabbages and kales. If you have not raised your own from seed, buy young plants and plant them where summer annuals will be cleared in autumn. Give them a good start by adding a little general fertiliser when you plant them.

Preparing the ground

A newly planted border should always be dug over and cleared of perennial weeds. If you intend to grow edible plants amongst the ornamentals, it is a good investment to work in some well-rotted organic matter at the same time.

When adding edible crops to an established border, you will need to take into account that the existing plants have a head start and will deprive your crops of sunlight, moisture and nutrients. To give them a decent start, fork the area over with a border fork to loosen the soil. Work in a little garden compost if it is available and add a scattering of general fertiliser. Water the area thoroughly before sowing or planting the vegetables.

Aftercare

Larger plants such as courgettes and bush tomatoes can be mulched to keep the soil underneath moist and to prevent weeds from growing. If you have sown vegetables from seed, hand-weed to prevent competition. Otherwise, edible plants in a border are cared for in the same way as they would be in a vegetable plot.

It is worth having extra plants waiting in pots, ready to be planted out as gaps appear later in the summer, when an early crop is harvested, for example.

Vigorous leafy plants will benefit from a top-up of a nitrogen feed in summer (see page 45).

Despite what you might read about pests not finding the crops because they are hidden by ornamentals, it is as well to be vigilant. Mobile insects such as cabbage white butterflies and aphids will still find them. However, natural predators, such as birds and ladybirds, should keep most pests under control. The main exceptions are slugs and snails. You may need to take some precautions against these (see pages 40–1).

Vegetables for borders

Artichoke, globe *

Asparagus *

Beetroot

Broad beans

Cabbage, winter

Cardoon *

Carrots

Chicory

Courgettes

Fennel

Kale

Kohl rabi

Leeks

Lettuce

Onions, salad

Oriental greens

Peppers/chillies

Pumpkins/squash

Rhubarb *

Seakale *

Spinach and chard

Sweetcorn

Tomatoes

For herbs, see pages 204–19

* Perennial plants

Planting broad beans in a spring border

Sow seed in shallow drills

Any late gaps can be filled with lettuce

VEGETABLE CLIMBERS

If you are short of space, grow vertically – many vegetables make attractive climbers. Runner beans were first grown as colourful ornamental climbers rather than for their beans. The tall pea variety 'Carouby de Maussane' is often mistaken for a sweet pea, and trailing marrows look wonderful as the ripe fruits hang down from arches and pergolas.

The vegetable climbers mentioned here are all annuals and grow very quickly from a seed to a plant 1.8–2m or so high in one growing season. The wall of foliage can be used as a temporary screen or garden divider, and many vegetables, the beans in particular, have eye-catching flowers.

Growing vegetable climbers in an ornamental garden rather than a vegetable plot has a couple of advantages. First, the climbers can be sited where they will not cast shade over other edible crops. Second, permanent existing supports such as walls, fences and trellis can be used instead of temporary supports.

The most useful permanent supports are south-facing. Have a look around your garden for possible sites: house walls, sheds, garage walls, boundary fences could all be candidates. If there is no soil to plant into, use large tubs filled with compost. A wall or fence will need horizontal wires, netting or trellis panels fitted to support the climbers.

In the open garden, a row of runner beans trained up bamboo canes

Top Pumpkin 'Baby Bear' trailing along a fence
Left Runner beans are the ultimate climbing vegetable – pretty and productive

or hazel poles could be used as a garden divider. A tripod of bamboo or willow fits well into a bed; either as a centrepiece or to add height to a newly planted border. For other methods of supporting climbing vegetables, see page 179.

Poor or dry soil can be improved by digging in plenty of organic matter and by generous mulching and watering after planting.

Left Wigwam of beans in a border **Above** Cordon tomatoes trained up canes

PLANTING AND TRAINING

Sowing seed in pots and planting out young plants is generally the most successful way to start plants off, but it is also possible to sow seed direct into the ground where they are to grow.

When growing climbing plants in a row, take out a trench and add organic matter to the bottom rather than digging individual planting holes. The supports should be in place before planting, as pushing canes and poles into the ground near growing plants can damage their roots. The growing plants may at least need to be tied to the supports to get them started. Use plant ties or make figure-of-8 ties with garden raffia.

Once the plants reach the top of the supports, pinch out their growing tips. Pick the fruits regularly.

Climbing vegetables
While all runner beans are climbers, this is not the case for, say, French beans. Many of the other vegetables have only a few varieties which climb, so do check you have a climbing variety. The variety guide in each entry in the A–Z of vegetables will tell you the best one to buy.
Climbing French beans
Cucumbers, trailing outdoor types (or greenhouse varieties in a sheltered spot)
Tall peas and mangetout
Trailing marrows
Runner beans
Squash (only the small-fruited winter squash)
Tomatoes (cordon varieties)

SALAD OR
HERB BEDS

There are times when all you need is
a little salad for a garnish or a pinch of
herbs for cooking. Even if you have a
vegetable plot at the end of the garden,
think how convenient it would be to
have a supply of fresh salad leaves or
herbs just outside the kitchen door.
Even a small patio or balcony can be
used to grow a constant supply of salad
leaves and herbs, either in large
containers or in a small raised bed.

MAKING A SALAD OR HERB BED

Any large tub or container will do, including hanging baskets and window boxes, but the bigger the volume of compost, the easier the plants will be to look after. On a balcony, choose lightweight containers such as plastic or fibreglass and use soil-less compost, as this is not as heavy as soil-based types.

Building a salad bar

An alternative to using a container is to build a wooden box to contain your herb or salad bed. The principle is the same as for making a raised bed (pages 26–7) in that planks or lengths of gravel board are fixed securely to corner posts, though the box is smaller.

A box that will stand on a patio or area of concrete should be made at least 45cm deep for vegetables, and 15cm for smaller herbs. Boxes built directly on to

soil could be shallower, but dig the soil over first and improve it by adding garden compost or well-rotted manure for salads. Top the box up with ordinary well-drained garden topsoil for herbs.

A box or bed just one square metre in size should provide ample supplies of fresh leafy salad or herbs throughout the summer. Herbs are best grown separated from one another. An easy and attractive way to do this is to lift a group of, say, four 45-cm square paving slabs from a sunny patio. Build a tiered raised bed using three squares. Rotate each layer by 45 degrees to give nine separate planting pockets for herbs such as chives, sage, tarragon, thyme and marjoram. Fill with free-draining soil or a grit and compost mix. A layer of fine gravel will keep the soil moist.

Feeding and watering

Whatever container you use, leafy salads are best grown rapidly without any check to their growth, so keep the soil moist by watering regularly. Even if you added organic matter at the start of the season, the bed may benefit from an occasional feed – use a liquid feed with a high nitrogen content.

Herbs are generally less fussy and will thrive without regular watering once they are established. Feeding herbs is only necessary if you crop them intensively, for example, cutting off handfuls of chives or parsley every couple of weeks.

Cut-and-come-again

This technique is used to produce a regular supply of young leaves for mixed salads and is described in detail on pages 180–3. If you regularly buy packs of mixed salad, copy the list of ingredients – chicory and endive, chervil, mizuna, chard, spinach and so on – and try growing your own.

Opposite A purpose-built raised bed holds a variety of salad leaves for picking over. An old cartwheel doubles as an edging for a collection of culinary herbs.
Above Pick individual salad leaves to make up your own designer salads.
Right Plastic storage boxes double as space-saving cut-and-come-again salad containers.

PLANNING A MINI-VEGETABLE PLOT

In a small garden, you will not have room for a conventional vegetable plot. Instead, you could have a mini-vegetable plot full of baby vegetables. Baby vegetables are often preferred for their appearance and tenderness, and if you buy them from a supermarket, they are more expensive than normal-sized vegetables.

You will be surprised at how much you can fit into a mini-vegetable plot: rows of root vegetables are just 15cm apart, and leafy crops such as cabbages, cauliflowers and lettuces are just 15cm apart each way.

Baby vegetables can be grown in the following three ways:

Grow conventional varieties, but pick them while they are young. This works for root crops such as beetroot, carrots (use an early variety), kohl rabi, leeks, parsnips and turnips.

Grow dwarf varieties, for example of cabbages and lettuces, which will not grow larger even if allowed more space.

Grow vegetables at closer spacings than normal. This technique was first developed for producing baby cauliflowers, but it works well with calabrese and all types of cabbages, too.

Although these techniques will work with most varieties, it is worth looking for varieties sold specifically for mini-vegetable production. Often, a combination of all three techniques works best: start with a suitable variety, grow it at a close spacing, and harvest when young and tender.

Other vegetables, such as courgettes and dwarf French beans, are picked small and sold as baby vegetables, but the plants take up as much space as conventional varieties. Cucumbers with naturally small fruit and cherry tomatoes also grow on normal-sized plants.

To make your mini-vegetable bed neater, consider edging it with boards (see pages 26–7). This will raise it above the surrounding garden, and enable you to improve the soil by adding organic matter and cut down on watering.

Opposite page, top Baby vegetables command a high price in the shops, but are easy to grow yourself; **left** The most efficient way to crop a small bed is to grow baby vegetables; **right** Pull roots when small
Top Summer squash can be picked when small, like courgettes, though the plants do reach normal size
Above A small vegetable bed can hold a surprising variety of baby vegetables
Right You can grow baby cabbages by spacing plants closer together – perfect for one meal

BEST FOR BABY VEGETABLES

For more details on specific varieties for mini-vegetable plots, see the relevant entry in the A–Z of Vegetables.

Beetroot

Cabbage

Calabrese

Carrots

Cauliflower

Kohl rabi

Leeks

Lettuce

Onions

Parsnips

Turnips

MODERN POTAGERS

One way of having a decent-sized vegetable plot, as well as a colourful garden feature, is to create a potager. In a potager, vegetables are grown alongside flowers, herbs and fruit. Beds are arranged in decorative, formal patterns, and separated by paths.

An area that provides vegetables, as well as being attractive to look at, has appeal for modern gardens. The idea of growing vegetables in formal, ornamental beds is not new. Indeed, the practice has reached high art in some French châteaux. But how practical is it? You need to accept that in order to look decorative all year, a potager may not be as productive as a dedicated vegetable plot. However, you will have a greater variety of produce, such as a mixture of flowers for cutting, herbs and even soft fruit, as well as vegetables.

The potager could be a simple rustic feature with rectangular beds and firmed earth or bark paths. Alternatively, you can introduce paving to divide up the beds and even raise the beds with edges of board or brick. Giving the potager a permanent structure will increase its appeal as a garden feature during winter. You could create a pattern using unusually shaped beds rather than squares or rectangles. Try to stick to a simple, symmetrical pattern and remember that you need to be able to reach into the centre of each bed from the paths. In addition, the higher the ratio of bed to path, the greater the yield of vegetables.

To make the beds in the potager look interesting, use the more ornamental vegetables (see list on page 17) especially those suitable for edging. Within the beds, plant bold blocks of the same plant. To keep the beds occupied all year, include overwintered vegetables in your planting scheme. As soon as you harvest a vegetable, fill the gap with fresh plants you have raised in small pots so the beds are kept full during the summer.

Wigwams, obelisks and arches all add vertical interest and impose a sense of symmetry, but be sure to site them where they will not shade the beds. For a seating area within or to the side of a potager, consider an arbour or a pergola.

Opposite Wigwams of sweet peas add height and colour to a potager
Above, top A mixture of vegetables and flowers gives a cottage-garden effect
Above, middle Geometric beds and gravel paths lend a strong structure
Above Bold planting of cabbages and kales
Right A colourful mixture of vegetables, herbs and flowers

BUILDING A RAISED BED

Raised beds are an efficient way of growing vegetables and can be used for mini-vegetable plots, potagers and no-dig systems. In such a bed, the volume of soil is increased by adding organic matter so it is higher than the surrounding paths.

You can have just a single raised bed with brick sides linking the patio with the rest of the garden, or a series of beds separated by permanent paths. The paths are never dug, watered or fertilised, but provide access to the beds for sowing, planting and weeding. This means that all the organic matter, fertiliser and water can be concentrated on the growing area.

Because the beds are higher than the surrounding soil, they will warm up earlier in spring, drain quicker after rain and have a greater depth of soil for plant roots. The soil in raised beds does not need to be dug every year and can easily be converted into a no-dig system, which does away with digging completely.

Small beds lend themselves to planting in blocks or sowing a succession of short rows to spread the harvest. They are also easy to cover with garden fleece or fine mesh to protect the plants from frost or flying pests.

By edging raised beds and making permanent paths between them, you can turn them into an attractive feature.

The choice of materials
Whether you opt for simple and practical rectangular beds or a more elaborate potager, there is a wide choice of materials to consider.

Nail edges to corner post

Build up the soil with organic matter

Paving slabs set on edge and half-buried will provide a permanent edging. Depending on the width of the slabs, you could build beds as high as 30cm above soil level.

Bricks or paving blocks, either laid loose or cemented in, can create an attractive feature, especially if linked to the rest of the garden.

Railway sleepers can be bought from specialist suppliers. They are heavy and hard to cut but provide solid edges to larger raised beds.

Gravel boards from fencing suppliers or builders' merchants are the easiest material to use for edging. Most are pressure-treated with preservatives;

if this worries you, look for untreated timber 15cm wide and 2.5cm deep.

Old floorboards make an acceptable substitute and can often be salvaged from demolition sites.

How big?
Make the beds narrow enough that you can reach the centre from either side without stepping on the soil. About 1.2m is a workable width for most people. Beds should be no longer than 3m so they are easy to get round. Rectangular beds are the most efficient use of space. The paths should be a minimum of 30cm wide; 45cm is wide enough to allow access for a wheelbarrow, but any wider uses up valuable growing space.

Raised beds for herbs
The majority of herbs need a well-drained soil. Where garden soil is heavy clay or is wet over winter, growing herbs in a raised bed is worthwhile. A raised bed can be incorporated into the patio or sited outside the kitchen door. Heavy manuring is not beneficial; dig some coarse grit, leafmould or spent mushroom compost into the topsoil to improve drainage.

HOW TO BUILD A SIMPLE RAISED BED

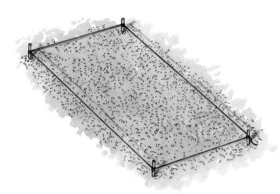

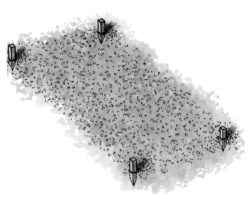

STEP 1 Level the site and remove any perennial weeds. Mark out the shape of the bed with pegs and string, making sure it is square and level.

STEP 2 Hammer the posts into the corners. 60-cm lengths cut from 5- or 7.5-cm square fenceposts are ideal. Leave about 12.5cm of the posts above ground. If the sides will be longer than 2.4m, you may need to join boards together – position a post to reinforce the joint.

STEP 3 Cut lengths of gravel board to size and nail them to the posts with galvanised nails. Settle them into the soil and check the tops with a spirit level.

STEP 4 To save weeding the paths, lay down porous polypropylene membrane, and top with a layer of bark or gravel. Dig the soil inside the bed and add well-rotted organic matter.

Aftercare

If you do all your planting and weeding from the paths and never walk on the bed, the soil should remain in peak condition and will not need digging each year. Add a generous layer of well-rotted organic matter every year or two. Mushroom compost is ideal, but stack it under a polythene cover for a couple of months to allow any chemicals in it to break down first. Not only will the compost suppress the weeds, but earthworms will mix it into the bed. Soon it will be possible to grow any crop without additional fertiliser.

Keep on top of weeds by hoeing or hand-weeding regularly. If you do not bring buried weed seeds to the surface by digging and prevent annual weeds seeding, the weeds should gradually decline. Keep beds occupied with vegetables, or use green manures (see page 47) to help maintain soil structure.

ALLOTMENTS

You do not even need a garden to grow vegetables – you can rent an allotment. If you are new to vegetable growing, you can rely on plenty of friendly advice and support too from a community of fellow gardeners.

Choosing an allotment

Find out about the allotment sites in your area. Some are run privately by a committee of allotment-holders, while others are run by the local council. Rent and the facilities provided can vary from area to area. A thriving site could have purpose-built sheds for each plot, a trading hut for cheap gardening sundries and even a clubhouse.

Talk to allotment-holders before you agree to rent a plot. Ask about the security of the site – vandalism and petty theft can be a problem on some allotments. Find out what the major pests are. Some sites have a problem with rabbits, which are hard to control.

A whole plot is normally about 250sq m – a large area to dig over in one go. Find out if you can rent a half- or quarter-plot to get started; you can always take on more later.

If you have a choice of plots, go for one that has been cultivated recently – breaking in an overgrown plot is a tough job (but see below). Check that there is a tap nearby and that access is easy for bulky deliveries such as compost. Established fruit bushes are a useful bonus.

Try to find out, from neighbouring plot-holders, about the recent history of your particular plot. For example, did the previous owner dig in lots of

Opposite Modern allotment with raised beds to reduce work

Right Autumn harvest on the allotment

organic matter, use fertilisers and pesticides excessively, or practise crop rotation. Does the site have a history of problem diseases such as clubroot on brassicas or white rot on onions?

Getting started

Getting off to a good start with an allotment can make all the difference. The best time to start is in the autumn or winter, as this will give you plenty of time to plan and get the soil right.

If the plot has been cultivated recently, it is worthwhile clearing any crop remains and digging it over roughly, removing any perennial weeds you come across. On heavy soils, aim to rough-dig before midwinter and leave the frost to create a crumbly soil structure. On lighter soils, you can get away with digging in late winter. Aim to work in a generous amount of well-rotted organic matter – a barrow-load to every two square metres should be plenty. Someone on the allotment site will be able to tell you where to get local supplies of bulky organic matter – farmyard or stable manure, or mushroom compost. The aim should be to have the whole plot ready to start sowing and planting by early spring.

An overgrown plot

You may have no choice but to take on a plot that has been left uncultivated for several years. This is a daunting prospect but the secret is to break down the task into manageable chunks. Take a small area and clear it thoroughly, rather than trying to tackle the whole plot at once.

If necessary, remove any undergrowth with a petrol trimmer – these can be hired, along with protective clothing,

by the day from a d-i-y hire shop. Cover any ground you cannot clear immediately with black plastic weighed down with large stones, or else use old carpet. This will weaken and eventually kill even perennial weeds. See pages 38–9 for more information on weed control.

Next steps

Start a compost bin immediately and recycle as much organic matter as you can, but do not include diseased plants or perennial weeds, or any weeds in flower. For advice on building a bin, see pages 32–3.

Find out about the soil (see pages 30–1). It is worth following a crop-rotation system on an allotment (see pages 36–7).

Your fellow plot-holders will be only too pleased that you are tackling an overgrown plot, so most will be more than happy to pass on their expertise and opinions. But do not be afraid to break with the traditional approach, for example, by building a couple of raised beds, and remember to grow what you and your family want to eat, not simply what everyone else is growing.

FINDING OUT ABOUT YOUR SOIL

While almost all soils can be improved to make them suitable for growing vegetables, you need to know what type of soil you have to start with.

Texture

To find out more about your soil, simply dig a couple of holes in the ground and look at the soil that comes up. Are there a lot of stones or lumps of chalk? Is it baked rock hard? Or is it like dust?

Take up a handful of soil from about 10–15cm down. Squeeze the soil in your hand: if it feels spongy, a bit like compost, it has a high organic content. Rub some soil between your fingertips – a gritty texture indicates that sand is present, while a smooth texture points to a loam or clay soil. Knead the soil in your hands – can you work it into a ball? A soil that cannot be moulded in this way and keeps breaking up contains very few clay particles. The ideal gardening soil is loam, which is a mixture of sand and clay particles. It can hold moisture in summer, yet water can drain through in winter. Where there is a high proportion of clay you can have problems with waterlogging. Try rolling the ball of soil into a sausage shape, then bending it into a circle in your hand; a loam does not have enough clay to make a circle but a soil rich in clay does.

Drainage

Dig a hole 45cm square and 45cm deep in late winter. Fill it halfway up with water and put on a waterproof cover. Check the level of water in the hole after an hour and again the next

Take a representative soil sample

day. If the water has disappeared within an hour, it is free-draining soil, but if it is still there the next day, the soil is wet or waterlogged.

Acid or alkaline?

A simple pH test that you can do yourself will tell you within a couple of minutes whether your soil is acid or alkaline. *Gardening Which?* trials found that the chemical kits for testing pH were better than pH meters available to gardeners. *Gardening Which?* offers a full soil-testing service for members (see page 224 for details).

Taking a soil sample

Soil tests are done in test tubes so the samples tested are a tiny proportion of the total soil you want to know about. For that reason, it is vital to get a soil sample that is accurately representative. Large areas are best divided into sections which are individually tested.
● Lay out four bamboo canes in

Mix it with water and the indicator chemical

a W-shape across the area.
● Using a clean trowel, dig down to about 15cm.
● Take out some soil at the end of each cane (five samples in total).
● Remove stones, weed roots etc. Mix the five portions together in a clean bucket. Take out the amount needed for the test (usually 500g for a full analysis).
● To test the soil for pH yourself, take a half-teaspoon of soil and drop it into the test tube of chemical supplied. Add water and shake well. Check the colour of the liquid against the colour chart supplied.

You should test the pH of your garden soil every two to three years. On the pH scale, 7.0 is neutral, a higher figure is alkaline and a lower one acid.

Most vegetables prefer a pH within the range pH 6.5–7.5, with brassicas preferring the upper end.

Check the colour and read off the pH

Liming

Acid soils can be corrected by adding ground limestone. The amount you add depends on the soil type and the initial pH.

Apply the correct amount of lime to each square metre of the plot

Amount of ground limestone added per sq m

pH	Clay	Loam	Sandy
6.0	420g	270g	140g
5.5	800g	540g	270g
5.0	1200g*	800g	420g
4.5	1200g*	1080g	540g

* Do not apply more than this in one go

Add the lime to the soil in autumn and wait until spring before applying manure or fertiliser. Nitrogen can be lost if lime is applied at the same time as manures and fertilisers.

Growing vegetables on different soils

Stony Use a garden fork to loosen the soil and put a lot of organic matter on the top of the soil, rather than trying to dig down with a spade.

Chalk Add lots of organic matter to improve the moisture-holding capacity of the soil; feed from spring to summer. Early sowings should do well.

Sandy These soils are usually acid, so may need liming regularly. They are also free-draining, so add plenty of organic matter. Spent mushroom compost is a good choice because it has a neutral pH. Water, mulch and feed from spring to summer. Early sowings thrive.

Loam This is ideal soil for vegetables but it may need lime, depending on the results of a pH test. It is still worth adding some organic matter but fertiliser is less vital.

Clay This is a fertile soil but it can become waterlogged and be slow to warm up in spring. Start plants off in pots of compost, use cloches to warm the soil and make raised beds. Digging will aerate the soil, but keep off the ground when it is wet and sticky or it will quickly become compacted. The best time to dig is either in late autumn before winter rains or as the soil is drying in spring. Organic matter will help to open up the soil but fertiliser may not be necessary.

ORGANIC MATTER

All soils benefit from organic matter, the only exception being peaty soils, which are rare in the UK. Well-rotted organic matter is a catch-all phrase for a number of materials of plant or animal origin that have been composted down to make a bulky soil improver. It improves the structure of soils that are waterlogged, compacted or too free-draining and feeds a hidden army of soil creatures and organisms that all contribute to the general health and fertility of the soil.

Unlike fertilisers, organic matter is added by the fork or barrow-load rather than being sprinkled on. As it is used up by the soil creatures, regular applications are needed.

Garden compost

Recycle as much organic matter as you can from your own garden and kitchen by turning it into garden compost. The most efficient way to do this is to collect all the material

Clockwise from top Leafmould, stable manure, garden compost, composted green waste

together in a bin and provide the right conditions for it to rot down.

Fill the bin with a mixture of woody material and green material. You can add a handful of nitrogen fertiliser or a shovel full of garden compost or garden soil to get the process going but do not bother with special compost activators.

Keep the contents damp but not sodden. A square of old carpet or sacking on the top will hold in moisture and warmth. A waterproof cover to keep heavy rain off is essential.

To encourage quick composting, turn the pile once every six weeks. After six months to a year, the compost will be dark and crumbly and ready to use.

Leafmould

Rather than putting piles of autumn leaves in the compost bin, stack them in their own wire enclosure to rot down into leafmould. They do not need warmth or a cover as the leaves are broken down by fungi rather than bacteria (as is the case with compost). Just water the leaves now and again, and in a couple of years the leaves will have rotted down. To speed things up, shred the leaves by running a mower over them before storing them.

Other sources

Most gardeners need more organic matter than they can make in their own gardens. Commercial products usually sold as soil improvers in 80-litre bags are ready processed and adequate for improving the soil of a small border or raised bed. For a larger area, you need a loose load of manure or spent mushroom compost.

Different manures

Well-rotted manure can be used straight away, but if it is fresh you

What to put in your compost bin

Fruit and vegetable waste, including tea bags and coffee grounds

Pet litter, e.g. from hamsters and rabbits

Shredded newspaper and corrugated cardboard (both in moderation)

Grass clippings and green prunings

Remains of bedding plants, top growth from perennials and used compost from containers

Woody prunings only if shredded first

Do not add
Cat litter
Cooked food waste
Perennial weeds
Annual weeds in flower
Diseased or virus-infected plants

will need to compost it. Make a heap and water it if it is dry. Cover it with a sheet of plastic secured at the edges; this will prevent nutrients being washed out. In about six months it will be ready for use.

Most manure these days contains a lot of wood shavings instead of straw. It needs to be stacked well before use so that the breaking-down process is completed before the manure is added to the soil, otherwise the wood can rob the soil of nitrogen.

Farmyard manure Horse or cow manure is preferable. Poultry manure is best regarded as a fertiliser (see pages 44–45).

Spent mushroom compost This is a mixture of horse manure, peat and lime, which is used to grow mushrooms commercially. After harvesting, it is sold off. It is an ideal soil improver because it is not as acid as other manures. Stack it under cover to allow chemical sterilants to break down.

Municipal compost Composted green waste is available in some areas. It contains a high proportion of shredded wood – use as a surface mulch.

Compost bins

Ready-made bins The best types are large plastic cylinders or cones with a lid. Make the compost in batches, then lift the bin off, leaving a composted heap that can be covered until it is used. Then start filling the bin again.

D-i-y bins The ideal size for an effective compost bin is about 1 cubic metre. If you have room, make two side by side so you can turn compost from one bin to another (to get air into the mixture).

Site the bin in a shaded area out of view but with access for a wheelbarrow. It should be on free-draining earth (not on concrete or paving) so that worms and insects can migrate in and help aerate the compost. If the soil is wet, put down a layer of twigs first. Leave gaps at the bottom of the sides for ventilation.

MAKING A COMPOST BIN

STEP 1 Use four fenceposts for the corners

STEP 2 Nail old planks or rough-sawn timber to make the sides

STEP 3 Use two lathes to make runners

STEP 4 Cut planks to slide between the runners to make a removable front

PREPARING THE SOIL

Digging is the traditional method for clearing a vegetable plot at the end of the season and preparing it for the next. But organic gardeners question the need for annual digging, pointing out that it destroys the soil's natural structure and can bring a fresh crop of weed seeds to the surface. Digging is often impractical when growing vegetables among other plants. Whether you dig every year, every few years or not at all depends on where you are growing your vegetables (see table, right), and on the underlying soil (see pages 30–31).

Breaking new ground
When starting off a new vegetable plot or constructing raised vegetable beds, it is advisable to prepare the ground thoroughly. Digging breaks up compacted soil, improving drainage and aeration. At the same time, you can remove perennial weed roots and incorporate bulky organic matter.

It is worth taking your time digging over a new vegetable plot, and doing a thorough job. First dig a hole at least 45cm deep. If there is a hard layer below the surface that could impede drainage, this should be broken up by double digging (see page 35). If the soil is fairly loose and free-draining, single digging should suffice.

Annual digging
Some gardeners still prefer to dig over the vegetable plot each winter. On a heavy clay soil, aim to complete digging by Christmas. Try to invert each lump of soil to bury annual weeds, but leave the clods intact. The action of frost and rain will break down the clods to leave a crumbly soil by spring. On light, sandy soils, wait until spring before digging. Often a hard crust forms on the surface over winter, and this needs to be broken up before sowing or planting.

If you need to lime part of the plot (see page 31), do this in autumn/winter. It may be convenient to incorporate bulky organic matter in the autumn or winter, but most of the nutrients are likely to be washed out by winter rain.

It is better to add organic matter as a surface mulch in the spring, so the nutrients benefit your crops.

To look after your back, spread the digging over several sessions.

Mulching
Spread organic matter on the surface of the soil in a deep layer, preferably at least 5cm thick. If applied in spring (March), it will prevent weed seeds germinating and help to retain moisture within the soil. In time, earthworms will drag the mulch down into the soil, so you do not need to dig it in. You will need to reapply mulch every spring. Mulching cannot tackle underlying problems such as compaction, but it will help to maintain a well-structured and fertile soil.

Bed systems
If you divide the plot into beds, in which the crops grow, and paths, on which you walk, the soil does not get compacted, so you do not need to dig. Add organic matter to the surface of the soil (see Mulching). Light cultivation, such as raking and hoeing, are all you need to do each year (see page 26–7 for more on raised beds).

Trenching
Preparing a trench can help in two ways. It can increase the moisture

Site	Soil care when setting up	Ongoing soil care
Container	*Fill with fresh compost*	*Refill with fresh compost each year*
Established border		*Mulch each spring and apply general fertiliser*
Raised bed/ Potager	*Dig or double dig, incorporating organic matter*	*Surface cultivation only; mulch with organic matter*
Conventional vegetable plot	*Dig thoroughly (double digging for problem soil)*	*Crop rotation (see pages 36-7) Test soil, and add lime if required (see pages 30-1). Dig, mulch or trench*

DOUBLE DIGGING STEP-BY-STEP

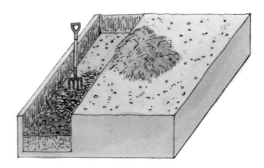

STEP 1 Dig a trench about 30cm wide and to the depth of the spade. You should only move the topsoil, not the underlying subsoil. Barrow the soil from this first trench to the other end of the area being dug.

STEP 2 Spread a layer of well-rotted manure in the trench and, using a garden fork, dig over the bottom of the trench to the depth of the fork. Break up any hard layer, loosen the subsoil and mix in the manure.

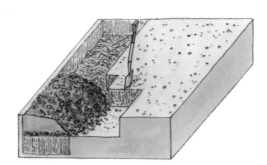

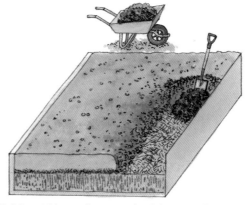

STEP 3 Dig a second trench parallel to the first. But this time throw the topsoil forward to fill in the first trench, then repeat step 2.

STEP 4 Repeat this procedure across the whole area, until you are left with a final trench. After completing step 2 for the final trench, use the soil from the first trench to top it up.

Single digging

Follow **Steps 1, 3 and 4** above but not step 2. If you want to incorporate manure at the same time, spread it on the surface so that it is mixed into the topsoil as you dig.

retention of the part of the vegetable plot where runner beans or other moisture-sensitive crops are to grow. It is also a convenient way to dispose of tough crop remains that are slow to rot down in the compost heap. Dig a trench about 60cm wide and about 30cm deep in the autumn.

Fill it over winter with crop debris, manure, old growing-bag compost, etc, and gradually replace the topsoil. Leave it to settle before planting in spring.

Planting holes

The same principle as trenching applies, but on a smaller scale. Dig a hole about 30cm deep and 30cm across for one plant, such as a courgette, and incorporate plenty of organic matter into the soil at the bottom of the hole before refilling with soil. This is useful when planting moisture-sensitive crops into an established border.

CROP ROTATION

Crop rotation means growing certain crops on a different area of land each year in a three- or four-year cycle. There are many benefits to this system.

Moving the crops around helps to prevent some troublesome soil pests and diseases from building up to damaging levels. Also, by swapping the main groups of vegetables around in a regular order, you can make the most efficient use of the nutrients in the soil because different types of crops require different amounts of nutrients.

Anyone who wants to grow crops with the minimum amount of chemicals and fertilisers should practise crop rotation.

The amount of organic matter available is often limited, so you need to make sure it goes to the hungriest crops. In a crop-rotation scheme, you

VEGETABLE FAMILIES

Here is a summary of the main members of each family, the problems that can be prevented by crop rotation and the care requirements they have in common.

CABBAGE FAMILY
Broccoli, Brussels sprouts, cabbages, calabrese, cauliflowers, Chinese cabbage and other oriental greens, kale, kohl rabi, radishes, swede and turnip. Sweet Williams, wallflowers and mustard are also related.
Potential problems clubroot. Pests such as cabbage aphid, flea beetle, cabbage root fly, cabbage caterpillars can be kept at bay with fine mesh. Rabbit netting and pigeon netting may also be needed for over winter crops.
Requirements alkaline soil – lime if acid (see pages 30–1); soil that was manured for a previous crop; a large amount of fertiliser (see pages 44–5).

ONION FAMILY
All types of onions, chives, garlic, leeks and shallots.
Potential problems eelworm and white rot. Leek rust cannot be controlled by rotation.
Requirements soil that has been manured for a previous crop. Needs only a small amount of fertiliser (see pages 44–5). Does not generally need watering.

PEA FAMILY
Garden and mangetout peas, broad beans, French and runner beans. Also many green manure crops.
Potential problems various root rots.
Requirements organic matter, e.g. manure, but little fertiliser.

POTATO FAMILY
Potatoes and tomatoes, also aubergines and peppers.
Potential problems eelworm, powdery scab (but not common scab). Potato blight (survives on unharvested tubers).
Requirements no lime needed, moderate amounts of fertiliser, organic matter if it can be spared.

All require protection from late spring frosts and may need spraying to prevent blight.

ROOT CROPS
Carrots, parsley, parsnips, salsify and scorzonera.
Potential problems various root rots, including parsnip canker.

Carrot fly can be prevented with a physical barrier of garden fleece or fine netting.
Requirements no fresh manure, little fertilizer; watering not usually necessary.

OTHER CROPS
These are not related to the main groups above and can be fitted anywhere in the rotation.

Beetroot, chard and leaf beet and spinach; they need fertiliser but not organic matter.

Celery and celeriac; they need a rich, moisture-retentive soil, with plenty of manure and regular watering.

Lettuces need organic matter, nitrogen fertiliser and regular watering; they are often grown with cabbage family crops.

Marrows, courgettes, cucumbers, pumpkins and squash benefit from a moisture-retentive soil, and can be grown on any well-manured area or on manure-filled planting holes.

Sweetcorn is generally not fussy about soil but is sensitive to frost, so should be planted late, when it can usefully follow early peas or beans.

Perennial vegetables such as rhubarb and asparagus are best kept out of beds used for crop rotation. Grow them in their own bed on the plot.

need only apply the manure to a third of the area in any one year.

It is also convenient to grow related crops together, so that, for example, members of the cabbage family can be protected from the insect pests that attack them all.

Green vegetables that require regular watering can be separated from root crops, which will survive without watering. See pages 46–7 for more about watering vegetables.

Smaller vegetable plots

On small vegetable plots, conventional crop rotation is not practical, so instead aim to separate the main crop groupings as far as possible. At the very least, try to grow vegetables such as potatoes, onions and the cabbage family, which are prone to soil pests and diseases, on a different area each year and fit any other crops around them. If you opt for growing in raised beds, it is relatively easy to confine each group of vegetables to one bed. You do not need to follow a strict rotation, but keep a record each year and try to ensure that key crops do not go on the same bed for at least another three years.

RECOMMENDED CROP-ROTATION SCHEMES

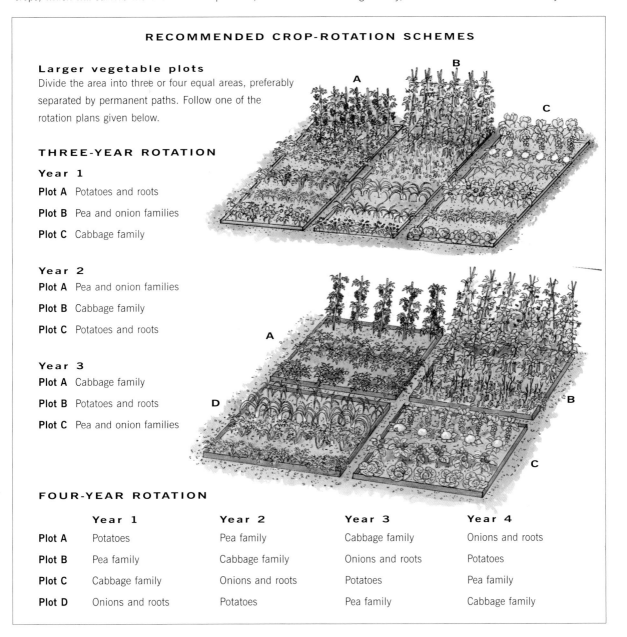

Larger vegetable plots
Divide the area into three or four equal areas, preferably separated by permanent paths. Follow one of the rotation plans given below.

THREE-YEAR ROTATION

Year 1

Plot A Potatoes and roots

Plot B Pea and onion families

Plot C Cabbage family

Year 2

Plot A Pea and onion families

Plot B Cabbage family

Plot C Potatoes and roots

Year 3

Plot A Cabbage family

Plot B Potatoes and roots

Plot C Pea and onion families

FOUR-YEAR ROTATION

	Year 1	Year 2	Year 3	Year 4
Plot A	Potatoes	Pea family	Cabbage family	Onions and roots
Plot B	Pea family	Cabbage family	Onions and roots	Potatoes
Plot C	Cabbage family	Onions and roots	Potatoes	Pea family
Plot D	Onions and roots	Potatoes	Pea family	Cabbage family

CONTROLLING WEEDS

Weeds compete with your plants for moisture and nutrients so you need to control them promptly, otherwise crop yield will be adversely affected. Some weeds can also harbour pests that then move on to growing crops.

Tackling a large, neglected plot full of perennial weeds such as a disused allotment is very hard work, and you may want to use a weedkiller to get a head start even if you plan to grow vegetables organically eventually. Once the cultivated ground is more or less weed-free, it can be kept that way without using chemicals at all.

Clearing weedy ground

When perennial weeds have got the upper hand, it is an uphill struggle to get rid of them. Even though you may have dealt with the top growth, the plants may regrow from tiny fragments of roots or stems left in the ground. A petrol rotovator can make the problem worse by cutting up the roots and spreading them around the plot.

There are three recommended ways of clearing weed-infested ground.

Covering Cut back the top growth of the weeds, then cover the ground with black polythene sheeting or old carpet. Provided the cover is kept in place for

Potatoes grown through black polythene

Swoe for weeding around plants

at least a year, the weeds will die. This is the easiest way to clear a plot if you can afford to wait a year.

Spraying A quick method is to use a systemic weedkiller such as glyphosate to kill weeds. This travels down to the roots and kills the weeds within a few weeks. You may need to apply the weedkiller more than once if the weeds re-grow. Glyphosate breaks down rapidly on contact with the soil so you will be able to plant within weeks. To improve the effectiveness of glyphosate, cut the weeds back, wait for a flush of young growth, then spray. The ideal time to treat weeds with systemic weedkiller is in late spring to early summer, when the weeds are growing rapidly. Take care to avoid spray drifting on to other plants.

Digging The traditional method of clearing a new vegetable plot is to dig it over and remove every piece of perennial weed root by hand. It is very time-consuming but if done thoroughly should remove most

Dutch hoe – good for annual weeds

perennial weeds. Deep-rooting weeds such as bindweed will need persistent removal over several years.

Keeping beds weed-free

Once you have cleared the beds of perennial weeds, you will still need to be vigilant. Annual weeds produce seed in vast quantities, and these lie dormant in the soil for many years. Cultivating the soil by digging will bring weed seeds to the surface, where they will germinate, grow and set more seed. Some annual weeds, such as chickweed, flower and set seed remarkably quickly, so it is vital to control them promptly. You can keep weeds down in several ways.

Loose mulches will prevent light reaching weed seeds and triggering germination. Covering the soil surface with a 5cm layer of loose mulch is recommended. Garden compost can be used, provided it is weed-free; well-rotted farmyard manure or composted green waste are economical alternatives

Draw hoe – used for chopping weeds

Hand weeding

A quick way to get rid of annual weeds before sowing or planting is to prepare the seedbed and cover it with a cloche or sheet of clear plastic. Weeds will germinate within a couple of weeks and can be hoed off.

Hand weeding is the best way to remove weeds growing in amongst rows of seedlings or in other confined spaces. You can pull up annual weeds with your finger and thumb. Remove perennial weeds with their roots, otherwise they will simply regrow. A hand fork can be used to ease them out, and a number of short-handled tools are available, such as onion hoes. Hand weeding is most effective if done when the soil is moist, when weeds are young and before they set seed.

for a vegetable plot. For an ornamental border, chipped bark or cocoa shells are attractive but rather expensive.

Sheet mulches are another way to keep beds and paths weed-free (see illustration, right). The sheet is laid over the soil and the edges secured. Sheet mulches are effective at keeping paths between beds weed-free in the long term. Use them on their own or under paving or gravel. Widely spaced crops such as courgettes, sweetcorn and potatoes can be grown through sheet mulch – cut a cross in the sheet, fold back the four triangular flaps, dig a hole and plant. Woven polypropylene sheet mulch is easy to handle and allows water through; black plastic is cheaper but you will need to put some holes in with a garden fork, otherwise rain will collect in puddles on the top. Double layers of newspaper work in the short term.

Hoeing is an excellent way to get rid of small annual weeds and is particularly useful for closely-spaced vegetables where mulching is not practical. As soon as a seedbed is prepared or the ground is dug over, a flush of annual weeds will appear. Even if these are removed, any soil left empty will be quickly taken over

by weeds. Use a Dutch hoe for weeding between rows or a swoe (this has a blade shaped like an elongated golf club) among wider-spaced vegetables. Keep the blade sharp so it skims along the surface of the soil, severing the weeds. The most effective time to hoe is early in the morning on a hot, dry day, when the hoed weeds will quickly shrivel up.

Essential tools

Dutch hoe or swoe
Hand fork
Hand weeders, e.g. onion hoe

Planting a courgette through plastic mulch

CONTROLLING PESTS

Plastic mesh keeps out many pests

Use an insecticide spray as a last resort

The pleasure of growing your own produce can be short-lived if slugs or rabbits get to your crops before you do, and greenfly on a salad is rarely appetising. However, not every crop gets ravaged by pests and diseases each year. In most cases, using barriers to prevent pests reaching the crop, and keeping an eye on plants so you can tackle pest or disease outbreaks early on, are the only regular steps you need to take.

Barriers
Early in the year, a layer of garden fleece will protect young plants from flying insects such as aphids, carrot fly and cabbage white butterflies. Later, in the summer, crops under fleece can scorch, so use very fine plastic netting instead. Both are easy to use if draped over hoops of stiff wire, as this gives the crop room to grow. Weigh down or secure the edges so pests cannot get in. Crop covers can be washed and re-used but check them over for holes at the start of the season.

Not all gardens are afflicted with pests such as pigeons or rabbits, but those that are will need protection. Pigeon netting is draped over supports to protect overwintering crops. Rabbits can be kept out by installing a barrier of chicken wire fencing 1m high above ground and buried 30cm below the surface.

Using pesticides
Pesticide is a term used to cover a number of products including fungicides that deal with diseases and insecticides that combat insect pests. As long as you follow the instructions, they are safe to use. Pay particular attention to the dilution rate, note which pest or disease they are recommended for and follow any advice on how long to wait before harvesting after spraying. Note that some pesticides are not suitable for edible crops or particular plants. Spray in the evening if possible to avoid harming pollinating insects.

You can buy pesticides in a ready-to-use form such as a spray gun. These are convenient to use but can work out expensive for a vegetable plot. Buying a concentrate that you dilute and apply with a pressure sprayer is more economical. Some insecticides are applied as a dust.

Organic gardeners prefer not to use pesticides at all, although some are used as a last resort (see pages 42–3).

Slugs and snails
A combination of vigilance and timely control methods should help to keep young crops safe from slugs and snails. Attacks are worse in the mild, damp periods of spring and autumn, and seedlings and young leafy crops are most vulnerable. Slug pellets are a popular control method as they are cheap and easy to apply. *Gardening Which?* trials have found them to be effective against slugs and snails. Nearly all slug pellets available to gardeners contain metaldehyde; this breaks down fairly rapidly, leaving very little soil residue. In addition, to limit the impact of slug pellets on wildlife, they contain

Crushed rock slug barrier

Sections of plastic bottle will deter surface slugs

an animal repellent and are coloured blue to deter birds. Scatter the pellets sparingly around the plants and re-apply after two weeks, sooner if it rains. For anyone with a sizeable vegetable plot, the low cost of pellets compared with other treatments is persuasive: alternatives cost over eight times as much per square metre.

Liquid slug controls will kill the small black slugs that live in the soil and there are no visible pellets to worry about. One liquid, based on metaldehyde, worked well in *Gardening Which?* trials, but those containing aluminium sulphate work out very expensive for vegetable growing.

A biological control based on nematode worms was effective for six weeks against slugs if applied before planting.

Young plants can be protected from surface slugs with rings cut from plastic bottles (see illustration above). Cut sections 10cm high and push them 2–3cm into the ground.

A promising new barrier method is powdered Australian rock. It was effective in *Gardening Which?* trials when applied as a continuous barrier about 8cm wide. Copper tape is worth trying around containers or small raised beds.

An entirely organic method is to visit the vegetable plot at night with a torch. Collect any slugs and snails you spot; repeat the visits several times to reduce the slug and snail population.

Aphids

Greenfly and blackfly are just a couple of the 500 or so aphids found in gardens. All aphids breed prodigiously and suck the sap from plants. Plants are weakened, and the yield can be affected. In addition, some aphids spread viruses from one plant to another, for example, mosaic virus can be introduced into a courgette plant, with fatal results.

Most insecticides kill aphids either on contact or by being absorbed into the plant sap and killing aphids that feed on the sap. Alternatives are to rely on natural predators such as birds and insects to eat aphids, or to use a crop cover.

Controlling diseases

With the exception of potato blight and clubroot, which can be prevented by pre-emptive fungicide sprays or liming, respectively, the gardener's options are limited. Vigilance, combined with scrupulous hygiene and good husbandry, will help. Advice on specific problems can be found in most entries in the A–Z of Vegetables.

GROWING ORGANICALLY

One of the best reasons for growing your own vegetables is that you can be absolutely sure how they have been grown and what has been sprayed on them. The aim of organic gardening is to work with nature, rather than trying to control it. So relying on natural predators to keep down pests plays a large part. There is little point trying to grow your vegetables organically if you regularly use aphid sprays on your flowers as you will remove the natural predators' source of food. Anything you can do to encourage a wide range of wildlife into the garden – by creating favourable habitats such as ponds, meadows and hedgerows, for example – will make it more likely that natural predators will help to control pests on your vegetables.

Feeding the soil

Organic gardeners aim to build up soil fertility over the long term, rather than supplying soluble man-made nutrients directly to plants. In practice, this means adding plenty of organic matter and caring for the soil in the ways outlined on pages 30–7. In addition, you might want to consider where manures have come from: for example, an organic farm rather than a conventional one.

Another environmental concern is that the nutrients are washed out of manure and garden compost while they are being stored and once they have been applied to the soil. In the past, nutrient-rich organic matter such as manure was applied during winter digging, but there is now a move to delay putting it on until after the winter rains. If applied in spring just before sowing or planting, or in summer to growing crops, the plants will benefit from the nutrients.

It is now recommended that more care is taken over the amount of manure applied: no more than about one barrow-load of manure or two barrow-loads of garden compost to ten square metres of ground each year. If you follow a crop-rotation system (see pages 36–7), apply manure to the crops that benefit most.

Organic fertilisers

If you do not have sufficient garden compost or bulky organic matter, you can use concentrated fertiliser, provided it is of animal or plant origin. For example:

Animal-based fertilisers Dried blood is a source of quick-release nitrogen. Hoof-and-hornmeal is a slower-release form. Bonemeal is a natural source of phosphate. Blood, fish and bone is a balanced fertiliser, but lacks potash.

Seaweed meal and **seaweed extracts** are useful sources of small amounts of minor nutrients or trace elements.

Home-made liquid feeds provide nutrients for plants in containers. Comfrey feed, for example, is made by packing fresh comfrey leaves into a water butt and collecting the liquor that runs from the tap at the bottom. It is the best natural source of potash so could be used instead of a tomato feed.

Natural predators such as ladybirds will help to reduce pest problems

Pest and disease control

There are many ways to prevent damage by pests or diseases:

- crop rotation (see pages 36–7)
- physical barriers such as fine-mesh netting and sections of plastic drink bottles (see pages 40–1)
- sowings timed to miss the most vulnerable period
- hand-picking larger pests such as slugs, snails and caterpillars
- encouraging insect predators such as ladybirds, lacewings and hoverflies, ground beetles, hedgehogs and birds, which will eat aphids or other pests
- in the greenhouse, biological control is an effective alternative to chemicals.

Acceptable pesticides

Generally, organic gardeners do not use pesticides, but some based on naturally occurring substances can be used as a last resort. Bordeaux mixture can be used to prevent potato blight.

Insecticides based on soft soap, plant fatty acids, derris and pyrethrum are all acceptable. Although these products are derived from natural materials, they will also kill beneficial insects, so should be used with care – in the evening when bees are not active, for example.

Weed control

Weeds are kept under control by mulches, hoeing and hand weeding. Not digging also reduces the amount of weed seed brought to the surface.

Green manures

Any ground on a vegetable plot that is unoccupied by an edible crop can be sown with crops that make up green manure. These are short-term crops that grow rapidly and often root deeply or fix nitrogen from the air. They cover the soil, preventing rain damaging the structure, and mop up any spare nutrients. When the land is needed for vegetables, the green manure is simply chopped up and dug in, so the organic matter is recycled back into the soil. They are particularly useful over winter.

A green manure crop of phacelia

Chopping green manure before digging it in

Green manure	When to sow	When to dig in (how long to leave)	Notes
Alfalfa (lucerne)	Apr–Jul	Any time (up to 2 years)	Deep rooting, cut 2–3 times
Bean, field	Sep–Nov	Before flowering (over winter)	Fixes nitrogen
Buckwheat	Mar–Aug	Before flowering (2–3 months)	Deep rooting, attracts insects
Clover, crimson	Mar–Aug	Before flowering (3 months or over winter)	Fixes nitrogen, attracts insects
Clover, Essex red	Apr–Aug	Any time (up to 2 years)	Deep rooting, fixes nitrogen
Fenugreek	Mar–Aug	Before pods form (2–3 months)	Easy to dig in
Lupin	Mar–Jun	Before flowers open (2–3 months)	Fixes nitrogen
Mustard	Mar–Sep	Before flowering (2–8 weeks)	Susceptible to clubroot
Phacelia	Mar–Sep	Before flowers open (2 months or over winter)	Easy to dig in, attracts insects
Rye, grazing	Aug–Nov	Before flowers open (over winter)	Deep rooting
Tare, winter	Mar–May/Jul–Sep	Before flowering (2–3 months or over winter)	Fixes nitrogen
Trefoil	Mar–Aug	Any time (up to a year)	Fixes nitrogen

USING FERTILISERS

General fertilisers: chicken manure pellets (in pot), growmore (loose) and blood, fish and bone (in trowel)

Vegetables grow fast compared with many other plants and need a readily available supply of nutrients while they are growing. Garden soil contains most of the essential minerals plants need for growth but the following three major nutrients are needed in relatively large quantities.

Major nutrients

Nitrogen makes plant proteins including chlorophyll, which gives plants their green colour. Lack of nitrogen slows growth and yellows the leaves; later, the stems may be an unnatural red or purple. The nitrogen used by plants is in a soluble form (nitrates or ammonium salts) so it is easily washed out of the soil during heavy rain. Free-draining soils such as sandy or chalky soils are most likely to leave plants short of nitrogen.

Phosphorus is important for growth and respiration. It is needed in the form of soluble phosphates for the formation of plant organs such as roots.

Potassium, in the form of potash, acts as a regulator in plant cells and also affects the size and quality of flowers and fruits.

Both phosphorus and potassium are usually present in sufficient quantities in garden soils. If in doubt, send a soil sample to be analysed (see page 30) – this will tell you if any is in short supply, as well as the pH, which can affect plants' ability to absorb nutrients. You can also ask for the soil's organic content to be analysed at the same time. The analysis should give advice on correcting any nutrient deficiencies.

Sources of nutrients

Organic matter added to improve the structure of the soil will also contribute to soil fertility. However, the quantities of nutrients present in organic matter is variable. Manure contains a reasonable amount of nitrogen; 1kg of cow or horse manure could contribute as much nitrogen as 25g of growmore. On the other hand, leafmould and bark chips contribute very little useable nutrient, and woodchips can actually remove nitrogen from the soil.

If you do need to add potash or phosphate, choose between the naturally occurring rock potash or

Herbs

Most herbs do well, often better, without added fertiliser. Just fork in some garden compost or leafmould when planting. Herbs in containers of compost will survive most of the season without additional feeding unless you are harvesting them in handfuls, in which case a dilute general liquid feed will encourage new growth.

bonemeal, which are acceptable to organic gardeners, or the man-made sulphate of potash or superphosphate.

The organic approach is to feed the soil with organic matter rather than rely on fertilisers. If your soil is low in nutrients and you cannot add sufficient

Making up a liquid feed

organic matter, fertilisers offer a quick and easy way to supply your plants' needs. It is important to supply sufficient fertilisers for heavy feeders, such as brassicas and maincrop potatoes, but not too much as nutrients can be washed out of the soil by rain and contribute to pollution.

Types of fertiliser

Balanced or **general fertilisers** contain more or less equal amounts of nitrogen, phosphate and potash. Examples of widely used balanced fertilisers include: growmore and blood, fish and bone. To find out if a fertiliser is balanced and what percentage nitrogen it contains, look on the packet for the nutrient ratio expressed as $N:P_2O_5:K_2O$ (nitrogen:phosphate:potash) – growmore has a ratio of 7:7:7. Balanced fertilisers promote general all-round growth but are especially useful for leafy crops.

Straight fertilisers add just one nutrient, so, if your soil has plenty of phosphorus and potash you can top

Applying fertiliser

up the nitrogen level annually by applying sulphate of ammonia or nitrochalk. Both of these add 21 per cent nitrogen, but nitrochalk is more useful for vegetable growing as it contains lime and so does not lower the soil pH.

Organic fertilisers are derived from plants or animals. Balanced fertilisers you may come across are pelleted chicken manure and blood, fish and bone (this often has extra potash added). Organic straight nitrogen fertilisers are dried blood or hoof and horn, both with 13 per cent nitrogen.

Applying fertiliser

Most fertilisers are sold as **powders** or **granules**. Rather than apply all the fertiliser to the growing vegetable in one go, spread the dose throughout the growing season. Typically, about half the amount is raked or forked into the soil before sowing or planting. The rest is then applied when the crop is halfway to maturity.

Liquid feeds are essential for crops growing in containers (see pages 12–13) or for getting nutrients to plants quickly. Liquid feeds for leafy crops are balanced, e.g. liquid growmore, but the most widely sold liquid fertiliser is tomato feed, which is high in potash to encourage fruit production.

Minor nutrients

The only other nutrient to worry about is magnesium. Lack of this shows up as yellowing between the veins on leaves of tomatoes, especially growing in containers. Look for a tomato feed which includes magnesium or water with a solution of Epsom salts (about 200g to 10 litres of water). Liquid feeds or fertilisers containing seaweed extract are a good source of all the other minor elements, manganese, boron and so on.

How much fertiliser?

For garden soil low in organic matter, apply fertiliser at the rates given below. For soils with plenty of organic matter, apply about half. The amounts given are for growmore (7 per cent N) but you can adjust these figures for other fertilisers, e.g. for nitrochalk (21 per cent N) divide the amounts by three.

High fertiliser requirement

Chalky or sandy soil 210–350g per sq m. Clay or loam soil 140–180g per sq m.

Beetroot, Brussels sprouts, cabbages (summer/winter), cauliflower, potatoes (maincrop), oriental vegetables, spinach

Medium fertiliser requirement

Chalky or sandy soil 180–210g per sq m. Clay or loam soil 90–140g per sq m.

Artichokes, asparagus, broccoli, cabbages (spring), calabrese, celery, chicory, French beans, garlic, kale, leeks, lettuces, onions, parsnips, potatoes (early), rhubarb, runner beans, salad leaves, shallots

Low fertiliser requirement

Chalky or sandy soil 70–140g per sq m. Clay or loam soil 35–70g per sq m.

Broad beans, Florence fennel, swede, turnips, sweetcorn

The following fruiting crops have a low nitrogen requirement but are fed diluted tomato feed to provide potash for fruiting.

Aubergines, courgettes, cucumbers, marrows, peppers, pumpkins, squashes, tomatoes

No fertiliser required

Carrots, peas, radishes

SENSIBLE WATERING

Some vegetables can crop even in a dry summer, while others need water throughout their growing season or at key stages for worthwhile yields. To cut down on the work and waste, concentrate on watering those crops that will benefit most.

What needs watering?

Vegetables can be divided into three main groups according to how much water they need (see box on page 47).

1 Vegetables that show no real benefit from watering once established. Some may produce excessive leaves at the expense of edible roots if they are watered too often. Water only at the seedling or young plant stage.

2 Vegetables that benefit from watering at a key stage in their growth, for example when they are producing fruits, pods or tubers. Watering before this will encourage only leafy growth.

3 Vegetables that benefit from regular watering in dry weather to produce lush or succulent leaves or stems. Even these need a generous soaking only once a week rather than more frequent light sprinklings.

How much water?

After several weeks without rain, the soil surface will appear dry. However, before watering, dig a hole 13–15cm down. The chances are, particularly if you have used a mulch, that the soil lower down will feel damp and so will not need water. Soils that are dry 13–15cm down will need watering.

The amount of water needed for most vegetables in the second two groups is 22 litres per sq m once a week. To convert this to a length of row,

French beans will benefit from a thorough soaking when pods are setting

Water leafy crops in well

divide one metre by the inter-row spacing for that crop – giving you the length of row to receive that quantity of water, e.g. lettuces with inter-row spacings of 30cm need 22 litres for every 3.3m length of row.

Water shortages

Water companies sometimes ban the use of sprinklers and hosepipes when water is in short supply, and some parts of the UK are particularly vulnerable. As a precaution, use an old water tank or barrel as a water reservoir near the vegetable plot. Keep it topped up before bans are imposed. During a water shortage, you can use cooled bath water and washing-up water as long as it is not too greasy. Water the ground and avoid getting it on the leaves.

How to reduce watering

● Increase the water-holding ability of your soil either by adding organic matter as a mulch in spring or by making a trench (see page 34) the autumn before. In a drought, avoid digging the soil, as doing so will just dry it out further.

● Adding plastic sheet mulch for widely spaced crops such as sweetcorn will help to conserve moisture.

● Hoeing will keep the surface of the soil dry and prevent evaporation from deeper in the soil.

● Draw up a ridge of soil around widely spaced crops. This helps water run into the ground rather than off the surface.

● Use funnels (made from plastic drinks bottles with their bottoms cut off) buried in the ground to direct water to the roots of crops (see illustration below).

● All vegetables in containers need to be watered. Move the plants to lightly shaded positions during periods of drought. Grouping them together and fitting them with automatic watering systems will help reduce the work.

Watering options

Young plants and seedlings can be watered using a **watering can with a detachable rose**, with the rose fitted so that the water comes out as a fine spray. More mature crops can be watered without the rose. Direct a steady stream of water on to the soil, giving it time to soak in. The average watering can holds 10 litres.

Lay a **leaky hose** on the surface of the soil. Water seeps out of the sides. Leaky hoses are more efficient than sprinklers as the water is not scattered on foliage and in the air. They are flexible enough to be laid in various shapes, so are useful for small beds. It is easy to forget to turn them off, so consider using them with a water timer.

When you are growing a lot of plants in containers (or in a greenhouse) and are not around to water them regularly, **automatic irrigation systems** are useful. These can be used on the patio or in a greenhouse, and consist of a network of plastic tubing with small nozzles or drippers for each pot. They need to be set up and checked to ensure they are delivering the correct amount of water, and can be automated by using a watering computer fitted to the tap.

How often to water

[1] Watering not usually necessary once the plants are established: *Artichokes, asparagus, beetroot, broccoli, Brussels sprouts, cabbages (winter and spring), carrots, cauliflower (winter), chicory, garlic, kale, onions, parsnips, pumpkins, rhubarb, shallots, swede*

[2] Water once, three weeks before harvesting: *Cabbages (summer), calabrese, cauliflower (summer)* Water regularly from start of fruit/tuber formation: *Broad beans, French beans, peas, potatoes (maincrop), sweetcorn*

[3] Water regularly, i.e. once a week: *Aubergines, celery, cucumbers, Florence fennel, leeks, lettuces, oriental greens, peppers, potatoes (early), radishes, runner beans, salad leaves, spinach* Water twice a week at half-rate: *Courgettes, marrows, tomatoes*

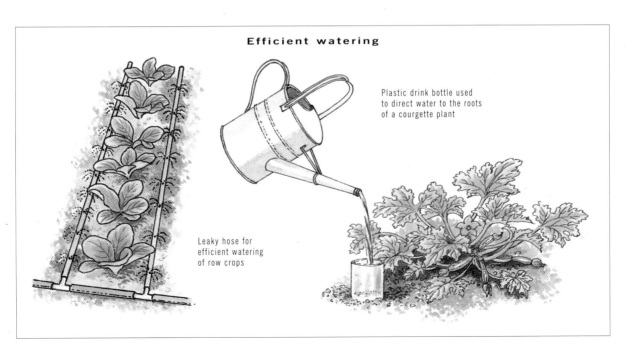

Efficient watering

Plastic drink bottle used to direct water to the roots of a courgette plant

Leaky hose for efficient watering of row crops

USING SPACE EFFICIENTLY

In a small vegetable plot it is particularly important that you use every space to its best advantage. Try not to leave areas vacant and plan ahead so that when one crop is harvested another can be planted out to reoccupy the space. The five main techniques for using space efficiently are listed below.

Sow little and often

Rather than sow all the seed from a packet in one long row, sow a small proportion of it in a short row, small patch or couple of pots and repeat this every two or three weeks. This will help to provide a longer harvesting season and avoid a glut.

Try to have young plants in pots ready to replace vegetables that are harvested. This is particularly useful in borders, potagers or containers, where gaps will be really obvious. You will need a holding area – a bit of unused concrete or part of the patio – where reserve plants can be kept until needed.

Double cropping

It should be possible to make efficient use of space by fitting two crops into the same area in one season. It also means that hardy crops which suffer from pests and diseases later in the summer (e.g. peas with pea moth grubs and broad bean with chocolate spot) can be replaced in mid-summer by tender vegetables that are generally pest-free, such as dwarf beans and sweetcorn.

Any crop that is harvested in June, for example, shallots, early potatoes, the first sowings of calabrese and cauliflower, can be followed by tender vegetables started off in pots. Courgettes, cucumbers, marrows and

A quick crop of lettuce occupies space between the rows of runner beans

squashes, tomatoes, sweetcorn and dwarf beans all fit the bill.

Later on in the summer, during July, overwintered vegetables can be planted to replace those harvested in early summer.

Early starters

Even the best-planned vegetable plots are likely to have bare soil in late winter and early spring. This is where cloches and the modern alternative, garden fleece, come in. By starting

the hardiest crops in February or March, you can be certain that you will be able to follow them with another crop in early summer.

Catch crops

Small, fast-growing crops can be used as temporary space fillers. Particularly useful are beetroot, carrots, lettuces and spinach, which can be picked immature. The following examples show how catch crops can be used to increase the productivity of an area.

Between slow root crops Parsnips are notoriously slow to germinate and take months to fill their allotted space completely. Use quick crops of radishes, spring onions or short-rooted carrots between the rows of parsnips.

Between large brassicas Even if you start them in pots or a seedbed and transplant them, Brussels sprouts, sprouting broccoli, autumn cauliflower and kale all take a long time to fill their space. Use a related crop such as radish, turnip or lettuce to fill the space. If you start them earlier in the spring you should be able to get a crop of summer cabbage, cauliflower or calabrese. In this case, leave sufficient space to plant the winter brassicas between them.

Before tender crops Tomatoes, cucumbers and courgettes are planted out after the last likely frost and do not fill their allotted space for a couple of weeks. Use hardy catch crops from March or April until June.

Between rows of runner beans Runner beans are not sown or planted until late May or early June in most areas of the UK, although the supports may already be in place. So there is plenty of time to grow a quick crop of peas, lettuce or spinach before the beans start to cover their supports and cast too much shade.

Between sweetcorn Even when fully grown, sweetcorn plants allow enough light through for a crop of lettuce, spinach, radish or spring onions to reach maturity. Sow these early and leave space to plant the sweetcorn later. You could even try planting dwarf French beans between the sweetcorn after the last frost. Or grow a crop of hardy broad beans and allow space to plant the sweetcorn among it. By the time the beans are cleared, the sweetcorn should

be well established and will benefit from the nitrogen fixed by the beans' roots.

Follow-on crops

By May, the vegetable plot is probably pretty full, but it is worth starting late or overwintered crops to follow those that will be harvested during June and July. All of them can be sown into small pots or a seedbed (see pages 50–1) and, provided they are kept well watered, will wait until you are ready to plant them out. The table below lists the best follow-on crops. In milder areas, you could also try overwintered peas (see pages 154–5) and broad beans (see pages 74–7). It is also possible to grow a second crop of early potatoes (see pages 162–3).

Best catch crops	When to sow	Time from sowing to harvest
Beetroot	Apr–Jul	8–11 weeks
Carrot	Mar–Jul	10–12 weeks
Chinese cabbage	Jun–Jul	10 weeks
Corn salad	Aug–Sep	12 weeks
Dwarf bean	May–Jul	8–12 weeks
Kohl rabi	Apr–Jul	8–12 weeks
Leaf beet	Mar–Jun	12 weeks
Lettuce	Mar–Jul	10-12 weeks
Onion, salad	Feb–Aug	8 weeks
Pea	Mar–Jul	12 weeks
Radish	Feb–Sep	4–8 weeks
Spinach	Mar–Jun	8–12 weeks
Turnip	Apr–Jul	6–10 weeks

Best follow-on crops	Sow	Transplant	Harvest
Broccoli, sprouting	May	July	Feb–Apr
Cabbage, autumn	May	June	Aug–Sep
Cabbage, winter	May	July	Nov–Feb
Cabbage, spring	Jul–Aug	Sep–Oct	Mar–May
Calabrese	May	July	Sep-frost
Cauliflower, autumn	Apr–May	June	Oct–Nov
Cauliflower, winter	May	July	Mar–May
Kale	May	July	Dec–Mar
Leek	Feb–Apr	July	Jan–May
Onion, overwintered	n/a	Oct	May–Jun

SOWING OUTDOORS

Check the soil temperature

Rake to produce a fine seedbed

Use a draw hoe to make drills

Some vegetables are always sown directly into the ground or compost where they are to grow, notably carrots and parsnips, radishes and spring onions. Most other vegetables can either be sown direct or started off in pots, then planted out.

In many ways, sowing straight into the soil is easier as it saves having to look after large numbers of small plants in pots. However, direct-sown seedlings are more vulnerable to soil pests and diseases so it can be risky for expensive seed. Also, you have to wait for the soil to warm up, and this can delay sowing.

Essential tools

Soil rake

Garden line (or two pegs and a length of string for straight rows)

Draw hoe (for making seed drills)

Soil thermometer

When to sow

Some vegetables are very hardy and can be sown outdoors early in the spring, while others are susceptible to frost and should not be sown outdoors until after the last frost normally occurs. Up to two weeks' extra growing time can be gained by sowing outdoors early under cloches (see pages 58–9).

Before sowing, it is worth checking the soil temperature using a special soil thermometer with a metal tip. Push the tip into the soil, to the same depth as you will sow the seed. It is the colder night temperature that is critical, so take the soil temperature first thing in the morning. Refer to the minimum temperature on the chart, right. When the thermometer shows this temperature consistently over a period of a week, it is safe to sow. Seed sown before the optimum temperature is reached will germinate, but much more slowly, and will be more vulnerable to soil diseases.

Preparing a seedbed

Remove large stones, weeds or weed roots and break up large lumps of soil, either with the back of a garden fork or using a chopping action with a soil rake.

Using a soil rake with a steady but gentle push-pull action, work the surface of the soil until it has a fine, even texture and is flat and level.

Set out a garden line or pegs and string to mark the position of the rows. Use the correct row spacing for each vegetable (see under the individual entries). When planting different types of crops next to each other, allow for the different spacing. For example, if one crop needs 30cm and the next 60cm, leave 45cm between them, so the larger crop does not swamp the smaller one.

Seed drills and bands

A seed drill is a narrow trough into which you sow. You can use a narrow trowel (a pointing trowel is ideal), a cane or stick, or the corner of a draw hoe or soil rake. The seed drill is usually 1.5cm deep.

Sow seed thinly

Space rows evenly apart

Sowing depths

Most vegetable seed should be sown about 1.5cm below the soil surface. Exceptions are:

4cm *broad, French and runner beans*

3cm *peas, sweetcorn*

2cm *courgettes, cucumbers, marrows, squashes swede and tomatoes*

out). Start by thinning larger clumps to one or two strong seedlings. Take care not to disturb the remaining seedlings too much. A couple of weeks later, remove all but one plant at about half or a third of the final spacing. For example, if the final spacing is 30cm, leave one plant every 10cm and pull two out later. With care, thinned seedlings can be replanted to fill any gaps. Thinnings of lettuces and carrots can be added to salads.

Transplanting

Some vegetables need so much space to mature that sowing them at their final spacings straight away would be a waste of valuable space. The following members of the cabbage family fall into this category: cabbages, Brussels sprouts, winter cauliflower, kale and sprouting broccoli. Leeks also transplant well. Such plants are often started in a seed bed, prepared as above but sown into short seed drills 15cm apart; the seedlings are thinned to 5–10cm apart. When the plants reach 15cm high they are dug up with as much root as possible and planted into their final position. These bare-root transplants may wilt at first but will quickly establish and grow to maturity. In dry weather, water the seed bed before lifting the transplants with a fork and water them well in their final position.

If the soil is very dry, dribble water into the bottom of the drill and allow it to soak in for a few minutes before sowing. Open the seed packet and the inner foil packet carefully. Tip some seed into the palm of your hand. Take a pinch at a time and sow as evenly as you can into the bottom of the drill.

Carefully draw soil over the seed drill to cover it. The soil should not need to be watered until the seedlings emerge.

Some vegetables, such as radishes, spring onions and peas, are best sown in bands rather than single rows. Use a draw hoe with a blade 10 or 15cm wide to draw out a shallow trough. Sow the seed thinly so that they are evenly scattered across the width of the band.

Thinning out seedlings

As soon as the seedlings are large enough to identify, start to pull out any that are surplus (this is called thinning

Minimum sowing temperatures

5°C *broad beans, broccoli, Brussels sprouts, cabbage, calabrese, cauliflower, kale, kohl rabi, lettuce, oriental greens, peas, radishes, swede, turnip*

7°C *beetroot and leaf beet, carrots, leeks, onions, parsnip*

10°C *celery*

12°C *French and runner beans, sweetcorn, tomatoes*

13°C *courgettes, cucumber, marrow, squash*

15°C *pepper*

Maximum sowing temperatures

Later in the summer most vegetables are unaffected by high soil temperatures. Exceptions are lettuce, which may fail to germinate above 25°C, onions and leeks above 21–24°C and celery above 19°C.

SOWING INDOORS

Sowing indoors frees you from the vagaries of the weather and gives you much more control over seed germination. A greenhouse is the ideal place to start off vegetable seeds. It needs to be insulated and heated to prevent the temperature falling below freezing, or preferably keep it at about 3–5°C. A coldframe is a cheaper alternative to a greenhouse for hardy vegetables that do not need high temperatures to germinate.

Tender vegetables are best started off on a warm windowsill where you can maintain a steady temperature of about 20°C. Ideally, it should get plenty of sunlight but preferably not full sun, which could easily scorch young seedlings. As the sunlight comes from one direction, the seedlings will bend towards it, so turn pots daily to keep the stems growing straight. Remember that if you draw the curtains at night, the windowsill temperature will drop considerably.

A heated propagator

A heated propagator consists of a plastic seed tray with a heating element built into it. This provides gentle bottom heat, which is usually capable of raising the temperature of the compost up to ten degrees above the room temperature. This is useful for a cool room without central heating, a windowsill that gets cold at night when the curtains are drawn, or in a greenhouse. A transparent plastic top keeps the atmosphere moist; the best have adjustable ventilators to increase or decrease the humidity.

The main drawback of a simple propagator is that you need to remember to turn it off on warm, sunny days.

Sowing small, expensive seed

Sow larger seeds thinly

Clumps of onion seedlings

Pull out excess seedlings

A propagator with a built-in thermostat will not get too hot, and with some propagators, the temperature can be adjusted to suit different types of seed.

Even the most powerful propagators will not be able to maintain 20°C if the room temperature drops much below 5°C, so background heating is essential in a greenhouse. It is worth checking the temperature in the greenhouse with a maximum-minimum thermometer.

Pots, trays or modules?

7-cm plastic plant pots are ideal for sowing most vegetable seed. Round pots are fine, but square ones can be fitted more neatly into trays if space is tight.

Modular trays are divided into square compartments and drop inside a standard seed tray. Those with 24 compartments are ideal for most vegetables, those with 40 will be more efficient for vegetables transplanted when quite small, such as lettuces.

When seedlings are large enough, pot them into individual pots

Sowing

Fill the pot with seed compost or multipurpose compost up to the level of the rim. Press the surface gently to firm it, so that it is 2cm below the rim.

Water gently, with a fine rose attached to the watering can, or stand the pot in a tray of water, to moisten the compost. Allow excess water to drain.

Sow small seeds on to the compost surface. Press larger seeds into the compost. Scatter loose compost over the seeds, leaving roughly 0.5cm below the pot rim for watering.

With expensive F1 hybrid seeds, sow one or two seeds per pot or module. If both germinate, you can either pull out the weakest seedling and throw it away or prick it out into another pot. With cheaper seed, sow a small pinch and thin out later.

Always label pots and trays with the variety name and date sown.

Pricking out

When a seed germinates, the first pair of leaves are actually part of the seed. The next pair to form are the first 'true' leaves and are more characteristic of the plant. Large seeds produce very large seed leaves and can be handled and pricked out as soon as they have fully opened. With smaller seeds, wait until at least one pair of true leaves has opened.

Prepare new pots full of firmed, moistened multipurpose compost for the seedlings. Use a dibber or something thin and pointed (a plastic plant label works well) to ease individual seedlings gently out of the compost with as much root intact as possible. Hold them carefully by the tip of a leaf, never the stem. Make a hole in the compost in

a new pot and drop the root in. The seedling should end up at the same depth as it was in the original pot. Push the dibber into the compost beside the hole to firm the seedling in. Return the seedlings to a warm spot to recover.

Potting on

Any vegetable that is likely to be in its pot for more than six weeks, or which grows very fast, is best transferred into a larger pot, say, 10cm. If the larger pot is also deeper, put a layer of compost in the bottom. Remove the plant with the ball of compost intact from the smaller pot. Do not pull the stem – put your hand over the top of the pot, with the plant stem between your two middle fingers. Tap firmly on the bottom of the pot. Drop the plant plus compost into the larger pot and fill around it with fresh compost.

GROWING VEGETABLES IN THE GREENHOUSE

Greenhouse, insulated with bubble polythene, used for raising seeds and growing tender crops

A greenhouse is not essential for growing vegetables, but if you want to grow a wide range of crops in reasonable quantities, it certainly makes life a lot easier.

Buying a greenhouse

Buy the largest greenhouse you can afford and can fit easily into the garden. Make sure it has several opening vents, preferably on both the roof and at floor level. Later in the summer, adequate ventilation is essential and a through-draught is important.

Stand the greenhouse frame on a solid base (e.g. 20-cm-deep concrete foundations). Leaving soil rather than concrete inside will make growing vegetables easier. When fitting the glass, try to ensure the entire greenhouse is airtight; any gaps will leak heat in winter. You will need at least one bench for seed raising and shelves for growing on seedlings. Ideally, benches and shelves should be removable to allow

crops to be grown in the greenhouse borders during the summer.

Electrical supply

Run an electricity supply to the greenhouse but remember that unless you are a competent electrician, this is a job for a professional. Take great care where cables are run across the garden. They should be buried, or run under concrete, and connected to a residual current device in the house. Any sockets in the greenhouse should be waterproof.

You can now run a heated propagator, which is essential for starting off tender seeds (see page 52), and an electric fan heater for background heat.

Keeping it frost-free

To grow vegetables throughout the winter, you will need to keep the greenhouse frost-free. The best way to do this is by using a thermostatically controlled electric fan heater to provide background heating. If you do not have electricity, use a bottled propane heater.

These are cleaner to run than paraffin heaters, and some can be thermostatically controlled. Set the heater to about 3˚C to ensure the greenhouse is kept frost-free.

If you use the greenhouse mainly from spring onwards for seed raising, you can screen off part of it with a curtain of bubble polythene and heat only that area. An electric propagator will not be able to maintain a suitable temperature if the ambient temperature in the greenhouse drops on cold nights. So provide some background heat and/or insulate the propagator on the coldest nights.

Fix bubble polythene insulation material to the greenhouse frame to help reduce heat loss. Drape a piece over the door and, if possible, run it across the roof space at head height to reduce the area to be heated. Start to remove the insulation material from the south side of the greenhouse in late spring to allow maximum light in.

Growing crops

The best place to grow greenhouse vegetables is in a soil border rather than on a bench. This gives them more headroom, which is particularly important for cordon tomatoes, and makes watering easier. The border soil should be enriched with a mulch of garden compost or well-rotted manure each spring. Rather than grow the same crop in the border year after year, alternate unrelated crops, such as tomatoes and cucumbers, between borders. This will help prevent the build-up of soil diseases. If you notice a fall in yield and the plants look unhealthy, you may need to switch to growing them in large pots or growing bags.

Growing bags contain a cheap and sterile growing media — usually peat, or a peat-free mix based on coir or bark. The flat shape of the growing bag means they dry out very rapidly in late summer and will need to be watered at least twice a day. Large pots are easier to keep watered than growing bags because of the greater depth of compost. Fill pots with multipurpose compost or the contents of a growing bag. Use a pot with a capacity of at least 10 litres, preferably more.

Both large pots and growing bags contain enough nutrients to support a vigorous plant (such as a tomato plant) for about four weeks from planting out, but after that, use a liquid tomato feed.

Automatic watering

Basic watering systems comprise a reservoir and tubing that trickles water into the pots or growing bags. More sophisticated systems are attached to a garden tap and feed water to plants via a network of thin tubing and adjustable nozzles. Some fine tuning will be necessary to ensure that each plant receives the right amount of water. Such watering systems can be completely automated with the addition of a timer or water computer. This means that even if you go away, the greenhouse will be watered each day.

Hygiene

Clear out the greenhouse once a year, in late autumn or winter, and clean it thoroughly. Scrub the frame and glass (including the gaps between the glass sheets) with a greenhouse disinfectant or hot soapy water to remove algae and grime. Cleaning ensures plenty of light reaches the crops but also removes overwintering pests inside.

Clean and disinfect all pots and trays used for raising seedlings, as well as

Lettuce and brassica plants ready for planting outside

the propagator and benches. Do this during the winter before the busy spring period. If you start the seeds in clean conditions you reduce the risk of damping-off disease. This fungus strikes vulnerable seedlings, which then fall over, often in patches.

If you can catch the disease early enough, watering with a solution of a copper-based fungicide such as Cheshunt Compound should prevent it spreading to healthy seedlings.

Other problems that affect greenhouse crops, such as aphids, spider mites and whitefly, can be effectively dealt with by using biological controls (see page 158 for more information).

BUYING PLANTS

When you want only a couple of tomato plants or a few lettuces for a container, it makes sense to buy them as young plants rather than raise your own from seed.

Most of the common vegetables are widely available in plant form, and the choice of varieties is generally good, especially for tomatoes. You may find only run-of-the-mill varieties in some garden centres. If you want new or unusual varieties, order young plants from a mail-order seed catalogue.

When to buy

In most garden centres, young vegetable plants are bought in and displayed throughout the spring. Like bedding plants, many tender vegetable plants are put on sale in March even though they cannot be planted out until the end of May. This makes caring for the young plants a lot more work than it needs to be as you have to keep them frost-free and will probably have to pot them on into larger pots at least once to prevent a check to their growth. However, if you wait until May before buying, you may be disappointed by the quality of the plants left in the shops. There is also the danger that shops will have sold out.

What to look for

Plants that you might want only one or two of (aubergines, courgettes, cucumbers, marrows, sweet peppers and tomatoes, for example) are sold singly in small pots. However, crops such as lettuces, cabbages and sweetcorn, where several plants are needed for a decent yield, tend to be sold in strips of about a dozen plants.

It is worth shopping around, not just to compare prices, but because some outlets have purpose-built facilities to keep plants well-lit yet frost-free, while others display them in outdoor areas, where they may get frosted, or indoors where light levels are inadequate. By following the advice below, you can make sure you obtain top-quality plants.

Above A good range of vegetable plants from a garden centre **Right** An instant vegetable plot

Always buy freshly delivered stock, as plants soon dry out and deteriorate when kept in small volumes of compost for several weeks.

Avoid cauliflower and calabrese that can easily suffer a check to growth and bolt.

Look for stocky or bushy plants with healthy green foliage. Straggly or leggy plants have been deprived of light and should be avoided. Also avoid plants with unnatural, discoloured foliage; this is a sign of stress, frost or lack of nutrients.

Avoid bringing pests into the garden: greenfly or blackfly can gather in the young growth. Speckled cucumber and courgette foliage is a sign of spider mite. Yellow or crinkled leaves could also indicate virus disease – avoid these, too.

Avoid buying bare-rooted brassica plants to reduce the likelihood of introducing clubroot into your soil.

Aftercare

Hardy plants (lettuces and brassicas, etc.) can be planted outside straight away unless they were displayed indoors, in which case they need to be hardened off (for about a week) before planting.

Tender vegetables (courgettes, marrows, runner beans, sweetcorn) need to be kept in a light, frost-free place then hardened off for ten days before planting after the last frost date. If planting out is delayed more than a couple of weeks, pot on into larger pots or apply a dilute liquid feed.

Greenhouse vegetables (tomatoes, cucumbers, peppers, etc.) should be kept in a light, frost-free place, ideally in a heated greenhouse. They do not need potting on, but aim to plant them into their final pots or growing bags by May. Feed with a tomato feed if you keep them in the same pots for more than four weeks.

A coldframe in use

Hardening off

A coldframe is the ideal place to get plants used to outdoor conditions gradually, over a period of seven to ten days.

First leave the plants in the coldframe with the top closed for a day, then open the top slightly the second day but close it at night. Repeat this, opening the top wider each day until it is wide open during the day. Then start opening the top slightly at night, increasing this until the plants are acclimatised to outdoor conditions (the foliage will look healthy and the plants will be growing).

Instead of a coldframe, you could use a double layer of garden fleece and a sheltered paved area near a greenhouse or on a patio. Leave first one layer then both layers of fleece off for increasing amounts of time during the day, then at night.

Buying plants in summer/autumn

It is often harder to sow seed in summer than in spring. Firstly, you need to remember to sow late crops and it can be difficult to keep the soil or pots of compost moist in hot weather. Fortunately, several seed companies will now despatch young plants of autumn or winter greens in summer. This is a useful way to catch up and ensure you have fresh produce during the autumn and winter months.

Late-cropping vegetables by mail order

CLOCHES AND FROST PROTECTION

Warming the air and soil around plants means you can start growing crops earlier in the year and continue for longer at the end of the season. This is especially useful if you live in a cold area or have to cope with a cold, wet soil. As an example, a *Gardening Which?* trial found that soil temperatures could be 2°C higher under a cloche than outside, and this means that crops such as lettuces were about ten days more advanced. Cloches also protect plants and soil from heavy rain and wind.

The two main structures used to protect plants are cloches and coldframes. Cloches can be moved about to protect seeds and plants growing in the ground, while a coldframe provides conditions that are halfway between those in the greenhouse and those outside. It is used to protect plants prior to planting out. Garden fleece is now widely used

A Victorian lantern cloche

to protect plants from frost (see illustrations on page 59).

Both cloches and coldframes can be made of glass or various types of plastic. Glass and polycarbonate retain more heat than PVC or polypropylene. Polythene is the least efficient material. Enough light reaches plants grown under glass, PVC or polycarbonate, but light reduction can be a problem with polypropylene and polythene. Use cloches and coldframes in a sunny site and keep them clean. Plastics will scratch and discolour in time; paying more for a material that has been stabilised to protect it against ultraviolet light damage is worthwhile. Thin, unstabilised polythene usually needs to be replaced every year but thicker, stabilised polythene may last two to three years. Twin-walled polypropylene lasts three to five years whilst moulded polypropylene and stabilised PVC last five to ten years. Polycarbonate should last ten years.

Cloches

Put cloches in position two weeks in advance of sowing or planting, so the soil has a chance to dry out slightly and warm up.

You can buy a ready-to-use cloche or buy cloche clips then get your own glass cut to fit. If you have raised beds, it is well worth making your own cloche. Create a series of hoops (made from overflow piping) 60cm apart covering the width of the bed. Cover with polythene sheeting.

When choosing a ready-to-use cloche, consider the following points.

Match the cloche to your site. Only the bell jars and lantern cloches make

attractive features so these are the ones to use for borders, potagers or other ornamental areas. Other cloches are best in vegetable plots and allotments – most are designed to cover rows of vegetables. Some designs are prone to being blown away, so in windy sites look for a design that can be firmly secured to the ground.

Match the cloche to your crop. Small tent cloches 30–45cm wide are useful for getting seedlings and young plants off to a good start, but plants soon outgrow them. Tunnel cloches or barn cloches are a better shape for more mature plants.

A cloche should be convenient to use. It should be easy to tend the crop and to move the cloche. You will need to ventilate the cloche on warm, sunny days, either by removing the whole cover, taking off the sides or adjusting the panels or flaps.

Coldframes

A coldframe is like a large box or cupboard and provides an environment halfway between indoors and outdoors (see page 57). It is usually placed near a greenhouse. It saves you time as you do not need to keep moving trays of young plants outdoors during the day and back indoors in the evening, and so is worth considering if you grow a reasonable amount of tender plants (this could include bedding plants as well as vegetables).

Coldframes with an aluminium or wooden frame and a glass or plastic lid can be bought from larger garden centres or ordered from greenhouse catalogues, but d-i-y-minded people could make their own from recycled materials. Designs with sides as well as lids that let in light are better for cropping plants.

Garden fleece

Garden fleece is sold in packs or rolls and can be used in place of cloches or coldframes. Lay it over plants after sowing or planting or while getting them used to outdoor conditions. A double layer of fleece will protect plants from frost when the outside temperature is down to −4˚C. Fleece is more versatile than a fixed structure but it needs to be secured well at the edges and is prone to ripping. Remove the fleece once the weather gets warm. Top-quality fleece can be washed in the washing machine and re-used several times.

Extending the season

In the spring, if you use cloches, you can sow or plant a whole range of crops such as lettuces, carrots, spring onions and radishes earlier than normal, although you still need to check the soil temperature.

In summer, make an August sowing of summer lettuces in a cloche or coldframe. Start them off with the cloche ends removed or the coldframe top removed. Cover the crop when the first frost is forecast.

In autumn, cloches can be placed over growing crops to encourage ripening or to preserve leaf quality. For example, large cloches are put over tomatoes or courgettes in late September to extend cropping into the autumn. Cordon tomatoes need to be untied from their supports and laid on sheet mulch before they are covered.

Herbs such as parsley, chervil and chives can be covered to improve leaf quality. Likewise, hardy crops such as oriental greens, spinach, chicory and endive benefit from cloche protection from October onwards.

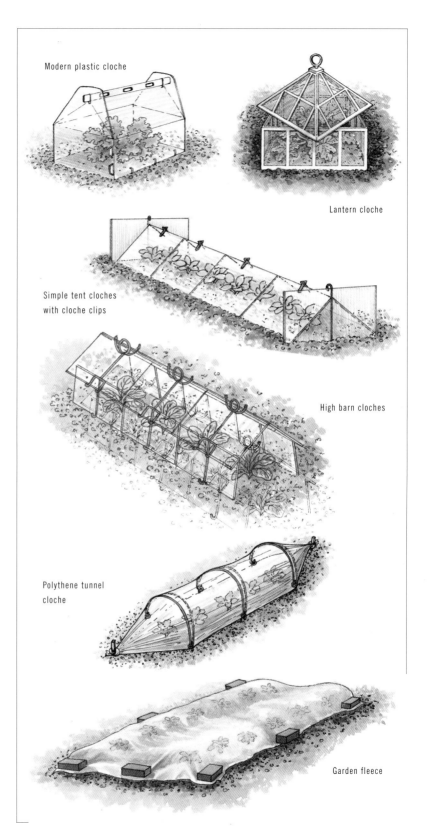

Modern plastic cloche

Lantern cloche

Simple tent cloches with cloche clips

High barn cloches

Polythene tunnel cloche

Garden fleece

HARVESTING AND STORING

What do you do if all your vegetables crop at once, or while you are away? To a certain extent, you can plan ahead to avoid gluts and holidays (see the calendar on pages 220–21) but most of us end up with excess produce, and it makes sense to store at least some of it, while retaining as much flavour and goodness as possible.

Harvesting

Set aside time to pick the crops that are at their peak and concentrate on eating or storing them while they are really fresh. If possible, water them the evening before and pick them when they are turgid very early the next morning. The second best time is in the cool of a summer evening. Once you have picked them, keep the vegetables cool; if you travel to your allotment, use portable cool boxes to transport the produce.

As soon as the vegetables are picked, their vitamin levels start to drop. The most vulnerable is vitamin C. This water-soluble vitamin is not only destroyed by cooking in water, but simply by being exposed to air and sunlight. Fresh vegetables will retain vitamin levels if they are eaten raw or lightly cooked, or are frozen on the day of harvesting.

Storing

Only store produce that is healthy and sound; any blemishes or softness will get worse during storage, and problems can spread to neighbouring vegetables. Most leafy crops can be stored in the short term (a week or so) in the salad compartment of a fridge. For longer-term storage, use one of the four methods discussed below.

Freezing

Plunging prepared vegetables into boiling water for a few minutes (blanching) is a worthwhile preliminary step for freezing most vegetables. Blanching kills bacteria and destroys enzymes that could, in time, taint food. A limited range of crops do not need to be blanched if they are consumed within a month or so. Once blanched, vegetables can be frozen for a year unless otherwise stated (see table below).

Aim to pick, blanch and freeze the produce on the same day. Put the freezer on fast freeze an hour before filling it. Prepare the vegetables as you would for normal cooking, i.e. clean and cut them into even-sized sections. Blanch them in batches of 250–300g in 2 litres of boiling salted water. Use a wire blanching basket so you can

FREEZING GUIDE

Vegetable	Blanch (minutes)	Comments
Asparagus	2–4	Pack in rigid boxes to prevent tips getting broken Use within 9 months
Broad beans	2–3	Blanching essential
Broccoli/calabrese	3–5	Pack in rigid containers to prevent damage
Brussels sprouts	3	Blanching essential
Carrots	5	Do not blanch, can be stored for 12 months either way
Cauliflowers	2–3	Add a squeeze of lemon juice to blanching water No need to blanch if eaten within 4 weeks
Courgettes	2–3	Pick young and freeze whole, use within 6 months
French beans	1–2	Freeze young ones whole, slice older ones No need to blanch if eaten within 4 weeks of freezing
Mangetout peas/ peas	1–2	Only freeze young ones. No need to blanch if eaten within 9 months
Peppers	3	Slice and freeze unblanched, use within 6 months
Runner beans	2–3	No need to blanch if eaten within 4 weeks of freezing
Spinach	n/a	Cook, rather than blanch. Squeeze out excess water and freeze in balls
Sweetcorn	4–6	Keeps 6 months after blanching (4 weeks unblanched)

FREEZING HERBS

It is also worth freezing herbs at their peak. Chop them finely and sprinkle into ice-cube trays. Add water and freeze. Use a cube each time you want 'fresh' herbs in winter. There is no need to blanch herbs.

move batches quickly in and out of the boiling water. Cool the blanched vegetables in a large bowl of iced water for a few minutes, then transfer them into freezer bags. Remove excess air, then seal and label the bags.

Storing dry

To store potatoes you need double paper sacks and a place that is dark and cool, but above 4°C. An outbuilding, cellar, garage or a cupboard under the stairs should do. Other vegetables that will keep in a dry, cool, frost-free place are onions, garlic, shallots, marrows, pumpkins, winter squashes and winter cabbages. Peas and beans can be left on the plants to dry out and then spread out on trays in an airy shed or greenhouse. When the pods are dry and brittle, crack them open and store the seeds in screw-top jars.

Leaving in the ground

Brussels sprouts, winter cabbage and leeks will stand outside until needed. Root vegetables such as carrots, parsnips, swede, turnips and, for a time, beetroot can be left in well-drained ground until they are needed. Mark the root crops so you can find them once the foliage has died down. Cover the soil with a layer of straw, then black plastic; this will stop the soil freezing and make the vegetables easier to dig up.

Storing in sand

Harvesting root crops in mid-winter is not pleasant, so put some of the crops in boxes of sand and keep them in a shed, cellar or garage. Remove any foliage and lay the roots on a layer of moist sand, then cover with sand. Put the large roots at the bottom as they will store for longer than the smaller ones.

Crop yields

These yields assume the crop has been left to mature – crops harvested young, e.g. early carrots, baby beet, will produce considerably less. For radishes and salad onions, expect a couple of bunches per metre.

Yield per metre of row

Beetroot	*2.5kg*
Broad beans	*3kg*
Carrots	*3.5kg*
Dwarf French beans	*1.5kg*
Leaf beets	*2kg*
Leeks	*3kg*
Onions	*2.5kg*
Parsnips	*5kg*
Peas	*2.5kg*
Shallots	*1.5kg*
Swedes/turnips	*2kg*

Some vegetables, lettuce for example, are not normally sold by weight.

Yield per plant

Brussels sprouts	*2kg*
Broccoli	*1.5kg*
Cabbages	*2–3kg*
(depending on type)	
Cabbages, spring	*0.5kg*
Calabrese	*0.5kg*
Cauliflowers	*1–2kg*
(depending on type)	
Courgettes	*15 fruits*
Marrows, squashes	*3kg*
Potatoes, early	*0.5kg*
Potatoes, maincrop	*1.5kg*
Runner beans	*1kg*
Sweetcorn	*1–2 cobs*
Tomatoes	*2kg*

A – Z OF VEGETABLES

Food for thought . . .

(from top left)

Dwarf French beans, in green or purple, are expensive to buy but can be grown in containers

Coloured lettuces are easy to grow and are especially good in mixed-leaf salads

Yellow courgettes and stripy beetroot 'Chioggia' make a change from the more conventional green and red

Sweetcorn is best really fresh and therefore worth growing for a late summer treat

Early carrots are a good choice for borders and containers and can be available fresh all summer

Fresh garden peas taste so much better than frozen peas; tall varieties can be trained as climbers

Round courgettes and yellow beetroot have novelty value, are easy to grow and productive

Red and silver chards are attractive enough for the ornamental border or patio containers; the stems are edible as well as the leaves

Mangetout peas are easier to prepare than garden peas and some can be used as decorative climbers too

Cherry tomatoes taste best when fully ripened on the plant and can be used as sweet substitutes for children

Shallots are a gourmet vegetable that could not be easier to grow; simply plant one bulb and harvest up to a dozen

All these and many more are described in detail in the following pages.

As you read through this A–Z of vegetables, you will come across the following symbols at the top of most entries.

Vegetables suitable for growing in containers. See list on page 13.

Vegetables that are attractive enough for growing in borders. See list on page 17.

Vegetables that are particularly suitable for beginners to grow. See list below.

Vegetables that give a high return on the area of ground used. These are ones to grow if you are short of space. See list below.

Easy vegetables

Beetroot

Broad beans

Cabbage (summer & winter)

Courgettes, marrows

French and runner beans

Garlic, shallots, onions

Kale

Leeks

Lettuce, salad leaf

Peas (mangetout)

Potatoes

Radishes

Rhubarb

Spinach (leaf beet)

Tomatoes

Turnips

High-yielding vegetables

Beetroot

Cabbage (all types)

Courgettes, marrows

Cucumber (indoor)

French and runner beans

Garlic

Kale

Leeks

Lettuce and salad leaves

Onions and shallots

Parsnips

Peas (mangetout)

Potatoes

Spinach (leaf beet)

Swedes and turnips

Tomatoes

ARTICHOKE

The globe artichoke and the Jerusalem artichoke are two unrelated plants referred to as artichokes. Both offer a rare treat in the kitchen, but also have a place in the ornamental border. Globe artichokes are statuesque focal points with huge blue thistle flowers. Jerusalem artichokes are less spectacular in flower but can be used as a tall temporary hedge for the vegetable plot or as a foliage backdrop in the border.

Varieties

GLOBE ARTICHOKE

Globe artichoke and cardoon are related to the thistle.
'**Green Globe**' is the variety most commonly available for growing from seed. You may also come across varieties with purple-tinged leaves and stalks.

JERUSALEM ARTICHOKE

These originated in North America and have no connection with the Near East. The common name is probably a corruption of the Italian *girasole* meaning 'following the sun'. It is a relative of the sunflower.
'**Fuseau**' is a newish variety, noticeably less knobbly and therefore easier to use in the kitchen than older varieties.

CARDOON

No named varieties.

Fleshy leaf bases

Blanching cardoon

CARDOON

An ornamental relative of the globe artichoke, cardoons are grown for the fleshy stem bases, which are blanched, rather than for their flowers. Established plants can grow to 1.8m in height and take up a lot of room. If you want to eat them, treat them as annuals, growing them from seed. Follow the growing advice for globe artichokes. Give them about 45cm per plant in rich soil.

Blanch them from September onwards by tying the tops of the leaves together with soft string. After six weeks, remove the blanched hearts and use them raw or cooked as you would celery. They are best eaten fresh.

Globe ready for picking

Digging Jerusalem artichoke

Calendar

GLOBE ARTICHOKE

FEBRUARY

Sow seed in trays in a greenhouse or on a warm windowsill.

MARCH–APRIL

Prick the strongest seedlings out into individual 7-cm pots when large enough. Grow on and gradually harden off the young plants.

Mulch established plants with plenty of well-rotted manure or garden compost.

MAY

Plant out when they are 10cm high. Globe artichokes need a sunny but sheltered site and a very rich soil. Allow at least 75cm diameter per plant and dig in plenty of garden compost.

JUNE–AUGUST

Keep newly planted artichokes well watered. On established plants, flower buds should start to appear from June onwards. A well-grown plant should yield up to 12 flowers a year, but will reach 1.5m in height.

Multiply your stock by taking offsets (sideshoots with roots) from the most productive plants and use these to replace existing plants after about three seasons. Although you can start more plants from seed, the resulting plants can be variable. It is much easier to take cuttings from the strongest plants.

SEPTEMBER

Flowers may form on newly planted artichokes, but these are best removed to allow the roots to build up reserves for the following year.

NOVEMBER–DECEMBER

Cut the dead stems back to the ground. Except in the mildest areas, protect the crowns with straw or cloches.

HARVESTING

Cut the flower heads of globe artichokes with a little stalk when the outer scales have opened flat. Boil them whole for 20-30 minutes until the scales are tender. Serve with melted butter or a hollandaise sauce. The best part is the fleshy base under the bud or 'choke'. The 'choke' is discarded. You can also eat the fleshy bases of each scale by scraping them with your teeth.

JERUSALEM ARTICHOKE

FEBRUARY–APRIL

Mail-order suppliers will provide small tubers. Plant them 10-15cm deep and 30cm apart. Larger tubers can be cut into sections, as long as each has at least three buds. Jerusalem artichokes are not fussy about soil and will tolerate partial shade, though yields will be better in an open position.

MAY–JULY

Jerusalem artichokes are good candidates for a temporary windbreak to protect more tender vegetables. However, in exposed sites, you may need to stake the stems or pile soil around the bases. When the plants reach 1.5–1.8m in height, pinch out the tops. You will not get the flowers, which look like small sunflowers, but this will encourage tuber formation.

SEPTEMBER–OCTOBER

When the stems have blackened in the autumn, cut them back to ground level, but mark the position so you can find them easily later.

NOVEMBER–SPRING

Dig the tubers up as needed. They should survive light frosts, but in colder areas, cover the crowns with straw. Try to remove every fragment of tuber, or you will end up with a thicket. Replant one sound, egg-sized tuber for next season.

HARVESTING

The tubers of Jerusalem artichokes look like small, knobbly potatoes. They have a sweet flavour and, unlike potatoes, contain no starch. They are difficult to peel when raw. Scrub to remove the soil and cook in their skins, removing these carefully just before serving. They can be boiled, baked or roasted and make excellent soup or purée.

ASPARAGUS

Asparagus is a luxury vegetable that is not hard to grow but does need patience. A decent-sized bed (one that contains at least ten plants) takes up a lot of space. If you have room for only a couple of plants, grow them at the back of a border to provide a feathery foil for other plants during summer.

Once established, asparagus will crop year after year with little effort, other than a mulch of organic matter. The fresh spears taste delicious when cooked straight from the garden.

PLANTING AN ASPARAGUS BED

As a very rough guide, ten established plants should yield about 3kg of spears over a six-week period each year for up to 20 years.

The simplest way to start a bed is to buy crowns in April. These are the dormant bases of one-year-old plants. The ideal site is well-drained, with neutral or slightly alkaline soil and free of perennial weeds. If necessary, create a raised bed. Dig in plenty of well-rotted organic matter – spent mushroom compost is ideal. Allow 45cm between plants and 90cm between rows.

Dig a trench or a hole wide enough to spread the roots of the crowns out. Lay the crowns gently on to a ridge or mound in the centre of the trench or hole with the roots spread on either side (see diagram, right). The top of the crown should be 10–13cm below the soil surface. Cover with loose soil. Asparagus will grow on the flat, though traditionally a ridge of soil 10cm high was drawn up around the plants to aid weed control, increase drainage and prevent seeding (not a problem in all-male varieties). Do this in the early spring, two years after planting and before you cut the first crop.

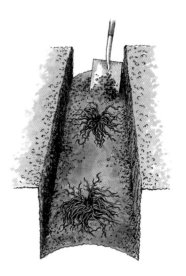

GROWING FROM SEED

Raising asparagus from seed is a cheap alternative to buying crowns, but be prepared to wait three years before starting to crop them.

Sow the seed in a seed tray in March. Note that seed of modern hybrids is expensive, so you may only get ten seeds. Maintain a minimum temperature of 24°C. After three weeks or so, prick the seedlings out into individual 7-cm pots and grow on at a temperature of 15°C. Harden the plants off and feed weekly with a balanced liquid fertiliser. Plant out in early to mid-June into the bottom of a furrow 10–13cm deep. Fill it in in the autumn and treat the plants as you would those from crowns.

HOW TO PREVENT PROBLEMS

Asparagus beetles are the only serious pest. The adults are small, yellow and black beetles with red heads. They and their buff-coloured grubs eat the ferns, sometimes defoliating and weakening the plants. Pick off adults and grubs from early May. Dust with derris, if necessary, to prevent serious damage during the summer. Clear plant debris, where they hibernate in the autumn.

Calendar

MARCH
Scatter a balanced fertiliser on established beds or mulch with well-rotted organic matter. The latter will also help to prevent weeds.

APRIL
The best time to establish a new bed or plant in a border is in early April (see left).

The first spears should be ready to cut in late April on established plants.

MAY
Stop cutting spears on two-year-old plants to allow the ferns to develop and build up the plants' underground reserves for the following season.

JUNE
Stop cutting established plants towards the middle of the month. Apply a high-nitrogen fertiliser to encourage the ferns. Plant out young plants raised from seed (see left).

JULY–SEPTEMBER
Keep asparagus beetle under control (see left). Weed by hand to prevent weeds, especially perennials, gaining a foothold. In exposed areas, vigorously growing ferns may need some support with canes and string.

OCTOBER–NOVEMBER
Cut the dead ferns to ground level.

Cutting asparagus spear

Asparagus beetle

HARVESTING
Use a sharp knife to cut the spears about 2.5–5cm below the soil. The white base can be trimmed off in the kitchen or used as a handle when eating. Spears should be at least 10cm long with a tight bud. Check twice a week, as they can grow very rapidly.

Asparagus is best eaten straight away, but can be kept up to two weeks in a fridge. (Do not wash before storing and keep in salad chiller.) It may be necessary to store spears until you accumulate sufficient for a meal. Asparagus also freezes well, if you are lucky enough to have a surplus. Blanch spears for 2–4 minutes, depending on their size.

Varieties

Asparagus is unusual in that it produces separate male and female plants. Male plants produce more spears. Female plants produce fewer but bigger spears and also self-seed which can be a nuisance. Hybrids are now widely available that will produce only male plants.
'Connovers Colossal' is an old variety that can be grown from seed or crowns. It is long-lived, but produces both male and female plants. It is not as productive as modern varieties.
'Franklim', 'Geynlim', 'Theilim' are modern all-male Dutch-bred F1 hybrids available as crowns. Try mail-order firms if you cannot find them in garden centres. You may come across seed of some of these varieties too. They all produce a good crop of quality spears.

'Franklim'

AUBERGINE

Although we now know them by their French name, aubergines were originally called eggplants – look at the small white fruits of the variety 'Ova' to see why. It is not easy to grow them in the British climate, but you are more likely to succeed if you live in southern Britain, or if you have a greenhouse or polythene tunnel. In high summer, the plants can stand on a patio where the attractive leaves and flowers can be appreciated.

Garden centres are likely to stock a few conventional varieties, but look to the specialist vegetable catalogues for a huge choice of exotic types – purple, green, white and striped oval, round and sausage shaped.

'Slim Jim'

'Long Tom'

'Ova'

Varieties

'Moneymaker' is the best variety if you want big purple fruits like those in the supermarket. In the *Gardening Which?* trial, it produced seven fruit per plant. 'Long Tom' and 'Vista' are other standard purple varieties.

'Ova' is well-named because the white fruits are about the size of a hen's egg. The crop may not be huge, but makes an interesting

talking point on a patio.

'Slim Jim' produces bunches of finger-sized fruits, like miniature versions of the typical supermarket variety. The purple-tinged foliage is attractive enough to justify its position on a sunny patio.

'Violetti di Firenze' is one of a growing number of exotic varieties finding their way into the specialist catalogues. Although low-yielding, it has spiny leaf stalks and purple-and-white striped fruits.

Calendar

MARCH

Sow two seeds per 9-cm pot. The seed is similar to tomato seed. You will need a heated propagator or at least a warm windowsill, where you can maintain a constant temperature of 20˚C.

APRIL

Gradually wean the seedlings, reducing the temperature to a minimum of 14˚C at night. If both seeds germinate, remove the weaker ones.

MAY

If you have not raised plants from seed, buy small plants from a garden centre and pot into larger pots.

As the plants begin to fill their small pots, pot them on into 2-litre pots of multipurpose or growing bag compost.

JUNE

Pot the plants on into 5-litre pots. This size pot should be sufficient to produce neat, manageable plants. When the plants reach about 20cm high, pinch out the growing tip to encourage them to branch. Vigorous varieties may require further pinching to keep them bushy.

This method worked well in a *Gardening Which?* trial. Aubergines can also be planted directly into a greenhouse border or growing bags and trained as cordons in the same way as cordon tomatoes (see page 199).

Remove the first flower that forms to encourage further flowers – and fruits.

JULY–AUGUST

Use split canes to support the main stem and each main branch, before the fruit starts to swell. During this period, you may need to water the plants twice a day on hot days. After the first flowers start to form, feed regularly with a tomato fertiliser, according to the manufacturer's instructions. It is also worth moving the plants out of a greenhouse to a sunny position outside.

SEPTEMBER

Aubergines are very sensitive to frost. If the fruits are still developing, move outdoor plants under cover at night.

HARVESTING

Pick fruits when they reach full size and have developed their rich purple colour.

Aubergine flower

Aubergine plants in a greenhouse

HOW TO PREVENT PROBLEMS

Introducing predatory mites on tomato plants

Aubergines are a magnet for greenhouse pests, especially spider mite. Maintaining a damp atmosphere by wetting the greenhouse floor will help to prevent **spider mite**. It is worth inspecting the undersides of leaves for the characteristic flecking and webbing, though the mites themselves are hard to see with the naked eye. If they do appear, use the biological control agent *Phytoseiulus*. These larger predatory mites feed on the pest and will deal with the problem for you.

After a few weeks new growth will be pest-free. Whitefly and aphids may also attack aubergines, and can also be controlled biologically (see page 158).

Outdoors, biological control is less likely to work, because temperatures fluctuate too much. Use a non-persistent insecticide spray based on soft-soap solution.

Aubergines also suffer from **blossom end rot** (see page 198). This condition can be prevented by regular watering through the hottest period.

BEETROOT

We are all familiar with the bright-red beetroot pickled in malt vinegar, but you can do much more with this versatile vegetable. It can be grated raw, roasted, served with sauces, and is delicious hot or cold.

In a small garden, beetroot offers variety, diversity and colour. There are varieties with white, yellow and striped roots, round roots for baby beet and long roots which are easy to slice. Beetroot is ideal for mini-vegetable beds, grows well in containers, and the leaves can be decorative enough for the flower border.

Young beetroot leaves can be used raw in salads and the older leaves can be cooked as spinach. However, if you do not favour the roots, you would be better off growing chard, a close relative of beetroot that produces fleshy edible leaf stalks rather than roots (see pages 186-9).

Left to right: 'Forono' (long roots), 'Boltardy', 'Burpees Golden', 'Albina', 'Chioggia' (striped)

Calendar

Beetroot is a greedy feeder, so grow it on soil that has been well manured over the years, or work in a general fertiliser (e.g. growmore, pelleted chicken manure or blood, fish and bone) before sowing.

FEBRUARY

Make the earliest sowings under cloches. Put the cloches in place at least two weeks before sowing to allow the soil to warm up. Follow the procedure below.

MARCH–APRIL

In milder areas make the first outdoor sowing in March, but continue using cloches in colder areas. By April it should be safe to sow directly outdoors in all parts of the UK.

Make a seed drill 1.5cm deep. Sow a short row and repeat at fortnightly intervals for a continuous supply of tender baby beet. If early sowings are allowed to become too large, the beetroot will be woody and lose their flavour. Space rows about 15cm apart.

If the soil is dry, dribble water into the drill and leave it to soak in. The seed clusters (see page 73) are large and easy to handle. Place one every 2.5cm or so along the drill. Cover with soil and water in dry spells until the seedlings emerge.

When sowing in containers, aim for a seed roughly every 5cm each way. Cover with a 1.5-cm layer of compost. In a border you can sow directly, as you would hardy annuals, or transplant multi-seeded beetroot (see page 73) as you would bedding plants. Work in plenty of fertiliser first.

MAY–JUNE

This is the best time to sow for a main crop for harvesting from August or September onwards. Sow as above, pull every other root as a baby beet and leave the remainder to grow on for winter storage.

Continue sowing short rows for a regular supply of baby beets. The first sowings are ready to harvest as baby beet.

JULY–AUGUST

Do not water beetroot unless the soil is likely to dry out completely. Over-watering will simply produce more leaves rather than roots. Watering or even heavy rain after a very dry spell will cause the roots to split. Water beetroot in pots regularly.

Make a final sowing in July for baby beets.

OCTOBER–NOVEMBER

Lift maincrop beetroots for storing indoors. Roots can be left in the ground, but remember that they may be attacked by soil pests, and since some of the roots project above the soil, they can be damaged by severe frosts. If you prefer to leave them in the ground for winter use, cover them with straw or soil to prevent them freezing.

Beetroot seedlings

Harvesting baby beets

HARVESTING

For baby beets, pull the roots before they reach golf-ball size. Take care not to disturb any immature plants growing nearby. Try not to break the thin tap root, or the beetroot will bleed. For the same reason, do not cut the foliage off. Twist the leaves off about 2.5–5cm above the root to limit bleeding.

To store maincrop beetroot indoors, place a layer of barely-moist sand in a wooden box. Inspect the roots carefully and reject any damaged ones. Lay them on the sand so that they are not touching. Cover completely with sand and start another layer, and so on until the box is full. Keep the box in a cool, dry but frost-free place.

Rinse off soil and remove the skins after cooking.

Varieties

RED

'Boltardy' is an old variety that is reliable for the earliest sowings. As its name implies, it is less likely to bolt (or throw up a flower shoot at the expense of the root) than some others.

'Bull's Blood' and **'McGregor's Favourite'** are both old varieties that have been reintroduced for their ornamental value. The leaves are bright red rather than the dark green of other varieties. They are excellent for combining with bedding plants and for edging ornamental potagers, and the young leaves could be used as a garnish for salads. The roots are likely to be disappointing.

'Pablo' is a modern variety with top-quality bright-red roots which have no obvious rings when cut. A good choice for baby beets.

'Forono' is a cylindrical variety – the one to choose if you prefer large roots to slice.

OTHER COLOURS

Avoid red beetroot juice stains by growing a white or yellow variety.

'Albina' has absolutely no colour, and although the cooked roots look rather anaemic, they are sweet and tasty.

'Burpees Golden' has golden-yellow roots which keep their colour when cooked. An interesting

'Boltardy'

'Albina'

alternative to red beet.

'Chioggia' is a very old Italian variety that has become popular again. The roots look unspectacular on the outside, but when cut open reveal concentric rings of red and white. Disappointingly, they cook to an insipid pink.

'Burpees Golden'

Sowing beetroot in a container

Multi-seeded beetroot in a modular tray

BEETROOT 'SEED'

The large corky 'seeds' are in fact a type of fruit, each containing up to four seeds. This explains why it is so hard to sow beetroot evenly! Breeders have produced varieties with a single seed per seed cluster which has advantages for commercial growers. These are often prefixed with 'Mon-' as in 'Monaco' and 'Monopoly'. They are more expensive and offer no particular advantages for gardeners. Sowing in clumps or multi-seeding is a useful technique (see below).

Beetroot seed clusters also contain a chemical that inhibits germination until it is washed out by rain after sowing. To give your plants a quick start, try soaking the seed clusters in warm water overnight before sowing. This will also give more even germination.

MULTI-SEEDING BEETROOT

Multi-seeding is a technique that works well with a number of root vegetables. The idea is that you grow 6–8 seedlings in a small pot and plant the whole clump out together. As the plants grow, the roots will push each other apart to produce a clump of small but perfectly round roots. Beetroot is the ideal vegetable for multi-seeding because each of the large corky seed capsules contains up to four seeds.

Sow two seed clusters in a 7-cm pot, 1.5cm deep. Keep the pots somewhere cool but frost-free. Beetroot germinates at temperatures as low as 7°C. Keep the compost moist.

When the clump of seedlings has developed the first 'true' leaves (the first pair of leaves are actually part of the seed) you can plant it out.

Dig a hole with a trowel and carefully tap the rootball out of the pot. Plant clumps level with the soil surface, 15cm apart each way.

HOW TO PREVENT PROBLEMS

Beetroot is generally pretty trouble-free, and any leaf problems should not affect the yield of roots. You may come across:

Leaf spot Brown, roughly circular spots develop on the leaves and sometimes the centres drop out, giving a 'shot-hole' effect.

Leaf miner Tiny grubs burrow in the leaf, causing transparent patches. Pick off badly affected leaves. Sometimes heavy rain following periods of drought causes the roots to split, so it is worth watering to prevent the soil from drying out completely.

BROAD BEANS

It can be difficult to buy good-quality fresh broad beans in the shops. But this needn't worry the vegetable gardener, as broad beans are easy to grow and, unlike runner beans, they are hardy, so there is the option of sowing in either autumn or spring. The dwarf varieties are free-standing so they can be grown in gaps in beds and borders where the blue-green foliage and white flowers are an attractive feature early in the season.

Broad beans grow early in the year, so they need an open, sunny site with shelter from strong winds. As their roots fix nitrogen from the air, they are a useful part of a crop rotation and can be followed by a greedy feeder such as one of the cabbage family (see pages 34–35).

ASPARAGUS PEA

This is an unusual but very decorative plant that would make an interesting addition to an ornamental border. It grows into a low bush covered in dark red pea-like flowers, which are followed by strange, crinkled green pods. These pods rapidly turn woody, so to taste them at their best, you need to pick often, and before they reach about 2cm in length. Like all pod-forming vegetables, as soon as the first pods start to set seed, further cropping drops off. Their small size makes asparagus peas awkward to pick, but steamed or lightly boiled, they have a pleasant taste, not unlike asparagus.

Sow the seed outdoors in late April or May, or start individual seeds off in 7-cm pots under cover. Allow 30cm between plants. There are no named varieties.

Calendar

FEBRUARY–MARCH

Make the first outdoor sowing in March, as soon as the soil is workable. You could start earlier in February by sowing under cloches or garden fleece. In cold areas, or to give the plants a good head start, sow seed, one per 7-cm pot, in a greenhouse or coldframe.

Before sowing or planting out, rake in a general fertiliser such as growmore.

On a vegetable plot, broad beans are usually grown in double rows with plants 20cm apart each way. A path of 60cm between double rows makes for easier picking. If you prefer, you can grow single rows 45cm apart, with plants 13cm apart. Broad beans can also be grown in a block, with plants 20–30cm apart each way. When growing a row, it is quicker to use a draw hoe to take out a seed drill 5cm deep. Sow more than you need at the end of each row. You can then transplant these to fill in any gaps.

In a border, plant informal drifts of three to five plants 15–20cm apart. Use a trowel, or push the seeds in 2cm deep with your finger. Alternatively, start the seeds in 7-cm pots for planting out later.

Broad beans can be grown as container plants by simply pushing four seeds into a 10-litre pot in spring.

APRIL–MAY

April is the last chance to sow spring-sown beans. In theory, it is possible to sow broad beans later for a summer or autumn crop. But in trials we found that these late crops suffered from severe attacks of chocolate spot, and yields were very poor.

Plant out beans that were started in pots, after careful hardening off.

Dwarf varieties do not need support but tall varieties may lean over, so a length of string along the rows secured by canes or stakes makes access easier.

Broad beans do not need watering before the flowers appear but it is worth hoeing to keep the weeds down when the plants are small. If it is very dry when the flowers are forming, a good soak once a week (22 litres a sq m) will improve the quality of the final crop.

JUNE

When the plants are in full flower, pinch out the top 10cm. This encourages the pods to form and reduces problems with blackfly. The first crops can be ready in June if you sowed in February or the previous autumn (see November).

JULY–AUGUST

This is the main harvesting time (see page 77). If growing in a border, plants can be removed after harvesting and replaced by late-flowering perennials such as penstemons.

SEPTEMBER–OCTOBER

On a vegetable plot, dig spent plants into the soil to provide green manure.

NOVEMBER

If you have a sheltered garden or live in a mild area, hardy varieties such as 'Aquadulce' can be sown now (or up to December) for an early crop next year. In a members' trial for *Gardening Which?* some gardeners succeeded with an autumn sowing of one of the new small-seeded varieties. This may be worth a try, but keep half of the seed for a conventional spring sowing in case the winter is cold and damp.

Another option in colder parts is to start broad beans off in pots under cover for planting outside in early spring.

Young plant ready for planting

Ready-to-harvest beans

Overwintered plants

Varieties

There are two main kinds of broad bean. **Longpods** have long, slender pods, each with up to eight kidney-shaped beans. These are the hardiest of the two types, used for autumn sowing. The second is **Windsors**, for spring sowing. They have short, fat pods containing four flat, round beans, and are said to have the best flavour. Both types can have either white or green beans.

'Witkiem Major'

'Stereo'

'Crimson-flowered'

'Witkiem Major' in flower

'Red Epicure'

'Witkiem Major' is a tall (1.2m) plant that is high-yielding and early.

'Aquadulce Claudia' is very hardy and the best for autumn sowing. It is 90cm tall and has white beans.

'The Sutton', a bushy dwarf variety reaching only 60cm, produces lots of pods containing three to four white beans.

'Red Epicure' has green pods but red beans. You can retain this red colour by steaming the beans, though they can turn yellow when cooked.

'Jade' is a small-seeded variety, but the beans have a uniform green colour that is retained throughout cooking.

'Stereo' and **'Optica'** are new varieties with normal-sized plants, but they bear many more small pods containing small white beans.

'Crimson-flowered' is a very ornamental variety with red flowers, that looks stunning in a border. The beans are green. To obtain the seed, try heritage seed catalogues, or contact seed libraries.

76

HOW TO PREVENT PROBLEMS

Blackfly breed rapidly and will eventually weaken the plant and reduce yield. You are likely to come across blackflies clustered around the growing tips from May onwards. You might also find leaves that are sticky and covered with a black sooty mould. Ladybirds and other predators may eventually control blackfly, indeed, they seem to decline from July onwards, but that will not help early crops like broad beans. Pinching out the growing tips once five flower trusses have developed will help. Using a suitable aphid killer or systemic insecticide is another option. Treat as soon as the flies appear and repeat if necessary.

Chocolate-coloured streaks or spots on the leaves and stems are a sign of **chocolate spot**. It is most likely to occur on overwintered plants during a wet spring. Plants that are crowded or on poor soil are the most vulnerable.

Broad bean rust looks superficially similar, though the brown spots are powdery and more likely in the summer. With both diseases, pick off and destroy badly affected leaves. Do not compost affected plants.

Occasionally, you may come across a few other problems at the seed or seedling stage. Have a few spare plants to replace any losses.

Bean seed beetle grubs can make holes in the seed. Once seed has been holed, it is a waste of time sowing it.

Bean seed fly maggots live in the soil and can damage the young seedlings. While you can dust seed drills with soil insecticide, it is easier to replace any lost plants.

Mice relish broad bean seeds. Traditional ways to deter them include dipping the seed in paraffin and putting layers of prickly leaves, such as holly, over the seed drills. Plants started off in pots indoors are less likely to be damaged.

Pea and bean weevil cut semi-circular notches out of the edges of the leaves. Plants may look ragged, but usually outgrow the damage. Controlling the pest using chemicals is not really justified, although you could use derris if the damage is severe.

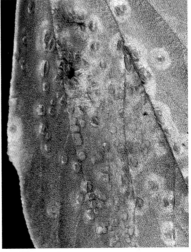
Broad bean rust

Chocolate spot

HARVESTING

Pick the lower pods first as they mature. For shelling, pick the pods when the seeds inside are just showing and are still soft. You can also pick the young, tender pods and eat them whole, like French beans. To test the pods are at the right stage for shelling, open one up and look at the scar where the seed is joined to the pod – it should be green or white. The beans are past their best if the scar is discoloured. Pull the pods downwards (try twisting them at the same time), but if they prove difficult to break off revert to cutting them off, otherwise you may damage the main stem or even uproot the plant.

Surplus broad beans can be blanched in boiling water and frozen. Any pods that are left to dry on the plant can be opened and the dry beans stored and used in stews. You can also save seed for planting next year (from healthy plants only). Note that they may cross-pollinate with other broad beans growing nearby.

BROCCOLI *Sprouting*

Broccoli is often used as a catch-all term for a number of vegetables, ranging from coloured types of cauliflower to calabrese. But true or sprouting broccoli produces lots of smaller buds at the ends of side shoots rather than fewer, larger heads. Sprouting broccoli is more of a 'cut-and-come-again' vegetable, so you can pick small amounts of it over a period of several weeks or months.

Sprouting broccoli comes into its own in the winter, when fresh green vegetables are most welcome. It needs a fair amount of space (each plant needs an area 60x60cm and you will need several plants) over a long growing season, so it is only really worth growing if you have a vegetable plot. However, it does occupy ground in late winter and early spring which would otherwise be unproductive.

Varieties

PURPLE SPROUTING

Until recently, there were no named varieties, though you could get early or late selections. Some seed suppliers offer a mixture which gives a spread of harvest dates from March to May.

Modern, named varieties and the even newer F1 hybrids produce better-quality crops, though the seed is more expensive. **'Claret' F1** is a late variety, cropping in April but with very good quality spears. **'Red Arrow' F1,** an early

'Red Arrow'

variety, crops from February. **'Rudolph'** is a very early variety that may begin to crop before Christmas.

WHITE SPROUTING

Again, until recently you had

the choice between early and late selections. Breeders have started to produce normal varieties, such as **'White Eye'** an early cropper, or **'White Star'** which is later.

'Early White Sprouting'

Calendar

APRIL–MAY

Make a single sowing of sprouting broccoli. Bear in mind that the plants need plenty of space, so do not sow too many. The seed should keep for several seasons, if resealed immediately and kept in a cool, dry place.

Sow two seeds per 7-cm pot. Broccoli is a hardy plant and will germinate at low temperatures, provided it does not fall below freezing. If both seeds germinate, pull out the weaker one.

Unlike calabrese, broccoli does not suffer when transplanted from a seedbed. Prepare a seedbed by digging over the soil and rake the surface to a fine texture. Sow the seed thinly into drills 1.5cm deep and 10cm apart (see pages 48–9). Aim for a seed every 10cm or so. Water the bottom of the drill if the soil is dry. Unless it is exceptionally cold, cloches are not necessary, though you may need to take precautions against slugs and flea beetles.

JUNE–JULY

Transplant the young plants into their final position. Water the seedbed or pots well first and try to retain as many roots as possible on bare-rooted transplants. Space plants 60cm apart each way. Until the plants reach full size you can grow a catch crop in the spaces between them (see pages 48–9). Lettuce, turnips and spinach should all crop before the broccoli plants fill out.

Broccoli requires a fairly rich soil with plenty of nitrogen. Depending on the previous crop, apply a top-dressing of a nitrogen fertiliser (e.g. nitrochalk or dried blood). Water this in if it does not rain the next day.

AUGUST

Keep an eye out for cabbage white caterpillars on the leaves. If you cannot hand-pick them all, spray with an insecticide based on pyrethrum, or use the biological control BT (based on a bacteria that attacks caterpillars but not other creatures).

SEPTEMBER–OCTOBER

The plants should be large and leafy as they go into the winter. In exposed gardens, earth up the base of the plants or stake them to stop them blowing over. Take precautions against pigeons, which can spoil the young shoots over winter.

Cut side shoots with the stalk

HARVESTING

Pick the flower shoots as they develop between January and May. The purple or white flower buds should still be tight with no sign of the yellow flowers. Leave the small tender leaves around the flower buds and the flower stalk, all of which are edible. Spears may develop over a long period from just after (sometimes before) Christmas until well into May. Keep picking regularly to prevent the plants flowering.

HOW TO PREVENT PROBLEMS

Sprouting broccoli can suffer from all the usual problems associated with the cabbage family – **clubroot**, **whitefly**, **mealy aphids**, **cabbage caterpillars**. See pages 86–7 for how to prevent these problems on growing plants. However, because the spears are produced at a time when cabbage white butterflies are inactive, they are never infested with caterpillars, unlike summer calabrese.

As long as the plants are big and healthy when they go into the winter, the only major pest is likely to be **pigeons,** which attack the young shoots. Cover plants with pigeon netting if this is a problem.

Whitefly can be a nuisance rather than a serious problem. Spray the broccoli with an insecticide based on pyrethrum. Wash spears thoroughly before cooking.

BRUSSELS SPROUTS

It is possible to have fresh Brussels sprouts from August until the spring, but it is as a winter vegetable that they come into their own. Brussels sprouts require rich soil and a lot of space. Since only a small part of the plant is eaten – just the lateral buds formed on the thick single stem – you need a vegetable plot for a reasonable yield. However, even in a small garden, a couple of plants can provide a useful crop for Christmas dinner.

Varieties

Most Brussels sprout varieties are F1 hybrids. These are used by commercial growers and have been bred to produce a heavy crop of small firm sprouts that can be picked in one go. Some people still prefer more traditional open-pollinated types, either for taste or for the bigger sprouts. Even among the F1s there are differences in yield, cropping time and sprout quality.

'Braveheart' is a reliable, tall variety, cropping from Christmas into the spring. It was the overall favourite in a *Gardening Which?* taste test and has sweet sprouts. It is resistant to powdery mildew and ring spot.

'Falstaff'

'Braveheart'

'Cascade' is a tall variety with a high yield of quality sprouts that crops from Christmas onwards. It is resistant to powdery mildew. **'Peer Gynt'**, an old F1 variety, still has a lot to offer as it is dwarf and crops early, sometimes as early as September. For sprouts that will crop from August to September, sow towards the end of February and protect with a cloche.

'Falstaff' is a dwarf, red-leaved plant with red sprouts. These lose their colour when boiled, and the yield may be disappointing compared to other varieties. But this variety makes up for it in ornamental value. **'Trafalgar'** is a recent introduction and the one to choose if you prefer a sweeter, milder-flavoured sprout. It crops in time for Christmas.

Calendar

Like all brassicas, sprouts prefer a neutral or slightly alkaline soil, which makes them less prone to clubroot. Do a simple pH test early on, because if you need to apply lime, this needs to be done at least a month before adding organic matter. For more details see pages 30–1.

MARCH

Sow seed from mid-March to mid-April for a winter crop.

For just a few plants, sow seed in 9-cm pots. You do not need a greenhouse; the pots can be kept outside in a sheltered spot or in a coldframe. You need to keep an eye on them to make sure the compost is moist but not sodden or dry.

For more than a dozen plants, it is worth using the seedbed technique to start them off (see page 79). Sow seed 1.5cm deep in rows 15cm apart.

Seed will germinate in 1–2 weeks. Thin the seedlings to 8cm apart or one per pot. Use a hoe to keep the weeds down and put up netting if sparrows are a problem.

Dig over the ground where the sprouts will eventually be planted. Add plenty of garden compost or other well-rotted organic matter. An alternative is to grow sprouts where you last grew peas or beans, as the roots of these plants use nitrogen in the air and fix it in the soil as a nutrient. This is beneficial to crops grown in that soil the following year.

APRIL

There is still time to sow seed for a winter crop so long as you do it before the middle of the month.

Prepare soil for planting if not yet done and leave the ground to settle.

MAY

The plants will be in the ground a long time so they will need feeding. Fork or rake in 100g a sq m of growmore, then tread down soil gently before planting. Early sowings should be ready for planting out by early May; later sowings by mid-May to early June.

When the seedlings are 15cm high they are ready to be moved on to their final planting site. Water the rows the day before and ease up the young plants with a trowel, taking care not to damage or dry out the roots. Dig a hole with the trowel and plant so the lower leaves are just above the soil surface. Firm down well and water them in well. Allow 50–90cm between the plants.

JUNE

Aim to complete planting by the beginning of this month.

Keep the ground around the plants weed-free and pick off any caterpillars from the foliage. A month after planting, a fertiliser such as nitrochalk can be sprinkled on the soil surface at 35g a sq m. This adds nitrogen without lowering the pH. Water in if the weather is dry. This is also the time to draw soil around the base of late varieties or to stake plants in an exposed garden.

JULY

Apply a second dose of nitrochalk and water in if the soil is dry.

OCTOBER

If you prefer to harvest and freeze sprouts in one go, cut off the leafy head at the top of the plant. This will encourage the sprouts to mature all at once. However, there is no reason to do this if you want to pick little and often. The leafy tops can be left and used as spring greens.

Net crops against pigeons.

Young plant

De-leafing a sprout plant

One plant per square yard (90cm each way) is the traditional spacing. You can plant modern varieties closer, at 50–60cm apart each way, but yield drops if you plant any closer, and you increase the risk of fungal diseases. If you are prepared to pick over a shorter period, try an early variety at 50cm apart each way.

Alternatively, use the space between young plants for another crop. Lettuce, radish, summer spinach, beetroot and early carrot will be ready before the sprouts need the space. In a border, a dwarf variety needs a spread of about 50cm and grows 35cm high.

Brussels sprouts can suffer from all the usual problems associated with the cabbage family – **clubroot** and **cabbage root fly** can attack the roots, and a host of insect pests and diseases can attack the leaves. See pages 86–7 for how to prevent these problems. The mature plants are top-heavy and prone to falling over (known as **lodging**). This adversely affects yield and sprout quality but can be prevented. A firm soil helps to anchor the plant, so tread it down before planting and plant deeply. Pile soil around the base of late varieties to anchor them. Only tall, late varieties in exposed gardens need staking.

Blown sprouts

Sprouts that are open and leafy rather than tight buttons are said to have 'blown' and do not cook so well. Prevent this by looking for a variety that stands well, digging in plenty of organic matter and firming the soil well before planting. Also, water during dry spells.

HARVESTING

Harvesting time is not critical with sprouts; they will stay on the plant until you are ready to pick them and most can be picked over a three-month period. Some varieties are particularly noted for their 'standing time', a characteristic worth looking out for if you want to pick little and often over the winter.

Harvest when the sprouts are tightly closed buttons. Starting at the bottom of the stalk, either pull them off with your fingers or cut them off with a sharp knife. While you are harvesting, you can also remove and destroy any yellowing foliage or open sprouts.

Picking sprouts after they have thawed from a frost is said to make them taste sweeter, but you can pick them before if you want to. In cold weather, uproot whole plants and leave them outside the kitchen door. The sprouts can then be picked off indoors when they are needed. Picked sprouts will keep for a couple of days in the salad compartment of a fridge, but if you have a lot it is worth freezing them.

CABBAGE *Summer and Autumn*

Cabbage may not be your first choice for a patio container or an ornamental border, but it can offer the gardener variety and colour in a number of attractive plants. For example, consider red cabbages with their mauve-tinged outer leaves and tight red hearts, or one of the many hardy winter cabbages (see pages 88–9). Both types tend to grow quite large, much wider than the edible hearts themselves. If lack of space is a problem, consider a crop of baby cabbages (see below) or spring cabbage (see pages 90–1). The latter takes up little room, keeps the ground occupied over winter and will produce a flush of tasty greens in the spring. It will also grow well in an otherwise unoccupied container.

HOW TO GROW BABY CABBAGES

Rather than having cabbages that are too big for one meal, you can manipulate the spacing of the plants to produce cabbages that are just the right size for your household's needs.

Traditionally, cabbages were spaced about 45cm apart, though 30cm is better for smaller modern varieties. *Gardening Which?* trials have shown that by reducing the spacing between plants to 25cm you can get perfect heads 8–10cm across. Reducing the spacing to 15cm will produce even smaller cabbages – around 8cm across. Although this technique worked for different types of cabbage, for the closest spacing use the varieties recommended on page 85.

To be successful with baby cabbages, you will need a fertile soil with plenty of organic matter. If you do not have this, apply a generous amount of a balanced fertiliser before planting or sowing. Keep the plants well watered and give them a good soaking once a week in very dry spells.

A baby cabbage

HOW TO GET A BONUS CROP

With summer and autumn cabbages, this trick is worth trying if you do not need the space for another crop. When the head is ready to harvest, cut it off, leaving as much stalk as possible. Make a cross-shaped cut across the cut end and about 1.5cm deep. Give the plant a boost with a sprinkling of a nitrogen fertiliser (e.g. nitrochalk or dried blood). After about six weeks, four small but otherwise perfect heads should have formed from the old stalk.

Cut a cross in the stump

Calendar

SUMMER AND AUTUMN CABBAGES

Cabbages are greedy feeders and will be disappointing on poor soil. They will grow well on heavy clay soil, provided it is not waterlogged, and especially if it has had plenty of well-rotted manure dug in over the years.

They also prefer a slightly alkaline soil. If yours is acid (check with a soil test kit from the garden centre) you will need to apply garden lime over winter to gradually raise the pH (see pages 30–1).

On light, sandy soils, an annual application of well-rotted manure or garden compost will help to increase fertility and retain soil moisture. Work up to 170g a sq m of growmore or a similar balanced fertiliser into the soil before sowing or planting out. Four to eight weeks from planting out, scatter a little nitrogenous fertiliser beside the plants and water it in if it does not rain (see pages 44–5). Reduce the amount of fertiliser to about half if the soil is already well-manured.

FEBRUARY

For the earliest crop, sow a quick-maturing variety in pots. The seed is easy to handle and the germination rate is high. Aim to sow one seed per 7-cm pot or one seed per compartment of a 24-module seed tray. Keep them in an unheated greenhouse or other sheltered but frost-free spot, and water regularly.

MARCH

Make the main sowing this month. Choose between a single sowing of an early, a mid-season and a late variety to provide a succession of crops, or monthly sowings of an early variety. Sow seed in pots as for February or start the plants off in a seedbed. In this case, prepare a small patch of ground, by forking it deeply and raking it down to a fine, level surface. Make seed drills 15cm apart and 2cm deep. Sow the seed thinly, aiming for one every 5cm or so. If the soil is dry, dribble water into the drills before sowing. Cover over with soil and keep the seedbed well watered. Watch out for slugs and flea beetles.

APRIL–MAY

Plants raised in pots or seedbeds earlier can be planted out now. They should be about 12cm tall, with at least four leaves. Water the pots or seedbed well and handle bare-rooted transplants from seedbeds carefully. Plant so that the base of the first pair of leaves sits on the soil surface, then firm and water in.

For conventional-sized cabbages, allow 45cm diameter per plant in a border or one plant to a 20-cm pot. In a vegetable plot, plant 45cm apart each way. Space smaller varieties 30cm apart.

Cover newly planted cabbages to prevent pests (see page 86–7).

Make a further sowing of an early variety, if you have opted for this method of extending the season.

JUNE–JULY

Harvest early varieties as soon as they produce firm heads. Cabbages in the open are now vulnerable to mealy aphid and caterpillars.

AUGUST

Mid-season varieties and late-sown early varieties should start to mature.

SEPTEMBER–NOVEMBER

Late or autumn cabbage varieties should start to come into their own. Most will stand well in the garden until you need them, but do not leave them if severe frosts are forecast.

Sowing directly in the ground

Planting pot-raised plants

HARVESTING

Cut heads when they feel firm and trim off outer leaves. Most varieties will stand outside until needed.

Varieties

'**Castello**' F1 is a round variety that matures in late summer and stands well until needed.

'**Derby Day**' and '**Golden Acre Primo**' are old but reliable non-hybrids that are both quick to mature in early summer and produce heavy, solid heads on compact plants.

'**Hispi**' F1 is a very early-maturing variety with small, pointed heads. It will not stand for long, but is a good choice for sowing little and often, or as a baby vegetable. '**Spitfire**' is similar.

'**Minicole**' F1, a naturally small autumn type with solid round heads, will stand for months until needed. It is an excellent choice for a baby vegetable.

'**Stonehead**' F1 is a summer-maturing variety with large, solid heads that stand well until late summer.

RED CABBAGE

'**Metro**' F1 is a modern variety with solid hearts that is ready in autumn, but can be stored indoors for winter use (see page 89).

'**Primero**' F1 is a small red cabbage, ideal for containers, ornamental borders and as a baby vegetable.

'**Ruby Ball**' is an older variety that matures in early autumn and will stand for several months until needed.

'Ruby Ball'

'Primero'

'Stonehead'

'Hispi'

Top Clubroot damage **Middle** Caterpillar damage
Bottom Check for mealy cabbage aphid

Cabbages and their relatives (broccoli, Brussels sprouts, calabrese, cauliflower, kale, oriental greens, swede and turnip) can suffer from a large number of pests and diseases. Fortunately, most can be prevented by non-chemical methods and good planning.

Cabbage root fly grubs live in the soil and feed on the roots of young plants. Severe attacks can stunt or even kill the plants. You can prevent the adult flies from laying their eggs by pushing young plants through cabbage collars (see picture on page 87). These are 15-cm diameter circles of flexible material, e.g. carpet underlay, which lie flat on the soil.

An easier method on a vegetable plot is to cover the whole bed with garden fleece, or fine netting supported on plastic hoops. Provided the edges are well secured, this will prevent the flies getting anywhere near your crop. It will also stop other flying pests such as the flea beetle, mealy cabbage aphids and cabbage white butterflies.

Cabbage white caterpillars feed voraciously on the leaves of all members of the cabbage family from mid-summer onwards. Check leaves regularly before infestations of caterpillars have a chance to build up. Rub off the tiny eggs or pick off the caterpillars (for the bird table). Caterpillars can be killed by spraying with a contact insecticide. One based on pyrethrum is acceptable in organic gardens. The biological control BT is a solution of a bacterium that kills caterpillars, but is harmless to all other creatures.

Clubroot affects not only all the edible members of the cabbage family, but related ornamentals too, such as wallflowers and stocks. It is caused by a fungus that can survive in the soil for up to 20 years. Despite feeding and watering, leaves of infected plants will turn red or purple and the plants will wilt on hot days. Dig up the plant and you will find the characteristic swollen and distorted roots.

While a three- or four-year crop rotation may help to prevent a build-up of the disease, once it appears in your garden this will not help to eradicate it. If the disease is restricted to one area, try growing members of the cabbage family on a different part of the garden. Be careful not to transfer soil around the garden, even on your boots. Destroy all affected plants, preferably by burning. Do not compost them.

Even if you have clubroot in your soil, there are several precautions you can take to ensure a reasonable crop:

● Clubroot is less severe in alkaline soil, so liming during the winter to raise the pH to 7.5 will help. Some gardeners take cabbage family plants out of the crop rotation and grow them on the same area year after year. By keeping the plot alkaline through regular liming, they manage to live with clubroot.

● Raise all plants in pots and pot on into 10- or 15-cm pots containing multipurpose compost. Plant these out; the plants should be sufficiently well developed before the roots contact the fungus, that you will still get a crop. Cabbages grown in containers should not be affected unless infected garden soil is used. Watch out for signs of the disease in ornamental borders; it will also affect related flowers growing there.

● No varieties of broccoli, Brussels sprouts, cabbage, cauliflower, kale or oriental greens are resistant to clubroot, though spring cabbage, which does most of its growing in autumn and winter, may avoid the disease. There are resistant varieties of calabrese and swede.

Flea beetles are small yellow and black beetles that pepper leaves with little holes. Seedlings and young plants are most at risk, in spring and early summer. Unless damage is severe, the plants generally grow out of danger. In severe cases, dust around vulnerable plants with derris. As the beetles hibernate in the soil, crop rotation combined with a covering of garden fleece should offer complete protection.

Leaf diseases that can attack the leaves of brassicas include:

Downy mildew appears as yellow patches on the upper leaf surface with a fluffy growth on the underside. It is worse in cool damp weather and is often a problem on crowded young plants. Remove and destroy badly affected plants. The remainder can be sprayed with a fungicide.

Powdery mildew appears as white powdery mould on the leaves, especially in hot, dry summers and when plants are crowded or suffering from lack of water. Water in very dry spells or, in severe cases, spray with a systemic fungicide.

Ring spot may occur in cool, wet summers, showing as large spots of concentric rings on older leaves. Pick off and destroy badly affected leaves.

White blister can also occur in some years, disfiguring plants but not generally affecting yield. Leaves appear splashed with small white spots. Overcrowded plants are most at risk – thin plants out and remove the worst-affected leaves.

Some varieties have resistance to one or more of these diseases. Crop rotation should help to reduce the risk,

too. Clear away crop debris at the end of the season and do not compost diseased material.

Mealy cabbage aphid can build up rapidly on the undersides of leaves or in the hearts of all brassicas from July onwards and especially in hot summers. The aphids are grey and covered in a waxy excretion, which makes them hard to spray with insecticides. Severe infestations will weaken plants and may also spread virus diseases. Unchecked, they can ruin sprouts and the hearts of cabbages. Spray plants, especially the undersides of leaves, with a systemic insecticide, or spray thoroughly with a contact insecticide based on soft soap.

Pigeons and rabbits relish the leaves of overwintered brassicas. Protect the plants by surrounding the plot with rabbit-proof netting, at least 1m tall and buried to a depth of 30cm. If pigeons are a problem, cover the crop with netting or humming lines. Make sure netting does not touch the plants, or pigeons will eat the tops.

Whitefly will attack all members of the cabbage family but are a particular problem on overwintered crops such as sprouting broccoli, where they can survive the winter to infest brassica crops the following spring. Light infestations may do little harm, but heavy infestations will cover leaves with a sticky excretion and a black sooty mould which grows on it. They will also reduce yields and can spoil sprouts. The larvae, or scales, feed on sap and are protected by a tough shell. Spray with a systemic insecticide or spray at weekly intervals with a contact insecticide such as pyrethrum to kill newly hatched scales.

Top Rabbit protection **Middle** Fine mesh to deter insect pests **Above** Brassica collars on cauliflower **Bottom** Ring spot disease

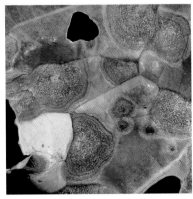

CABBAGE *Winter*

Winter cabbages are some of the largest and most ornamental of the cabbage family, and include blue-green Savoys and red-tinged 'January King'. Both are worthy of a place in a mixed border in their own right. Winter cabbages require plenty of space and a rich soil, but will reward you with a very heavy crop and are a useful source of fresh winter greens, too. They are grown in a similar way to summer cabbages, though they do not need to be sown until later in the spring. Some types are hardy enough to stand outside over winter, until you need them, while others can be cut in the autumn and stored indoors.

Varieties

You may come across three distinct types:

DUTCH WHITE

These are familiar as the huge pale-green balls you often see in supermarkets. They are best cut in November and stored indoors.

'**Holland Winter White**' is a large, round Dutch White type.

JANUARY KING

These varieties are prettily coloured and hardy enough to stand outdoors over winter.

'**January King – Hardy Late Stock No 3**' is an attractive plant with slightly frilly outer leaves and a flattened ball-shaped head, all tinged with purple. It should stand well over the winter.

SAVOY

These have crinkled outer leaves and are also hardy.

'**Celtic**' is a cross between a Dutch White and a Savoy cabbage. It is hardy enough to stand over winter, or can be cut and stored like other Dutch Whites. It was the best overall in a *Gardening Which?* taste test, with good texture and flavour, both raw and cooked.

'**Colorsa**' is an interesting newcomer – a cross between a Savoy and a red cabbage, with red-tinged, crinkled leaves. Plants should stand outside from September to January.

'**Rigoletto**' is a newer Savoy with very crinkled

'January King'

leaves. It is hardy and should stand through to March.

'**Tundra**' is claimed to be the hardiest of all winter

cabbages. The large, round heads should stand into April and had good flavour in a *Gardening Which?* trial.

Calendar

MAY

Sow winter cabbages, either in small pots or in a seedbed (see pages 83–4 for details).

JUNE

Plant out the young plants into their final position. Allow a space 45cm in diameter per plant, though in well-grown plants, the outer leaves may spread even further. Scatter a generous amount of fertiliser before planting. If the soil is dry, make a shallow depression, flood with water and when this has soaked in, plant the cabbages. It is worth planting a quick catch crop to occupy the space around them until they reach full size. Lettuce, radishes or turnips are all suitable.

Bear in mind that, at this time of year, pests are likely to be a nuisance, so cover plants straight away with garden fleece or fine netting, if possible.

JULY–OCTOBER

Watch out for pests and diseases (see pages 86–7). Water in dry spells.

NOVEMBER

Harvest Dutch White cabbages for storing indoors. Other winter cabbages will stand outside until required. Protect overwintered plants from pigeons and rabbits.

Young winter cabbages

HARVESTING

Cut the heads once they have reached full size and feel solid. Remove any outer leaves, and peel off damaged heart leaves to leave an unblemished ball.

Store cabbages on racks or trays, not touching, or suspended in net bags in a cool, dry, airy but frost-free shed or outbuilding. They should store for up to four months.

Above: 'Celtic'

Below: 'Dutch White'

'Colorsa'

CABBAGE *Spring*

It is possible to have fresh cabbage from the garden all through the year. Traditionally, spring cabbage (spring greens) spanned the gap from March to May, between the last of the hardy winter varieties and the first of the summer cabbages. You can also grow and crop modern non-hearting cabbages for most of the year, as a space-saving alternative to the hearting summer and winter varieties. In the garden, spring cabbage is a useful way of keeping the ground occupied after the summer crops are harvested, until the next round of spring sowings. Spring cabbage grows well in containers and can be picked over through the winter if grown under cover.

Varieties

SPRING CABBAGE

'April' is a larger variety that will heart up in the spring.

'Durham Early' is a reliable older variety for an early crop of spring greens, though it is unlikely to develop solid hearts. It is even hardy in the north of the UK, so is a good choice for cold areas.

'Pixie', a compact hearting variety, is worth trying at closer spacing or in mini-vegetable beds.

'Spring Hero' is the last spring cabbage variety to heart up. Unlike other varieties, it produces round heads, more like a summer cabbage. It can be sown as a summer cabbage in the spring, too.

ALL-YEAR-ROUND CABBAGE

'Advantage' is a 'synthetic hybrid' which makes it cheaper than a normal F1. It gives a crop of dark-green spring greens all year and may heart up if spaced wider apart.

'Duncan' F1 looks like a pointed summer cabbage but will also produce spring greens and will heart up later in the spring.

'Spring Hero'

HOW TO HAVE SPRING GREENS ALL YEAR

The lines between summer and spring cabbages are becoming blurred. Summer varieties such as 'Hispi' can be sown under cloches in October or November in mild areas and planted out the following February and March. They should give a crop by late April or May.

A new generation of truly all-year-round varieties can, in theory, be sown in succession from February through to late August. The earliest sowing will crop as a summer cabbage in late June; later sowings will produce spring greens and should heart up by the following June.

Calendar

JULY

If you live in the north of the UK, this is the best time to sow. You can start the seed off in pots if you want only a few plants.

Sow one seed per 7-cm pot or in a modular seed tray. Keep these somewhere cool and shady until the seedlings appear, and water frequently.

Sowing in a seedbed is easier for raising lots of plants. Work in a balanced fertiliser or well-rotted manure, especially if the spring cabbage follows an earlier crop. Give the area a thorough soaking if the soil is dry and prepare the seedbed a few days later.

In a seedbed sow into drills 2cm deep and 15cm apart. Sow thinly, aiming for a plant every 5cm or so. Do not forget to water the bottom of the drill thoroughly before you sow at this time of year. Sow in early evening, so that the seeds germinate quickly in moist soil. Water frequently until the plants are well established.

Cover with fine mesh netting to keep cabbage whites off the young plants – it may become too warm under garden fleece.

AUGUST

Sow (as above) by the middle of the month if you live in the south.

SEPTEMBER

Plant out in the north of the country and colder areas. Space rows 30cm apart and plants every 15cm. This allows for three out of four plants to be picked as greens and the fourth left to heart up. In pots, plant four plants to a 30-cm diameter pot. Spring cabbages are not the most ornamental vegetables, but if you have bare soil in borders, plant them in clumps of about five to a 30-cm square.

OCTOBER

Plant out in southern and milder areas.

NOVEMBER–JANUARY

The plants should be large enough to survive the winter. In particularly cold areas, covering with cloches will help to give an earlier crop. Cover the crop with netting if pigeons or rabbits are a problem. If you have space in the greenhouse or coldframe, make a late sowing in 30-cm pots for a crop of young leaves through the winter. Thin to about nine plants, pulling whole plants or individual leaves, until one is left to heart up in spring.

FEBRUARY

Apply a light dressing of a high-nitrogen fertiliser (e.g. nitrochalk or dried blood) as the plants start into growth.

MARCH–MAY

Start cutting alternate plants for spring greens as soon as they are large enough. Given enough space, most varieties will produce firm hearts by late April or May. You can get a bonus crop of greens six weeks later by cutting a cross in the top of the stump after cutting off the head (see page 83).

Ready for transplanting

Spring cabbage in a container

HARVESTING

Start by cutting immature plants as spring greens. You can also pick individual leaves of larger plants, or leave some to produce firm heads and cut them whole.

CALABRESE

Although it originated in Italy, calabrese or green broccoli — to distinguish it from white and purple sprouting broccoli (see pages 78–9) — is sometimes known, confusingly, as American broccoli or plain broccoli in the supermarkets.

By careful choice of variety and planting dates it is possible to have fresh calabrese from the garden for much of the year. It is not a difficult vegetable to grow and the smaller varieties are suitable for growing as a baby vegetable in even the smallest garden.

Calabrese will suffer a setback to its growth if it is transplanted from a seedbed, producing a poor-sized head. It is therefore best to start it off in pots, so that it can be planted out without disturbing the rootball.

Varieties

A few older varieties of calabrese are still available, but these have largely been superseded by F1 hybrids. They are more vigorous and produce larger, better-quality heads with tight buds. They are also more uniform in size, but tend to crop all at once. The solution is to make a succession of sowings to spread the harvest.

'Corvet' is a reliable older hybrid that produces a reasonable-sized main head, followed by a crop of side shoots.

'Jewel' and **'Roxette'** are small varieties that are good for growing as baby vegetables at close spacing. The main heads should be about 10cm across, ideal for individual portions.

'Marathon' is a large-headed modern variety.

'Romanesco' is, strictly speaking, a type of cauliflower, with lime-green, pointed curds, but it can be grown like calabrese. From a May sowing, it will mature in the autumn. As with more typical cauliflowers, it will not produce a secondary crop of side shoots.

'Trixie' is one of the few varieties in the cabbage family claimed to be resistant

'Romanesco'

to clubroot. Bred in Japan, it is not fully resistant to European strains of clubroot, but a good variety nonetheless.

HOW TO PREVENT PROBLEMS

Calabrese suffers from the whole range of cabbage family pests and diseases (see pages 86–7).

Covering the crop with garden fleece when you plant out the young plants should prevent most insect pests.

Later in the season (from late June onwards) cabbage white butterflies home in on calabrese plants, and the caterpillars can rapidly damage the leaves. Worse still, the tiny caterpillars can get into the developing heads, only to emerge, cooked, on the plate. A covering of fine netting, anchored to provide a complete barrier and not touching the foliage, should frustrate any butterfly intent on egg-laying. Cabbage white caterpillars can be controlled by spraying with a non-persistent insecticide such as pyrethrum or the biological control BT. If the caterpillars get through, cut the heads into small portions and soak them for half an hour in salty water before cooking.

Calendar

Like other members of the cabbage family, calabrese grows best in a rich soil. If possible, dig in well-rotted manure or garden compost before planting. If this is impractical, work in a balanced fertiliser instead. A light dressing of a nitrogen fertiliser can be given when the young plants have 6–8 leaves, to boost yields.

FEBRUARY–MARCH

Make the first sowing in pots in a greenhouse or somewhere you can maintain a temperature of at least 13°C. Sow two seeds to a 7-cm pot. If both germinate, pull out the weaker one later. Keep the plants growing somewhere frost-free. The compost needs to be moist but try to avoid wetting the leaves, as they are very susceptible to downy mildew.

APRIL–MAY

Plant out the first sowing after six to eight weeks. In cold areas, plant them under cloches or garden fleece.

For baby vegetables, space plants 15cm apart each way. For larger main heads, space plants 15cm apart in rows 30cm apart. This spacing will give the optimum yield of main heads. For a follow-on crop of side shoots, space them 30cm apart each way.

Water plants while in their pots and try not to disturb the rootball when planting out. Plant them deeply, so the first set of leaves are level with the soil surface.

Sow further small batches throughout April and May for a long harvest. As the weather warms up, you can start plants off in pots in a sheltered spot outdoors or sow seed directly where they are to grow.

JUNE

In dry summers, you can improve the yield of calabrese by giving the plants a good soaking about a month or so after planting out.

Sow another batch of seeds in pots. Bear in mind that cabbage white caterpillars start to become troublesome during mid-summer and will severely damage young plants given the chance, so cover the plants with fine netting.

JULY

Continue to sow small batches of seed and plant out earlier sowings, protecting them at all times from cabbage whites.

Cut the main heads of earlier sowings and pick over the side shoots of the earliest batch before the flower buds start to open.

AUGUST

Make a last sowing for a crop before Christmas. Note that the plants will be killed by severe frost.

SEPTEMBER

Plant out the late-sown plants and continue to pick over early crops.

OCTOBER–DECEMBER

Cover late crops planted out last month with tall cloches or garden fleece. Continue to cut main heads and side shoots of later sowings.

HARVESTING

The flower buds that make up the head should be tight and completely green. Yellow flowers will start to show if the heads are left too long before cutting.

Cut the heads with as much stalk as possible. This and any leaves can be trimmed off before cooking. At this stage, you can remove the plants and replace them with another crop, or leave them to develop several flushes of smaller side shoots.

Sowing seed

Young plants

Planting out

Cutting mature head

CARROTS

Forget the giant roots favoured by allotment gardeners and think sweet, crunchy, baby carrots — and you will appreciate how carrots are a perfect crop for the smallest garden. Their fresh, green, feathery foliage makes carrots a good foil for flowers whether in a border or a container. However you grow them, the taste of fresh carrots is incomparable with the supermarket offerings.

In a small garden, in flower borders or in containers try several sowings of a quick-maturing early variety (see page 96). Maincrop varieties are better on a vegetable plot if you want a single crop for storing over winter.

HOW TO PREVENT PROBLEMS

Carrot fly is the bane of carrot growers. It is endemic on allotment sites and even if carrots in your garden escape at first, the flies will find them eventually. Tell-tale signs are reddening or yellowing of the foliage and, in severe cases, individual plants may wilt and die, due to carrot fly grubs eating the side roots. Later in the summer, a second generation of grubs starts to burrow into the main tap root.

Carrot fly is more likely to be a problem on a vegetable plot. Carrots planted among flowers and in containers should be harder for the pests to find. Below are several strategies to outwit them. It is the grubs that do the damage, by tunnelling into the roots. Because the adult flies usually fly close to the ground in their quest for carrots, any physical barrier need not be very high to prevent them laying their eggs next to the young carrot plants. (See page 97 for how to build a carrot fly barrier.)

At least two generations of flies occur during the summer, so it is possible to minimise the damage by timing your sowings carefully. Carrots sown after late May or dug before early August should miss the main attacks.

No variety is completely resistant to carrot fly. However, some are less likely to be attacked and less likely to be damaged as a result. Resistant varieties are well worth trying if carrot fly is an annual problem (see page 96). Early varieties pulled young are less likely to suffer than maincrops left in the ground until autumn.

Splitting of mature roots is a sign of extreme variations in soil moisture. Typically, heavy rain followed by a drought. Aim to keep the soil moist during prolonged dry spells.

Rots of various types can strike during storage. Always inspect stored roots carefully and remove any rotten ones promptly.

Carrots under garden fleece

Carrot fly damage (on left)

Calendar

Carrots do best in a deep but well-drained soil. For good crops on a heavy soil it is worth digging the soil over with a garden fork to open it up, especially if the ground is compacted. Do not add any organic matter – this can cause the roots to divide (this type of growth is known as 'forking'). Break the soil surface down to a crumbly texture with the back of the garden fork and then use a garden rake to get a level seedbed. On sandy soils, if a hard surface crust has built up, break this up by raking into a fine seedbed. On a typical garden soil, carrots will grow well without additional fertiliser.

FEBRUARY

For the earliest crop of new carrots, start some under cloches or garden fleece. Put the cloches in place at least two weeks before you make the first sowing, to warm the soil up. Follow the advice for sowing outdoors below.

MARCH

Make the first outdoor sowings on lighter soils and in milder areas. Sow carrots directly into the ground. Starting them in pots may cause the roots to fork.

For a continuous supply of baby carrots, sow a short row or two and keep sowing at regular intervals through the summer. In a vegetable plot, draw out a shallow (1.5cm) seed drill. Space adjacent drills 15cm apart. If the soil is very dry, dribble water into the drill and let this soak in. Sow as thinly as you can to avoid having to thin the young plants later. Aim for a seed every 2.5cm or so. Cover the drill with dry soil, but to avoid disturbing the seeds, do not water.

In an ornamental bed or border, sow in patches just as you would hardy annuals. Draw out a pattern of short drills to sow into. This will make it easier to distinguish carrot seedlings from weeds later on.

To grow carrots in containers, scatter the seed thinly – aim for a seed roughly every 2.5cm on moist, weed-free compost. Cover with a further 1.5-cm layer of compost.

If you find handling the seed difficult, try seed tapes (see page 150).

APRIL

Make the first outdoor sowings on heavier soils. Carrot seed may fail in cold, wet soil, so be prepared to re-sow if this happens.

MAY

As soon as the seedlings are big enough to handle, gently pull out excess seedlings to leave a plant every 2.5cm. If they are too crowded, individual roots may be smaller, but they will push each other apart as they grow. Restrict thinning to a minimum and, if possible, thin out seedlings in the evening to reduce the risk of attracting carrot fly.

Sow maincrop varieties later this month. You need make only one sowing if you intend to store the roots for use over winter.

JUNE

The first baby carrots should be ready for pulling.

JULY–AUGUST

Keep sowing short rows of an early variety for a continuing supply of baby carrots. And keep pulling earlier sowings before they get too large. As they grow, the roots start to lose their initial sweetness and develop a more 'carroty' flavour. If you cannot keep up with picking them, leave them in the ground and dig them up in the autumn.

Once they are established, carrots do not need watering unless it is exceptionally dry, so save valuable water for more sensitive crops. Carrots in pots, however, will need regular watering.

Thin out maincrop varieties to leave 5–7.5cm between plants, to encourage good-sized roots.

SEPTEMBER

Harvest maincrop carrots, if carrot fly and slugs are starting to attack them. Store the untouched ones and use any damaged carrots straight away. Do not leave infested roots in the garden; bin or burn them. Otherwise, leave unaffected carrots in the ground until needed. Mark the position of the rows. In very cold areas, cover with a layer of straw or dry bracken to stop the soil from freezing solid.

OCTOBER

A greenhouse with soil borders is the ideal place for a catch crop of early carrots. Sow after the tomatoes and cucumbers have finished and again in the early spring before the next crop.

Varieties

Early varieties produce a usable root quickly and are therefore the best types to sow in spring for the earliest crop of new carrots. They can also be sown regularly through the season for a succession of baby carrots, or left to mature for winter use. Maincrop varieties are slower growing but store better through the winter.

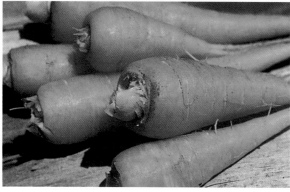

'Chantenay Red Cored'   'Early French Frame'

VARIETIES FOR STONY SOIL

'Early French Frame' and **'Parmex'** produce round roots, best pulled before they reach golf-ball size. They will not fork if they hit a stone, unlike conventional, pointed varieties. They also thrive in containers.

VARIETIES FOR SHALLOW SOIL

'Redca' or the more widely available **'Chantenay Red Cored'** produce short, fat, wedge-shaped roots. These are less likely to become stunted if your soil is shallow or you are growing them in a container.

EARLY VARIETIES

'Amsterdam Forcing 2 Sweetheart' or any selection of **'Early Nantes'** are good choices for light, sandy soil. **'Primo'** and **'Suko'** did better on heavier clay soil in the last

'Early Nantes'

Gardening Which? trial.

MAINCROP VARIETIES

'Autumn King – Vita Longa' is a good selection of a well-established garden variety and produces heavy, stump-rooted roots. **'Bangor'** was quick-growing

on both sandy and heavy soil in a *Gardening Which?* trial. **'Boston'** is an alternative for sandy soil.

VARIETIES RESISTANT TO CARROT FLY

'Flyaway' is the best choice. The roots are medium length

and cylindrical and, because of its tolerance to carrot fly, it can be grown as a maincrop.

'Sytan' and **'Parano'** are early varieties that are reasonably resistant to carrot fly.

'Primo'

HARVESTING

The roots should slide easily out of moist soil when the base of the leaves is pulled gently. If not, use a hand fork to ease the roots out.

To store carrots, cut the tops off just above the root and layer the carrots in slightly moist sand in wooden boxes. Keep them in a cool shed until required in the kitchen.

HOW TO BUILD A CARROT FLY BARRIER

By growing carrots in blocks of several short rows rather than one long row, it is easier to protect them with a barrier.

Method one Fix a stout post at each corner of the block of carrots. Wrap thick-gauge, transparent plastic sheeting round them to form a wall at least 75cm high. Bury the bottom of the plastic and secure it to the posts, e.g. by stapling. Make sure the structure will stand up to wind if your garden is exposed. For a more permanent barrier, construct frames from wood and fine plastic mesh to form four panels.

Method two Insert hoops over the width of the carrot bed and drape fine plastic netting over the top. Provided this is well anchored at the edges, it should prevent small insects getting in but allows light, air and rain to reach the crop.

Hoops can be made of wire or plastic (alkathene tubing sold in d-i-y stores is ideal). The netting should be well anchored with bricks or stones, or buried to prevent carrot flies finding their way inside.

Carrot fly barrier made from four mesh panels

CAULIFLOWER

Cauliflower is not the easiest vegetable to grow well and it can tie up a lot of space in your garden for quite a time. However, if you want a challenge, it is a crop that can be enjoyed over a long period. A modern approach is to grow closely spaced baby cauliflowers. As well as producing individual portion-sized curds, it will also leave you room for other crops.

Cauliflowers are not decorative enough for the border and are tricky to manage in pots, but they can be fitted into a vegetable plot alongside other members of the cabbage family. Like all their relatives, cauliflowers are greedy feeders and need a slightly alkaline soil.

HOW TO PREVENT PROBLEMS

Cauliflower suffers from the same problems as cabbage (see pages 86–7) and calabrese (see pages 92–3).

The best way to prevent insect pests, such as cabbage root fly, flea beetle, mealy cabbage aphid and cabbage white butterflies, is to cover the new transplants with garden fleece or fine netting. Cabbage caterpillars are a particular nuisance when they burrow inside the developing curds. Provided the fleece or net is securely anchored and held clear of the plants on wires or hoops, the adult butterflies should not be able to lay their eggs.

Cauliflower is also susceptible to clubroot disease and there are no resistant varieties. A combination of crop rotation and liming should help to prevent this disease.

Small curds can be caused by a check to growth when the flower was initiated. Cauliflowers bolt readily. To prevent this, feed and water the seedlings well, transplant them no later than six weeks old, and water in well if it is dry.

Cover cauliflowers with fine netting

CAULIFLOWERS ALL YEAR ROUND

Summer types are sown from early spring for a crop in mid- to late summer. They can also be sown in succession through the summer for cropping into the autumn. These are the best types for baby cauliflowers.

You can also sow them in the autumn and overwinter them under cover for an early crop the following spring.

Autumn types are sown in mid- to late spring for a crop in autumn, usually into November.

Winter types are also sown in late spring. They are winter-hardy but take longer to mature, producing a head in March to May the following spring.

Calendar

Cauliflowers will do well on heavy clay soil, provided it is not waterlogged. On light soil, dig in lots of well-rotted organic matter. Lime acid soil over winter to give a pH of 7.5 (see pages 30–1). Cauliflowers will also benefit from a generous amount of balanced fertiliser (e.g. growmore, chicken manure or blood, fish and bone). Work this into the soil before planting out. Before sowing, decide when you want to harvest the cauliflowers and pick an appropriate variety.

FEBRUARY–MARCH

Summer types You can sow summer cauliflowers in small pots or outdoors in a seedbed. Ideally, sow in 7-cm pots (or modular trays) – they are less likely to suffer a check in growth which could affect the size and quality of the final curd. A seedbed is easiest if you are raising a lot of plants, however. Protect early sowings with cloches.

Provided plants are kept well watered and are lifted with the roots as intact as possible, they should not suffer a check. Keep pots or trays in an unheated greenhouse, coldframe or sheltered spot outside.

APRIL–MAY

Summer types Plant out cauliflowers raised in pots. For conventional-sized curds, space the plants 45–50cm apart each way. For baby cauliflowers, see page 101.

Water young plants in well. Once they are established, do not water unless the soil becomes very dry, as this will encourage lush leaves rather than curds.

Further sowings of summer varieties will crop from August to early October. Make further sowings of baby cauliflowers in raised beds.

Autumn types Sow now for harvesting in autumn. Start plants in pots, and plant out after a month or so.

Winter types Start off hardy winter cauliflowers for a spring crop.

JUNE–JULY

All types If the plants are in the open garden, look out for insect pests. If aphids start to build up, spray with a pyrethrum- or soft soap-based insecticide. Caterpillars can be picked off and destroyed.

Summer types Curds should be ready from the earliest sowings. It can be worth making a final sowing of baby cauliflowers in early June, for a September crop.

Autumn types These should be growing strongly, but may still benefit from a scattering of high-nitrogen fertiliser along the rows.

Winter types Plant out winter varieties, 60cm apart each way. Grow a catch crop between them (see pages 48–9).

AUGUST

Cauliflowers may bolt or produce undersized curds if the soil gets too dry. A good soak once a week will be more effective than more frequent light watering. Failing that, one really good watering about three weeks before you expect to harvest will boost the size of the head.

Keep checking the plants regularly for pests.

SEPTEMBER–OCTOBER

Sow summer types for an early crop next year. Sow in 7-cm pots and keep in an unheated greenhouse or frost-free coldframe over winter.

SPRING

Summer types Overwintered plants should be ready to plant out as soon as the soil is in good condition in March and should be a couple of weeks ahead of the earliest spring sowings. Use cloches in colder areas.

Winter types Boost hardy winter varieties with a dusting of a nitrogen fertiliser (e.g. nitrochalk).

The curds should start to form from March to May, depending on the variety. To protect them from frost, tie the inner leaves together or break off a couple of the innermost leaves and lay them on top of the developing curd.

HARVESTING

Check the plants weekly, carefully peeling back the inner leaves. Cut them as soon as the heads reach a decent size. The curds should be white and individual flower buds indistinguishable. Occasionally, small leaves grow out of the curd. This is caused by fluctuating temperatures, and they are still perfectly edible.

If cabbage whites have been active and you have not taken any control measures, break the curds into pieces and check for caterpillars. Soak the curds in warm, salty water to flush out any hidden caterpillars.

Varieties

The best choice for a small garden is a quick-maturing summer cauliflower, sown in succession. These can also be overwintered under cover for the earliest crop. Winter-heading varieties used to be grown in the south-west of the UK, but are no longer popular. In milder areas, winter varieties might be worth trying. They are hardy enough to survive outdoors over winter, to crop the following spring.

SUMMER TYPES

'All Year Round' is an old, open-pollinated variety. It can be sown in spring for summer cropping, or in autumn for planting out the next spring.

'Purple Cape'

'Limelight'

'Marmalade'

'Dok Elgon' F1 is a well-established and reliable summer variety.

'Snowball' is another popular and versatile summer variety for spring or autumn sowing.

AUTUMN TYPES

'Barrier Reef' and **'Wallaby'** are older Australian-bred autumn

'Armado April'

HOW TO GROW BABY CAULIFLOWERS

Cauliflowers respond to closer spacing by producing smaller curds. Unless you particularly want huge curds, reduce the spacing to suit your household's needs. A spacing of 15cm between plants should produce curds about 7.5cm across – perfect for an individual portion. On the other hand, a spacing of 45cm should produce 15–20cm curds, but only one instead of nine from the same area of ground.

Sow the seeds directly into a well-prepared seedbed in seed drills 1.5cm deep and 15cm apart. Sow thinly and thin out seedlings to leave a plant every 12.5–15cm. For uniform-sized curds, it is best to grow baby cauliflowers in blocks, or in short rows across a raised bed.

You can also raise the plants in small pots or modular trays. Keep them well watered and plant out when they are large enough to handle.

Choose a naturally small, early summer variety but otherwise grow them like normal cauliflowers. They should mature about ten weeks after sowing. As each batch will mature over a short period, keep sowing baby cauliflowers in small batches throughout the summer.

varieties that are equally reliable in the UK.

'Castlegrant' F1, a modern hybrid, produces big heads in autumn. It is said to be tolerant of less-than-ideal conditions.

WINTER TYPES

'Walcheren Winter' is an older variety. There are several selections that mature at different times in the spring, for example **'Armado April'** in April, **'Markanta'** in late April and **'Maystar'** in May.

BABY CAULIFLOWERS

'Candid Charm' and **'Idol'** are both quick-maturing, early-summer varieties that can be grown in succession as baby vegetables.

UNUSUAL VARIETIES

Best regarded as interesting novelties, as the curds can be disappointing compared to conventional cauliflowers.

'Limelight' has pale-green curds. Matures September-October from a spring sowing.

'Marmalade' F1 is an early-maturing summer variety with cream or pale-orange curds. Higher carotene content than other cauliflowers.

'Purple Cape' is a very old purple-headed winter variety.

'Romanesco' has unusual, pointed lime-green heads (see 'Calabrese', page 92).

'Violet Queen' F1 is an autumn-maturing variety with purple curds, that turn bright green when cooked.

CELERY

Celery is tricky to grow so is not worth attempting unless you have plenty of space and you are prepared to pamper it. However, it is not as demanding as it used to be, thanks to modern self-blanching varieties. These have done away with time-consuming jobs, such as digging trenches and earthing up, that were needed to grow traditional trench celery.

Celery is best grown in a vegetable patch. It prefers an open site with a fertile soil that holds moisture well. If the soil is acid, you will need to add lime (see pages 30–1) to raise the pH to 7.0 (neutral).

Self-blanching celery is grown in a block. The plants are spaced close together so the crowded plants shade each other and thus lengthen and blanch the stems.

HOW TO PREVENT PROBLEMS

Bolting, where the plant produces a flower stalk instead of edible leaf stalks, is a common problem in dry summers. The secret is to keep the plants growing steadily from the seedling stage onwards. So do not let them go short of water or wait in their pots too long before being transplanted. Self-blanching varieties are less prone to bolting than the old-fashioned trench varieties.

Celery leaves can be disfigured by a number of pests, diseases and nutritional problems.

Celery fly grubs tunnel into the leaves and cause them to develop yellow-brown blotches. Pick off and destroy badly affected leaves.

Puckered leaves with yellow veins have been affected by the **mosaic virus**, spread by aphids. Lift and destroy plants, as there is no cure.

Brown spots on the leaves are caused by a seed-borne disease called **leaf spot**. Look out for this from the seedling stage and destroy affected plants. Remaining plants can be sprayed with a systemic fungicide. Most celery seed is treated to prevent leaf spot.

Carrot fly can tunnel into the roots and stalks causing stunted growth and yellow foliage. There is little you can do but destroy the plant. It can be prevented by planting after mid-June.

CELERY FLAVOURS

Celeriac is a related plant grown for its celery-flavoured root (see pages 116–7).

Par-cel, or celery leaf, is an easier option if you want the taste of celery for flavouring. It looks similar to parsley and you treat it in much the same way, picking individual leaves as required. It will not produce edible stalks (see page 213).

Calendar

MARCH – APRIL

Start the seeds off in a greenhouse or somewhere you can maintain a temperature of 15°C. Use a seed tray or a modular tray. The seeds need light to germinate, so sow them on the surface of the compost. Cover them lightly with vermiculite or place a sheet of glass on top of the tray. There is no point sowing too early; count back 10–12 weeks from the last frost date for your area.

Mist the seeds with a hand-held spray; they should germinate after about two weeks. Keep the seedlings frost-free and the compost moist. Pull out any weak seedlings or those with blistered or spotted foliage and grow on the rest until they have four to six leaves. Get the plants used to outdoor conditions gradually by hardening them off.

MAY – JUNE

If you forgot to sow any seed, it is possible to buy celery plants.

Prior to planting, rake in a general fertiliser. Plant out after all danger of frost has passed. Self-blanching types are planted in blocks with plants 23cm apart each way.

Water the plants in well and use a cover of garden fleece overnight for the first couple of weeks. Water once to twice a week after planting.

Celery plants are very prone to slug damage so it is worth using slug pellets.

JULY

Continue to water each week. Be prepared to apply 10 litres a sq m twice a week in dry spells. Re-apply slug pellets after rain.

AUGUST

Continue to water and feed the plants occasionally with a high-nitrogen fertiliser.

Start harvesting the plants on the outside of the block first. Straw can be tucked in between the remaining plants to enhance blanching.

SEPTEMBER

Continue to harvest as required.

OCTOBER

Aim to finish harvesting before the frosts.

HARVESTING

Remove any straw or earth. Ease a garden fork down into the ground and lift the celery plant out. Cut off the roots and discard any damaged outer stems. Replace any straw or earth around nearby plants. Separate the individual stalks and wash thoroughly to remove any soil.

Any surplus can be lifted and stored in a cool, frost-free place for several weeks. Once cut, it will keep in the fridge for up to a week.

Seed needs light

Planting out

Watering in

Varieties

Self-blanching varieties are less work than old-fashioned trench celery but are not as hardy.

'Golden Self-Blanching' is a yellow variety that is quick to mature and so ready for picking from August onwards.

'Celebrity' is a fairly new yellow-white variety with long sticks. It is said to be less prone to bolting and less stringy than other varieties.

'Victoria' is a British-bred F1 hybrid, quick to mature and with a good flavour. It stands better than most self-blanching types and has green stems.

'Victoria'

CHICORY *and* ENDIVE

These continental salad plants are a major ingredient in the bags of exotic salad mixtures available in supermarkets. They are fairly easy to grow and can be harvested late in the season. Both are very decorative in an ornamental border, with a choice of frilly and red types. They can be blanched to reduce the characteristic bitter taste, and certain types of chicory can be forced. Both crops are also useful additions to a mixed-leaf salad, and grown as cut-and-come-again crops (see page 180).

Varieties

GREEN CHICORY
'Bianco di Milano' is a variety with loose heads of pale-green leaves rather like a cos lettuce. The leaves of the inner heart should be much milder than the outer leaves.

RED CHICORY
'Palla Rossa' produces tight balls of red leaves in the autumn. They start off green but turn red as the temperature drops.

Some of the variegated Italian varieties are worth seeking out. Look for **'Rossa di Treviso'** in the more specialist catalogues for truly ornamental plants.

FOR CHICONS
'Witloof Zoom' is the standard green variety for forcing.

You can also try the red varieties 'Palla Rossa' and 'Rossa di Treviso' for the striking pink and white chicons.

ENDIVE
There are two types: frilly endives are more suited to summer sowing, and are more decorative. Broad-leaved endives are hardier and better for an autumn sowing, though less attractive.

The older varieties **'Moss Curled'** and **'Wallone'** were the best in a *Gardening Which?* trial. Both are self-blanching to a certain extent, but if you find them too bitter, try blanching them. **'Jeti'** is a broad-leaved or escarole type which is very hardy and will provide cut-and-come-again leaves all winter, especially if given some protection.

Chicory 'Palla Rossa'

Chicory 'Rossa di Treviso'

Endive 'Wallone'

Calendar

FEBRUARY–APRIL

Sow chicory and endive little and often as a cut-and-come-again crop (see page 180 for more details).

APRIL–JUNE

Sow frilly endives for a summer crop, either in pots for planting out later, or direct. Allow 20–30cm between plants.

JULY–AUGUST

Blanch frilly endives sown earlier once the hearts are full-sized (about the size of your fist) by covering them for a week or two with something heavy and round, such as a dinner plate, to exclude light.

Sow chicory and endive (especially broad-leaved varieties) for winter salads and for forcing. You can sow into a seed bed for transplanting later on. If you want only a few plants, sow a couple of seeds in a 7-cm pot. Keep well watered and pull out the weaker seedlings later if more than one germinates.

AUGUST–SEPTEMBER

Plant the young plants outside. Allow roughly 25cm per plant if you want them to develop large heads, closer if you want a supply of loose leaves. Red and variegated varieties will start to develop their distinct colouring as the temperature begins to drop.

A late sowing of hardy endive is worth considering under cloches or in an unheated greenhouse during September.

Blanching an endive

Young endive

> **HARVESTING**
>
> Harvest roots for forcing as chicons in November (see below). Pick leaves of hardy chicory and endive as required for winter salads.

HOW TO GROW CHICONS

These are the blanched young shoots of certain types of chicory. The taste is much milder than outdoor chicory.

Lift the roots in November. You want unforked roots with a diameter of 2.5–5cm across the top. Cut the foliage to within 2.5cm of the root and trim the root to 15–20cm. If there has not been a frost, lay them outdoors before storing. A frost will break their dormancy and make them easier to force later. Store horizontally in boxes of damp sand [1].

Take three or four roots at a time and plant them in 25-cm pots filled with multipurpose compost, so that the crowns are just visible [2]. Cover them to exclude all light (you could

Step 1

Step 2

Step 3

Step 4

use another pot with the drainage holes covered) [3]. Put them somewhere warm, with a temperature of at least 10–13°C. After three or four weeks, a chicon should grow from each root [4].

You can also force chicory outdoors by covering the trimmed roots with a low mound of soil 20cm high. Cover this with cloches or straw and wait until early spring, when the chicons should break through the soil surface.

COURGETTES

Courgette plants take up a lot of space, spreading at least 1m across. But, if you can find room for them in a border or a patio tub, you will be rewarded with a constant supply of tender courgettes throughout the summer months. The large, silvery-flecked leaves and bright-yellow flowers are attractive, too.

Do not make the mistake of growing a marrow variety (see page 138) and picking the fruits when they are still small. It is much better to start with a variety bred specifically for courgette production, or the total number of fruits may be disappointing.

A good choice of varieties is available, with long fruits in various shades of green and yellow. You could try an unusual round variety, or summer squashes, which are grown and cooked just like courgettes. Unfortunately, all courgette varieties produce bush plants, so if you want a plant with a climbing habit, it will have to be a trailing marrow.

HOW TO PREVENT PROBLEMS

Virus symptoms

Powdery mildew

The biggest potential problem is **mosaic virus**. This is spread by aphids and causes the leaves to become puckered and mottled. In severe cases, plants become stunted and the fruits inedible. Remove badly affected plants to prevent it spreading. Certain varieties succumb less easily to the disease and will continue to crop for longer if it strikes.

Powdery mildew frequently attacks courgette plants, particularly in hot, dry summers. Regular watering and correct spacing of plants to prevent overcrowding will help to offset mildew. Make sure you remove and destroy any infected debris to prevent the fungus overwintering.

Calendar

MAY

Courgettes are very sensitive to frost, so it is not worth planting them outside until all risk has passed. In most areas, this means waiting until early to mid-June. They are, however, very fast-growing plants. In very mild parts, and if you can provide a sheltered, sunny position, you could sow directly outdoors. But it is simpler to sow the seed in pots in a greenhouse or on a warm windowsill for planting out in June.

The seed is large and easy to handle. Sow it on edge into 7-cm pots and cover with compost. As the young seedling germinates it needs to push the whole seed out of the compost, otherwise it will rot. Given a minimum temperature of 18°C, plants germinate and grow very rapidly. Keep them well watered and if you cannot plant them out within four weeks, pot them on into bigger pots.

Gradually harden them off by putting them outside on warm days and moving them under cover on cooler nights.

JUNE

It should be safe to plant out in mid-June in all but the coldest areas. Delay until later in the month if there is any chance of a late frost.

Unless the soil is already rich in organic matter, prepare a planting hole first. Dig a hole up to 30cm wide and deep. Refill with a mixture of soil and well-rotted manure or garden compost. This will leave a low mound. Water both the hole and the plant well and plant into the top of the mound. This will direct excess rain away from the base of the plant and help to prevent stem rot.

In a border, allow an area at least 1m in diameter for each plant. Although the plants grow as a bush, they tend to go in one direction, so give them plenty of room to avoid swamping neighbouring plants.

The best way to prevent weeds later in the summer is to cover the area with permeable plastic mulch before planting out. Cut cross-shaped slits in the plastic and plant through them.

Alternatively, mulch the soil around each plant with well-rotted manure, chipped bark or garden compost to suppress weeds and conserve moisture.

To grow a courgette plant in a container you will need one that can hold at least 30 litres of compost (or the contents of a standard growing bag). You will also need to water and feed regularly (see July).

Water sparingly at first, aiming to keep the soil moist. Do not overwater or you will simply encourage too much leaf.

JULY–AUGUST

Once flowering starts, a good soaking once a week will be more effective in dry weather than regular light watering. Try burying a length of plastic drainpipe, or a large plastic bottle with the bottom cut off, about 20cm from each plant to direct water to the roots (see page 47). This is especially worthwhile if you applied a mulch earlier.

Feed plants, especially those in containers, with a dilute tomato feed once a week.

Pick fruits regularly to encourage further cropping.

SEPTEMBER–OCTOBER

Most varieties will continue cropping until the first frost. To extend the season in areas prone to early frosts, surround the plants with a barrier of polythene sheeting at least 45cm high, supported by canes, or cover with garden fleece.

Sowing seed on edge

Planting out

Picking courgettes

HARVESTING

Check fruits at least twice a week, and pick when they reach 15cm. Any you miss will rapidly turn into marrows. If you are going away for a couple of weeks, remove all of the flowers and fruits, to prolong cropping.

Varieties

Gardening Which? carried out a trial of 27 varieties of courgette and summer squash, including expert taste tests.

STANDARD LONG GREEN

'Defender' gave a big crop of average-tasting mid-green fruits. It does have some resistance to virus disease.

'Kojac' gave lower yields and was only average in taste tests, but the plants were small, which makes this variety suitable for a small garden or patio tub. They are also spine-free, which is useful if you find the spines on other varieties irritating when you are picking them.

'Patriot' is a new variety with reasonable yield and the best taste and appearance in the *Gardening Which?* trial. Other varieties that scored well for both yield and eating quality included **'Bambino'**, **'Elite'** and **'Sardane'**. **'Supremo'** was slightly better tasting

Some of the more unusual varieties of courgette and summer squash

than 'Defender', but had a lower yield. This variety also has some resistance to virus disease.

'Leprechaun'

'Goldrush'

ROUND GREEN

'Eight Ball' gives a reasonable crop of round, dark-green fruits on large, semi-trailing plants. The fruits grow close to the stem and are quite hard to pick. They quickly become too large if not picked regularly.

'Triple Five' is similar, but gave lower yields of better-tasting fruits.

'Leprechaun' is, strictly speaking, a summer squash rather than an immature marrow, but treat it like any other courgette. The

'Sunburst'

bright-green, slightly flattened, round fruit have a strong, distinctive flavour, which tasters either loved or hated.

OTHER COLOURS

'Goldrush', like other varieties with bright-yellow fruit, gave a disappointing yield and was not rated as highly for taste as the green varieties. Yellow varieties are very decorative in the garden and on the plate.

'Clarion' is a Lebanese squash that produces pale-green, club-shaped fruit on large plants.

SUMMER SQUASHES

These have soft skins and will not store into the winter. Pick them young and treat them like normal courgettes. If left to grow large, they can be cooked as winter squash (see page 168).

'Early Yellow Straightneck' is yellow-skinned and club-shaped. A variation with

'Early Yellow Straightneck'

curved fruits called 'Yellow Crookneck' is available. In the *Gardening Which?* trial, neither cropped as heavily as conventional courgettes, but 'Early Yellow Straightneck' was popular in the taste test.

'Peter Pan' is an unusual summer squash with pale-green, flattened and scalloped fruits, known as 'patty pan' squashes in the USA. Pick them regularly when they reach 5–10cm across and cook as you would normal courgettes.

'Sunburst' is a variation on the patty pan theme with bright-yellow fruits. In the *Gardening Which?* trial, it gave good yields.

EDIBLE FLOWERS

The huge flowers of the courgette plant, both male and female, are not only decorative but something of a gourmet treat. Pick them just as they are about to open and before the fruit has started to swell on the females; in the morning if possible. Keep them cool and moist until cooking later the same day. Dip them in a light batter and deep fry.

Courgette flower

HAND POLLINATING

Early in the season or in cold, windy periods, pollinating insects may be scarce and fruits may not set. If this happens, you can hand-pollinate the female flowers – those with a swelling at the base. Pick a male flower (with a straight stem), remove its petals and gently push it into the female flower.

A standard long green courgette

CUCUMBER *Greenhouse*

Summer would not be the same without cucumber for sandwiches and salads. If you have a greenhouse, cucumbers are fairly easy to grow, and a couple of plants will reward you with a constant supply of fresh fruits. If you have a sunny, sheltered spot on the patio, some greenhouse varieties are worth trying outdoors, too. For varieties that will succeed out in the garden, see page 114–5.

You can grow cucumbers from seed, but ready-grown plants are widely available in garden centres and are easier to look after if you do not heat your greenhouse earlier in the spring.

Varieties

Old, open-pollinated varieties produce both male and female flowers. The male flowers should be removed before they open to stop insects transferring pollen to the female flowers, resulting in bitter fruits with seeds in them.

Most modern varieties are all-female hybrids: they produce mostly only female flowers so the fruits develop without being pollinated. If the plants are stressed, a few male flowers will form, which need to be removed. In past *Gardening Which?* trials, there has been little to choose between most of the all-female hybrids.

'Carmen' F1 is worth looking out for. It was resistant to powdery mildew in the last trial and gave good yields. However, the seed is very expensive.

'Petita' F1, if grown like a greenhouse cucumber, will produce lots of half-sized fruits. Pick them when they reach 15–20cm. This variety is also worth trying outdoors, though yields may be much lower than under glass.

'Danimas' is another similar small-fruited variety.

'Telegraph Improved' is an old, open-pollinated variety that produces male and female flowers.

'Carmen'

'Petita'

Calendar

INDOOR CUCUMBERS

MARCH

If you start to heat your greenhouse through the spring, sow the seed in March, otherwise wait until April.

APRIL

Sow the seed now if you do not heat your greenhouse. Sow seed singly in 7-cm pots containing good multipurpose compost. Seed of the all-female hybrid varieties is very expensive, so use enough to raise a couple of plants and store the surplus seed for next year.

You will need a heated propagator to maintain a minimum temperature of 25°C, and somewhere warm to grow the young plants on. Cucumber seeds should germinate in about three days under ideal conditions. You can germinate them in an airing cupboard, but transfer them to a warm, well-lit windowsill as soon as the seedlings emerge. Pot them on into a larger pot (12cm is ideal), as soon as the first leaves have fully opened. This avoids disturbing the roots by potting on several times.

MAY

About four weeks later, when the young plants have four or five leaves, they should be ready to plant out. But wait until early June if the greenhouse is unheated. Harden them off carefully if you have raised them indoors.

Do not buy cucumber plants too early, unless you have somewhere warm to keep them.

Cucumbers are vulnerable to soil rots, so it is best to grow them in growing bags or pots filled with multipurpose compost. Plant two plants to a standard growing bag, or one plant to a 15-litre pot. If you choose to grow them in the greenhouse border, change the position each year, alternating with tomatoes to prevent diseases building up.

JUNE

Plant out in an unheated greenhouse in colder areas. Keep watering to a minimum water only in the morning to avoid wet soil overnight. It is easy to overwater cucumber plants at this stage. Cut slits in the growing bags near the base to drain off excess water.

Cucumbers prefer a temperature of at least 21°C. If you have automatic greenhouse vent openers, set them to this temperature. Start training the plants (see page 113).

JULY–AUGUST

As the plants grow, gradually increase the watering. If possible, use water at greenhouse temperature, rather than straight from the tap. To save time make a mini-reservoir for each plant out of a plastic drink bottle. Cut off the base and make a small hole in the cap. Push the bottle cap-end first into the compost and fill with water. The water will seep out over a couple of hours.

Growing bag compost should contain sufficient nutrients for about four weeks. Once the first fruits start to form, feed regularly with a tomato feed. Pick off dead or yellowing leaves from the base of the plant. Keep an eye open for pests or diseases (see page 112).

Young plants

Training up a cane

HARVESTING

Once a cucumber fruit has reached a decent size (around 30cm for a normal-sized variety), and both sides are parallel, cut it off and store in a cool place. Even if you cannot eat them all, pick mature fruit or further flowering and fruit initiation will cease.

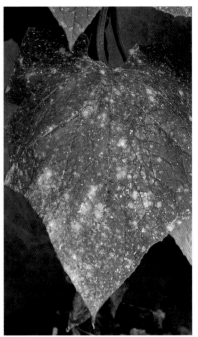

Spider mite damage

Powdery mildew

HOW TO PREVENT PROBLEMS

The main problems with growing cucumbers in a greenhouse are powdery mildew disease, spider mites and whitefly. Outdoors, powdery mildew and mosaic virus (see page 106) are the main problems.

Powdery mildew manifests as white powdery patches across the leaves. This disease is worst in hot, dry conditions and when plants are crowded and stressed.

It can be controlled with a systemic fungicide, but you may prefer not to use pesticides, especially near to harvest time. Keep the plants well watered in hot spells, but avoid wetting the leaves. Open the vents on hot days and give the plants plenty of room.

Some cucumber varieties are resistant to powdery mildew and are worthwhile if the disease is a regular occurrence.

Spider mites are minute, spider-like creatures that are only just visible to the naked eye. They can build up rapidly,

unnoticed, on the undersides of the leaves. The first signs are likely to be a speckling on the upper surface of the leaves caused by their feeding. A severe infestation will result in masses of fine webbing and the leaves will start to yellow and die.

You can spray with an insecticide based on pyrethrum, which is the only option if outdoor cucumbers are attacked. In the greenhouse you can also use biological control. This is quite expensive, but involves introducing a larger predatory mite (available from mail-order specialists). You need to introduce the control as soon as the first signs of the pest are seen. Thereafter, keep the greenhouse at a temperature of at least 21°C. Check new leaves with a hand lens – they should be free of spider mites.

Keeping the greenhouse humid, by regularly damping down the paths, will help to control spider mites.

Whitefly are tiny white flies that settle on the undersides of leaves. The larvae are immobile scales that feed on the sap and produce honeydew, a substance which makes the leaves sticky and encourages a black mould to grow. Whitefly are very persistent, so if you use a pyrethrum insecticide, spray every three days until the infestation is under control.

A biological control for whitefly is also available – a tiny wasp called encarsia that parasitises the scales. This can be ordered from mail-order suppliers. It usually arrives as parasitised whitefly scales glued to a small card or loose in a small tube. The parasitic wasps hatch out and start to lay their eggs in whitefly scales. When parasitised, the scales turn black, so you can follow the progress of the biological control with a hand lens over the next few weeks. Encarsia works best at a temperature of 18°C.

HOW TO TRAIN GREENHOUSE CUCUMBERS

Greenhouse varieties are easier to manage and produce a greater yield of clean fruit when trained up supports firmly attached to the greenhouse frame. There are two basic methods of training them.

Cordon system

This involves training each plant up a single cane or string. It is useful if you are short of greenhouse space.

Wind the young shoot round the support, tying in if necessary.

Remove the flower buds, tendrils and side shoots from the first 45cm of stem, leaving just one leaf at each joint. After this, keep removing any side shoots, but allow the flower buds to develop. As the fruits grow, they should be well clear of the ground.

Keep doing this until the leading shoot reaches the top of the support. With luck you should get one fruit per leaf joint. Make sure the top of the plant is secured to the greenhouse to stop it sliding down the support when laden with fruit.

Pinch out the growing tip but leave the last two side shoots and allow these to hang down, one on either side of the main stem. Stop them when they are about 60cm from the ground.

A variation on this theme is to lean the support at an angle of about 15 degrees, so that the fruits hang away from the stem.

Note that open-pollinated varieties such as 'Telegraph Improved' do not produce female flowers on the main stem. You must let side shoots develop one leaf before pinching them out. Or use the archway system.

Archway system

This involves training the plants on horizontal wires 20–25cm apart, fixed to either end of the greenhouse. This is better if you have more room and want a bigger crop from each plant.

Instead of pinching out the side shoots at each leaf joint, allow two to develop and train them horizontally along the wires.

Remove the flower buds on the main stem, but allow them to grow on the side shoots. Stop each side shoot when it has two leaves and allow two fruits to grow.

The horizontal support wires can be continued up and over the roof if you wish to create an arch.

CUCUMBER *Outdoors*

You can grow cucumbers even if you do not have a greenhouse. Try a greenhouse variety in a large container in a sunny, sheltered spot outside, perhaps trained up a trellis or against a fence. Follow the growing instructions for greenhouse cucumbers and plant outside after the last frost has passed. Or, grow an outdoor or ridge cucumber in a large container. The trailing varieties can be trained up a wigwam or a trellis.

Outdoor cucumbers are grown like courgettes, though it can be harder to get a decent crop. They need a site that gets maximum sun, yet is sheltered from wind. The large leaves are very vulnerable to wind damage. The soil should be well drained but moisture-retentive.

Varieties

'Burpless Tasty Green' F1 is a climbing or trailing plant with short, fat (by greenhouse standards) green fruits with good flavour. It is claimed to be resistant to powdery mildew.
'Bush Champion' F1 is a compact bush plant with dark-green fruits. It is a reliable choice for a large container or a limited space. It is claimed to be resistant to cucumber mosaic virus.
'Crystal Lemon' and **'Crystal Apple'** are old varieties with small, lemon-shaped, pale-yellow fruits on trailing stems. They are novelty climbers for a border or even a large pot. The fruits taste like ordinary cucumbers.

'Burpless Tasty Green'

'Crystal Lemon'

GHERKINS
You may come across two varieties: **'Conda'** and **'Venlo'**. Both are fairly similar, producing small, dumpy fruits on trailing plants.
How to grow gherkins
Gherkins are not just immature cucumbers. They are special, small-fruited varieties. Grow them as you would ordinary outdoor cucumbers, allowing them to trail, or training them as climbers. Pick the fruits when they reach about 10cm and pickle them.

Calendar

OUTDOOR CUCUMBERS

APRIL

Start the seeds in pots somewhere warm. Sow two or three per 7-cm pot about 1cm deep in good multipurpose compost. Keep them at a constant 18–21°C until the seedlings appear. If more than one comes up, pull out the weaker one. Grow them on at around 15°C and keep the compost moist, but do not overwater.

MAY

They will grow rapidly, but cannot be planted outdoors until all danger of frost has passed. If necessary, pot them into large pots to prevent a check to growth. In mild areas it should be safe to plant out in late May, but in colder areas, wait until early or mid-June.

JUNE

Greenhouse varieties can be planted outside into pots that hold at least 15 litres of compost. Outdoor bush or climbing varieties need a container that can hold 30 litres of compost.

In the garden, unless the soil is already very rich, prepare a planting hole. Dig a hole 30cm in diameter and 30cm deep. Fill this with a mixture of soil and well-rotted manure or garden compost. Replace the surplus soil to leave a low mound. Plant into the top of this mound to help prevent stem rot.

Allow a space of at least 75cm in diameter for bush or trailing varieties, or 45cm if they are to grow up supports.

In a border you can train them up wigwams or tripods of canes or bean sticks, about 1.5m tall. Or train them up trellis or on wires on a sunny fence.

An alternative approach in a border is to plant them on the flat and mulch generously with composted bark or compost. This will help suppress weeds and conserve soil moisture. Leave a gap of a couple of centimetres around the stem to prevent stem rot.

JULY

Water the plants regularly. Give them a watering-can-full twice a week in dry weather. When the first fruits start to swell, use a tomato feed once a week.

Watch out for pests and diseases, particularly spider mites, powdery mildew and mosaic virus (see page 112).

When climbing plants reach the top of the support, pinch out the tip to encourage side shoots. Similarly, when trailing plants have six or seven large leaves, pinch out the growing tip. Bush varieties need no such treatment. Outdoor varieties do not need training like greenhouse types.

Do not remove male flowers of outdoor cucumbers (the ones with no bump at their base), because pollination is necessary to produce fruits.

AUGUST

Start to pick fruits when they reach about 15–20cm.

Sowing seed

HARVESTING

Outdoor varieties are generally shorter and fatter than greenhouse varieties (and the sort you buy in the supermarket). The older varieties in particular have rough or spiny skins, and contain immature seeds. Pick the fruits regularly, even if you cannot eat them, or further cropping will cease.

FLORENCE FENNEL
and CELERIAC

These two unusual vegetables are rarely seen on the vegetable patch but are appreciated in the kitchen for their distinctive flavour.

Florence fennel is a type of fennel bred for its fleshy stem base. The feathery foliage is an attractive addition in the ornamental border. It has a subtle aniseed flavour and can be eaten raw, casseroled or braised.

Celeriac is a close relative of celery, with a thickened stem base which is edible. It is easier to grow than traditional trench celery (see pages 102–3) but requires the same rich, moist, organic soil to thrive. It prefers a cool, damp climate.

Florence fennel, on the other hand, prefers a Mediterranean climate, growing best in a warm site in light, well-drained soil. Work in plenty of well-rotted organic matter and water in very dry spells. Florence fennel can bolt if it gets too dry or too cold.

Varieties

FLORENCE FENNEL

'Cantino', 'Selma', 'Rudy' and 'Zefo Fino' all did well in a *Gardening Which?* trial, producing good-sized bulbs without bolting. There is little to choose between them. 'Selma' produced the biggest bulbs but is less widely available than the others.

CELERIAC

'Giant Prague' is an old variety. 'Monarch' is an improved modern variety that is said to be easier to grow.

Fennel 'bulb'

Celeriac roots

Calendar

FLORENCE FENNEL

Under ideal conditions – rich, moisture-retentive soil, regular watering and a Mediterranean climate – Florence fennel will grow rapidly, producing a 'bulb' in 10–12 weeks. In the UK climate, it is best to sow after late June. It is liable to bolt if sown too early or in a cold summer.

APRIL–MAY

For a summer crop, sow a couple of seeds per 7-cm pot. Plant the young seedlings when they have two pairs of leaves, 30cm apart. Florence fennel dislikes being planted out when it is larger (i.e. once a rootball has formed).

Keep the area well weeded and well watered to promote rapid growth.

JUNE–JULY

For autumn crops, sow the seed directly into a well-prepared seedbed and water thoroughly if the soil is dry. Germination can be erratic, but the seedlings will not suffer a check to their growth by being transplanted. Thin to 30cm apart. Keep the area well watered and weeded to promote rapid growth. When the stem base starts to swell, you can pile up soil around the stem to make it whiter, although this is not essential.

HARVESTING

When the swollen base is plump and fleshy, cut just above soil level. The stump may produce a crop of smaller shoots. Trim the larger leaves off the 'bulb'. While it is growing, the ferny leaves can be used for flavouring (see page 210).

CELERIAC

FEBRUARY–MARCH

Sow the seed in seed trays in gentle heat (12°C or less), then grow on in a greenhouse. The seed needs light to germinate so scatter it on the compost surface and do not cover it. Keep the compost moist by covering the trays with a sheet of glass. Germination may be slow and erratic.

Prick out the seedlings into small pots or modular seed trays when they are large enough to handle easily.

APRIL

Harden off the young plants carefully in a coldframe or a sheltered spot outside.

MAY

Plant out into their final position when they are about 5–8cm high. Give each plant a space of 30cm in diameter or plant 30cm apart each way.

JUNE–SEPTEMBER

Mulch between the plants with a 15-cm layer of old straw or well-rotted compost to help conserve moisture. Water well in dry spells and give a high-nitrogen feed

from time to time during the summer. Remove the lower leaves later in the summer to help the roots swell.

OCTOBER

Lift the large knobbly roots for storage.

Celeriac growing

HARVESTING

To prevent rotting, pull off all the leaf stalks except the innermost tuft. Celeriac can be stored in boxes of moist sand throughout the winter until needed. However, the flavour is likely to be better if they are left in the ground. Cover them with straw or dried bracken to protect them from severe frosts, and use slug pellets if slugs are a problem.

Scrub the root thoroughly before peeling and cooking. Cut the flesh into 2.5-cm cubes and cook in boiling water for about ten minutes or until tender. Celeriac can be used instead of celery in soups and stews, baked in a cheese sauce or grated raw in salads. The leaves should remain green all winter and can be used to add a celery flavour.

FRENCH BEANS *Dwarf*

If you enjoy those expensive needle beans imported from Kenya or exotic-sounding dried beans such as borlotti, why not try growing your own? Both types are easy to grow, take up little room, and some are ornamental, too. You can produce a succession of needle beans throughout the summer, and harvest your own haricot beans (dried beans) in the autumn.

Dwarf French beans are a trouble-free crop with several advantages over runner beans. They do not need insects to pollinate the flowers, which makes them ideal as early or late crops under glass. The plants are compact so only limited support is needed and they are small enough to grow under cloches if you do not have a greenhouse.

HARVESTING

Pick pods as soon as they reach 10cm for pencil-pod or needle bean varieties, or at no more than 15cm for larger, flat-podded types. Take care, when picking, that you do not pull too hard or you will loosen the plant.

To enjoy dwarf beans at their best, eat them straight away and take care not to overcook them. Surplus beans can be blanched and frozen for winter use. Fresh beans are one of the best crops for batch freezing, and if you choose the slim pencil-pod or needle beans, they can be blanched and frozen whole with little preparation. Haricot beans are even easier, because you do not need to pick the pods regularly. Simply leave them to dry off and ripen naturally, and scoop the whole lot up in one go for storing. Climbing varieties add height to a border or will cover a trellis.

For dried beans, leave them until mid-autumn. Cover the plants with cloches in wet spells and bring them indoors if frost threatens. You can continue drying in a sunny, airy room or in a greenhouse if necessary. Eventually, the pods will be dry and brittle and then seeds can be easily separated and stored in jars.

Harvesting dwarf beans

Calendar

MARCH

If you have empty greenhouse borders and are prepared to provide background heating to keep the temperature above 5°C at night, you should be able to get a quick crop of dwarf beans before planting out your tomatoes in May. Follow the general sowing advice given below and grow four plants in a 10-litre container.

APRIL

French beans are very sensitive to frost. It is not worth sowing outdoors until the risk of frost has passed. You can sow the seed in pots under cover about four weeks before it is safe to plant outdoors. In milder areas, sow the seed in 7-cm pots or modular trays for an early crop outdoors.

You could also sow directly into the soil under cloches. Put the cloches in place at least two weeks before to warm up the soil. Under cloches sow in blocks with 15cm between seeds each way.

MAY

In colder areas, make the main sowing in pots now for planting out into containers and ornamental borders as well as the vegetable plot.

In milder areas, plant out beans started in pots in April. You could also sow directly into the soil. Sow or plant in rows 30cm apart, with plants 7.5cm apart. Sow two or three seeds each time to allow for any failures. Pull out any surplus seedlings later.

French beans need a minimum soil temperature of 10°C in order to germinate. Check the temperature about 1.5cm deep with a soil thermometer before you risk sowing. Do this in the early morning and wait until a mild, settled spell is forecast before sowing.

JUNE

Plant out seeds started in pots in May in colder areas. In the vegetable plot, plant them 7.5cm apart in rows 30cm apart, or in blocks with plants 15cm apart each way. In borders, allow a diameter of 15cm for each plant. Give plants in containers roughly the same space too, i.e. about four plants to a 30-cm diameter pot.

When the first flowers start to form, regular watering will greatly increase the yield in dry periods. Give a thorough soaking once a week or fortnight to wet the soil to a good depth.

Sow a late crop directly into the soil in all areas. These will crop into September.

JULY

As soon as pods start to form, keep picking them regularly, twice a week if necessary. If seeds start to mature in unpicked pods, flowering will cease. Pick and discard any surplus pods to prolong the harvest.

Dwarf beans may need some support to stop them flopping over. If necessary, push twigs into the soil along the rows or use twine tied to canes pushed in at intervals.

Make a final outdoor sowing in milder areas if there is space in the vegetable plot. Give the seedbed a really thorough watering first.

AUGUST

Keep watering weekly in dry spells and harvesting frequently.

SEPTEMBER

In colder areas, cover the latest sowings with cloches or garden fleece to protect them against unexpected frosts.

OCTOBER

For dried beans, leave the plants as long as possible before harvesting.

French bean seedlings

Young dwarf beans

Plant with a trowel...

...or sow direct.

Varieties

FRESH BEANS

'Cropper Teepee' is unusual in that the bunches of pods are held above the foliage, making picking easy. The pods are round and green.

'Masterpiece Stringless' is one of the older varieties, yet it still produced the best crop in the last *Gardening Which?* trial. It has long, flat, green pods which are best picked young. **'The Prince'** is a similar variety which has also stood the test of time and was popular in the last *Gardening Which?* members' trial.

'Mont d'Or' has short, flat, yellow pods with a slightly waxy texture. They are best picked small before the black seeds start to develop.

'Purple Queen' has slim, dark-purple pods, which, like all purple beans, turn dark green when cooked. It is an attractive choice for an ornamental border.

'Purple Queen'

'Tendergreen'

'Purple Teepee' is a purple-podded version of **'Cropper Teepee'** with the same advantages.

'Safari' is one of many Kenyan-type beans (like the imported beans you find on sale in supermarkets), and produces slim, green pods. Pick them regularly before they exceed 10cm in length.

'Tendergreen' is an older variety with fleshy, round, green pods flecked with purple. It freezes well.

'Safari'

Beans for drying

DRIED BEANS

'Borlotto Firetongue' is a spectacular bean with flat, green pods flecked with red, which turn redder as they mature. Although sold as a dwarf variety, it can be rather straggly and will benefit from some support from pea sticks, for example. There is also a climbing version (see page 122). Grow either version for the dried beans, which are buff, flecked with red. These have become better known in recent years and are used in minestrone soup.

'Brown Dutch', with round, yellow-brown seeds, and **'Horsehead'**, with kidney-shaped, purple-speckled seeds, are other varieties grown for the dried beans.

'Canadian Wonder' is usually grown for its large, flat green pods, but leave them to dry and harvest the seeds as red kidney beans, for use in chilli con carne.

HOW TO PREVENT PROBLEMS

Blackfly (black bean aphid) starts to build up rapidly as the weather warms up, from June onwards. Often, they will be controlled by ladybirds and other natural predators. If they appear to be getting out of hand, spray with pyrethrum.

Bean mosaic virus is spread by aphids and causes the leaves to become mottled yellow or crinkled. Destroy affected plants to prevent it spreading further, and spray to control aphids.

Slugs will also attack the young plants and later the young pods. Use slug pellets as a last resort, if damage is unacceptable.

Mice are often responsible for gaps in rows of direct-sown beans. Set traps or sow extra seeds to allow gaps to be filled later.

OTHER DWARF BEANS

You may come across both soya and navy beans in specialist seed catalogues. Grow them in exactly the same way as you would dwarf French beans. The plants look very similar, but their seeds give them away. Soya beans produce small, flat pods with usually only two small round seeds. These can be green or black depending on the variety. Do not expect huge yields in the UK.

Navy beans are similar to other dwarf French beans, but the seeds are white and round. Once cooked, they are easily recognised as the familiar baked bean.

Grow both as novelties rather than as substitutes for the more productive green beans.

FRENCH BEANS *Climbing*

As a change from runner beans, try growing climbing French beans up a wigwam in the border or on a trellis or arch. Varieties with yellow-, purple- and red-flushed pods are available, as well as the plain green ones. Most have white flowers, though some have pale mauve blooms.

What is the difference between climbing French beans and runner beans? Both originated in South America and were brought back to Europe in the sixteenth century. The British favoured the runner bean (*Phaseolus coccineus*), while elsewhere in Europe, *Phaseolus vulgaris* was preferred, which led to the common name of French bean.

In *Gardening Which?* trials, French beans have given a better crop early in the season, but have been overtaken by runners later on. French beans are better in early summer or under glass because they do not rely on insects to pollinate the flowers.

Varieties

GREEN PODS

Most of these varieties are pictured on the opposite page.

'**Blue Lake**' (on the left) is the most widely available variety. It has white flowers and long, round pods with white seeds that can be dried as haricot beans.

'**Hunter**' (on the right) has long, flattened pods, superficially like a runner bean, but with bulges where the seeds are.

UNUSUAL AND COLOURED PODS

'**Borlotto**' (second from the left) has spectacular pods that start a light green flecked with red and turn bright red as they mature. You can eat the immature pods, but better still, let them ripen and harvest the round, mottled seeds as borlotti beans. Be careful, because there is a similar dwarf variety (see page 121).

'**Neckargold**' (centre) has white flowers, but the pods are flat and golden-yellow. The colour is retained after cooking.

'**Pea Bean**' is a novelty, with short green pods containing six or so round pink-and-white seeds the size of peas. You can eat the immature pods or shell them later.

'**Violet Podded Stringless**' (second from right) has slim, round pods that are bright purple, but turn dark green when cooked. The flowers are pale purple, too.

'Neckargold'

Calendar

APRIL – MAY

Sow the seed, two to a 7-cm pot, under cover (see page 121 for more details).

Prepare supports, unless you are using an existing garden structure. Simplest is a wigwam of bamboo canes or bean poles. Erect it so there is a base of at least 60cm diameter, with the supports spaced 15cm apart and tied securely at the top. French beans are not as vigorous as runners – supports 1.8m high should be sufficient. You can substitute strings for alternate canes if you prefer. They can also be grown in long rows like runner beans (see page 179). Enrich the soil by digging in well-rotted manure or garden compost, as for runners.

JUNE

Plant out after the danger of frost has passed. You can also sow seed directly into the soil this month. Sow two or three seeds, or one plant, 15cm apart. Ideally, each plant should have its own support.

JULY – AUGUST

As with runner beans, pick the pods regularly when they are still tender.

SEPTEMBER – OCTOBER

Towards the end of the season, leave some of the pods to mature. These will become dry and brittle and the beans inside can be harvested for use as haricot beans (see page 118) or saved for next year's crop. French beans do not usually have the nitrogen-fixing nodules of runner beans.

Shelling 'Borlotto' beans

> **HARVESTING**
>
> Snap a bean to check it breaks cleanly without any stringiness. Harvest while tender and before the beans inside have started to swell – if you let the beans mature, flowering and continued cropping will drop off. After picking, tie in stray shoots to keep plants neat.

From left: 'Blue Lake', Borlotto', Neckargold', 'Violet Podded Stringless', 'Hunter'

LABLAB BEAN

'Ruby Moon' is perhaps the most ornamental bean of all, and worth considering as an unusual border climber or as a container plant. Grow it as you would climbing French beans, planting out in a container or border in June, but do not expect a huge crop. It can grow up to 2m. The leaves are bronzed and the pale-

'Ruby Moon'

and dark-mauve flowers produce flat, curved maroon pods that go dark green when cooked.

G A R L I C

Garlic is one of the easiest crops to grow. No matter where you live in the UK, so long as you have a weed-free, sunny spot and well-drained soil, you can grow garlic just by planting a single clove and waiting until a whole bulb is ready to harvest.

Since ancient times, it has been known for its curative properties, and is used in almost every cuisine in the world. To some people, it is an indispensable cooking ingredient.

Varieties

Recent *Gardening Which?* trials comparing autumn and spring planting of garlic showed that some varieties produce a better crop from an autumn planting than from a spring planting, and vice versa. So choose the planting season that suits you best and pick a variety that does well then (see below). **'Cristo'** gave the biggest bulbs from both autumn and spring planting. They were strongly flavoured and this variety also has a reputation for storing well. **'Fleur de Lys'** and **'White Pearl'** both gave small but strongly flavoured bulbs from either autumn or spring planting. **'Fokhagyma'** and **'Snow White'** (also sold as **'Solent White'** or **'Mersley White'**) produced mild, medium-sized bulbs from both autumn and spring planting. **'Long Keeper'** gave big bulbs from an autumn planting.

'Sultop' produced mild, medium-sized bulbs but had better results from a spring planting. You may also come across **elephant garlic**, with its extra large cloves. It looks impressive and makes for easier peeling, but it is not as strong as normal garlic.

'Cristo'

GARLIC CHIVES

Garlic chives

These are attractive and useful perennials, also known as Chinese chives. The leaves taste like a cross between chives and mild garlic, and the flower heads can be used to decorate salads. They will grow in any well-drained soil or small containers. Sow the seed in spring, either indoors or in the ground in rows. Thin the plants to 15–20cm apart. In their first year, take a few leaves once the plants are 15cm high and do not allow them to flower. In the second year, the plants will form a clump and produce white flowers in late summer. The leaves die back in winter, but you could lift a plant out and pot it up for the kitchen windowsill.

Calendar

FEBRUARY

In milder areas, garlic can be planted now, if the soil is workable and not too wet. Loosen heavy or compacted soil.

MARCH

Plant out in colder areas as soon as the soil is in good condition.

Separate the bulb into individual cloves and plant each one upright, with the flat base of the clove facing downwards. Push them at least 3cm down into the soil with no tip visible or birds will pull them up. Leave 10–25cm between each clove. The bigger the clove, the larger the space needed.

APRIL–MAY

Garlic requires little attention while it grows. All you need do is pull up any weeds that come up near the plants. If the weather is very dry, it is worth watering to encourage leaf growth, as this determines the size of the bulb.

JUNE–JULY

Bulbs should start to swell underground. As soon as the leaves turn yellow, harvest the garlic. If left, the bulbs might re-sprout and not store so well.

OCTOBER–NOVEMBER

Garlic can also be planted in autumn (late October to early November). Push the cloves in firmly so that they are not lifted out by early frost. Otherwise they need no attention and should be ready to harvest the following June or July.

HARVESTING

Loosen the soil with a hand fork and ease the bulbs out gently. Dry them in the sun, but watch out for summer showers. In wet weather, dry them on a sunny windowsill. Put bulbs in a clean seed tray or plait the leaves and hang them up. Store them somewhere dry at a minimum of 5°C. Garlic should keep until the following spring this way.

Break up the bulb...

...and plant individual cloves

HOW TO PREVENT PROBLEMS

Garlic can suffer from the same soil-borne diseases as onions and leeks, especially leek rust (see page 128). Do not plant garlic where onions and leeks have been growing previously, and start with healthy cloves. You could plant garlic you have bought for cooking but you will get much healthier crops by buying special garlic from garden shops or from mail-order seed catalogues.

Garlic growing

TIP

Spare cloves can be planted in pots of multipurpose compost and the green shoots harvested and used like chives. If you have a large crop of bulbs, try planting a couple of whole bulbs in a pot, or leave them in the ground. Early the following spring they will produce a clump of green shoots which can be cut and used in the same way as chives.

KALE

Once confined to the allotment as a standby for the 'hungry gap' period of late winter and early spring, kale is now appreciated for its appearance, too. Modern and rediscovered heritage varieties are worth adding to ornamental borders and containers, especially as winter fillers. The greens are tasty and nutritious at a time when fresh, home-grown vegetables are scarce.

Kale can be grown as a cut-and-come-again salad crop (see page 180) and if left to bolt in the spring, the immature flower shoots rival sprouting broccoli.

Varieties

Some old garden books, and even some modern seed catalogues, still refer to kale as borecole. Do not confuse it with broccoli, which includes sprouting broccoli (see pages 78–9) and calabrese (or broccoli in the supermarkets) (see pages 92–3).

'Redbor' F1 is one of the most striking of the edible kales, and would be at home in either the flower border or a patio container. The bright red colour is lost in cooking.

'Black Tuscany' (**'Nero di Toscana'**) is a very ancient European variety now enjoying a come-back because of its interesting appearance. The strap-shaped, blue-grey leaves

would hold their own in the most stylish border. The young leaves have a mild flavour and can be used as a salad ingredient, too.

'Darkibor' F1 is a newer, tall variety (90cm) with dark-green curly leaves.

'Dwarf Green Curled', a dwarf, traditional variety with tightly curled blue-green leaves, is ideal for the smaller garden.

'Pentland Brig' is an older variety with large, slightly crinkled leaves. Pick the younger leaves in winter and the side shoots in spring.

'Showbor' F1 is a modern hybrid with a dwarf habit and tightly curled leaves. This is the one to grow as a baby vegetable.

'Black Tuscany' ('Nero di Toscana')

'Redbor'

ORNAMENTAL KALES

You can grow these and ornamental cabbages from seed, or buy young plants as winter bedding. Bear in mind that they suffer from the same pests as edible kales. You can eat them, but they taste bitter, so are best treated purely as ornamental.

Open-leaved varieties such as **'Red Peacock'** and **'White Peacock'** proved to be the most winter-hardy in a *Gardening Which?* trial.

Calendar

APRIL–MAY

Traditionally, kale is started off in a seedbed. Draw a shallow (1.5–2cm deep) drill in well-prepared soil (see page 50 for more details). Water the bottom well and sow the seed thinly, aiming for one every 5cm or so. Cover with soil.

If you want only a few plants for a container or border, start the seed off in 7-cm pots. The seed is quite large and easy to handle – sow two per pot and pull out the weaker one if both germinate. A cool but frost-free place in the garden or an unheated room is fine, with a minimum temperature of 5˚C.

JUNE

Grow the young plants in pots on in a sheltered spot outdoors. Protect them from pests such as flea beetles (which riddle the leaves with tiny holes, see page 87). Keep an eye out for aphids and, if necessary, spray with a product based on pyrethrum or soft soap. Covering seedbeds with garden fleece should prevent attacks from either pest. Slugs may also damage the young plants. If the leaves start to change colour, the plants may be running out of nutrients. Either feed them with a liquid feed, or pot on into a larger pot.

JULY

Plant out into their final position. First, water the pot or the seedbed well. Make a slight depression and plant into the bottom. This allows easier watering in a dry summer, until the plants are established. Lift the young plants carefully from the seedbed with as much root as possible. They may flop after planting even if well watered, but will quickly recover.

For larger varieties in a vegetable plot, space the plants 45cm apart each way. In a border, allow a space of about 45-cm diameter for the plant to develop. For container growing, use a pot that holds at least 5 litres of compost and site it where you can water it frequently. Smaller varieties can be grown as baby vegetables planted as close as 15cm apart.

AUGUST–OCTOBER

Consider a crop of kale as a gap-filler in August, after early crops have been harvested. Sow the seed directly into drills and thin out in stages to leave the final spacing. You can use thinnings in salad. Slugs and flea beetles should not cause further problems on established plants. But keep an eye out for mealy cabbage aphid (see page 87), which can build up very rapidly, unnoticed. Towards the end of summer, cabbage white butterflies will become numerous, and their caterpillars will attack the leaves. Pick them off or spray with a pyrethrum spray if they cause damage.

NOVEMBER–FEBRUARY

Cover the crops with bird netting or use bird scarers if pigeons start to damage the young leaves.

SPRING

The plants might start to look scruffy and the leaves unappetising, but leave them to bolt for the edible flower shoots.

Leaves ready for picking

Kale in containers

Edible flower shoots

HARVESTING

Pick individual younger leaves as required. Wash them carefully to remove any aphids or whitefly lurking in the wrinkles.

The immature flower shoots (before the yellow flowers start to show) can be picked and eaten like sprouting broccoli. You should also get a flush of tender young leaves before the plants bolt.

LEEKS

Leeks make a very useful winter vegetable. They are so hardy you can leave them in the ground until you need them. Baby leeks are easy to grow in containers and raised vegetable beds and provide a tasty crop through the summer and autumn. Grow some on into conventional-sized leeks for winter. In the border, the strap-shaped, blue-green leaves are an interesting addition throughout the winter.

Leeks are very easy to grow from seed and because you can transplant them without a problem they are very versatile. Start them in pots ready to plant out later in the season to follow other crops that have been harvested. Or grow them in a seedbed, use the thinnings as an alternative to spring onions, and plant them into their final position for a winter crop.

HOW TO PREVENT PROBLEMS

Leeks are generally trouble-free but do suffer from one disease – **leek rust**. This also affects garlic and chives. The symptoms are raised, rust-coloured spots or streaks on the leaves. In severe cases, leaves may turn yellow and die. There are no suitable fungicides for garden use, so remove and burn badly affected plants. However, the blanched underground stems of mildly affected plants are still edible and the plants will stand through the winter.

Destroying the remains of the crop (do not put on the compost heap) and growing on a new piece of ground each year should limit the damage.

Although no varieties are totally resistant, some are more resistant than others (see page 130).

Leek rust

Calendar

MARCH

Unless you want exhibition-sized leeks (see page 131) March is early enough to make the first sowing. The young plants will also be at the right stage to follow on early crops such as early potatoes, early peas or broad beans in late June or July.

If you want lots of plants for a vegetable plot, sow in a seedbed. Make seed drills 1–2cm deep and 15cm apart. Sow fairly thickly as the thinnings can be used for salads. Leek seeds will germinate at fairly low temperatures (around 7°C). In colder areas cover the seedbeds with cloches or garden fleece.

For borders, start seed off in small pots or modular trays. Sow seed about 2.5cm apart in seed trays. Keep them somewhere cool but frost-free. To grow leeks in containers, see page 131.

APRIL–MAY

After careful hardening off, move plants raised inside outdoors when temperatures start to rise in spring. At this stage the seedlings can be pricked out into modular trays (those with 40 cells are ideal) to grow on. Do not worry if you cannot separate every seedling; leeks are one of the crops that can be multi-seeded (see page 140).

Remove the cloche or fleece covers from seedbeds once the young plants resemble rows of grass. Thin seed rows out to leave a plant every 3–4cm.

JUNE–JULY

Depending on the growth of the young leeks and when space becomes available, plant out into the final position. The plants will wait until you are ready, but should ideally be about 20cm tall and as thick as a pencil.

After harvesting the previous crop, prepare the site by forking the soil deeply, especially if it is compacted. At the same time, work in some general fertiliser. Give the whole area a thorough soaking if the soil is dry and leave for a week to settle.

Plant leeks raised in pots or modules into the bottom of a shallow depression. Use a draw hoe to make a trench about 10cm wide and deep. This will make earthing up, to blanch the base of the plant, easier later.

Plants raised in a seedbed should be watered, then eased out of the soil with a fork. Separate them out and trim the roots to about 8-10cm. You can trim very long leaves too to compensate. Drop each plant into a hole made with a dibber – the end of an old spade handle is perfect. The deeper the hole, the longer the blanched stem will be, but make sure that some of the leaves are above soil level. Fill each hole with water to settle the plants in. They will flop at first but will soon pick up. The holes will fill in, too. An alternative is to plant deeply with a trowel. However you do it, aim for a plant every 15cm in rows 30cm apart for average-sized leeks. Increasing or decreasing the spacing will produce bigger or smaller leeks.

AUGUST–SEPTEMBER

Leeks planted with a dibber should have a long white stem. Other plants can be earthed up as they grow, by drawing soil along the row to increase the length of blanched stem.

OCTOBER–SPRING

Harvest the leeks as you need them through the winter (see page 130).

Using a dibber

Planting leeks

Watering in

Earthed-up leeks

Varieties

'Autumn Mammoth 3 Snowstar' is a mid-season variety for harvesting from November to February.

'Bandit' is a late variety that can be harvested until April. It has some in-built resistance to leek rust.

'Carlton' F1 was the first hybrid leek, though more are becoming available. Although the seed is more expensive, the plants grow more quickly and produce thick stems by autumn.

They are a good choice for an autumn crop, but may not be as winter-hardy as traditional varieties.

'King Richard' is an old garden variety that is ideal for a quick crop of baby leeks. It will also stand well into the winter and produce acceptable large stems.

'Musselburgh' is an old variety, reasonably resistant to rust, for mid-season – October to February.

'Musselburgh'

'Autumn Mammoth 3 Snowstar'

HARVESTING

Leeks need no protection from the cold, but bear in mind that lifting leeks from frozen ground is hard work. If very cold spells are forecast, lift a supply of leeks and heel them in temporarily in a sheltered part of the garden, near the kitchen. Always use a fork pushed deeply beside the plant to ease it out of the ground.

Trim off any diseased, rotten or excess green leaves and roots. In the kitchen, cut off excess green leaves and the bottom and peel off outer leaves to give the maximum length of white base. Wash thoroughly to remove soil and grit that has lodged between the leaves. Very dirty leeks are best washed, cut into slices, then washed again.

Harvesting leeks

BABBINGTON'S LEEK

A vegetable oddity, more closely related to garlic than true leeks. It is a perennial, producing bulbils around the underground bulb and in the flower head. These are used to propagate the plant because it does not produce seed. The bulbs have a mild garlic flavour.

HOW TO GROW BABY LEEKS

These have become popular in supermarkets and are the best option for containers and raised beds.

Sow short rows regularly from March to June in seed drills 15cm apart. Thin the seedlings, if necessary, to about 1cm apart. In containers, sow seed roughly 2.5cm apart and cover with a dusting of compost.

Keep the young plants well watered so that they grow rapidly and produce tender young plants about as thick as a pencil. Pull these in bunches and use them as a substitute for spring onions. They are a little milder and can be used in salads or braised. You can also leave them to grow on and pull them as baby leeks when they reach about 1–1.5cm in diameter.

'King Richard'

Baby leeks in a pot

EXHIBITION LEEKS

Two types of leek are popular with exhibitors. In some parts of the country, growing giant pot leeks is an obsession. And no local horticultural show is complete without its display of long white 'blanch' leeks. These two types are different in many ways.

Pot leeks are very short and squat and are grown for weight. You will not find pot leek seeds in normal seed catalogues. They can also be grown from 'pips'. These are small bulbs that actually grow in the flower heads, but

unlike the seeds, are clones, identical to the parent leek. Exhibitors select their own special strains of pot leek. If you want to compete seriously, you will need to buy seed or pips from a specialist supplier.

Blanch leeks are more like the typical garden leek, but are grown for the length of blanched stem. The stem is blanched by tying a paper collar round it or even by using sections of plastic drainpipe.

Both types are started

before Christmas using artificial heat and light to increase the growing season. They are given lots of space,

SAVING SEED

Leeks are one of the easier vegetables to save seed from. Leave one plant to bolt or run to flower the following spring. The huge white flowers on 1.5-m stalks may need supporting with a cane, and attract bees. When the flowers have dried off, the black seed can be shaken out.

often under cover, and fed and watered regularly to produce the maximum length or bulk possible.

L E T T U C E

Lettuce is the perfect crop for a window box or other container, and needs little care, other than regular watering. You can grow any variety of lettuce in an ornamental border or bed, though the loose-leaved and coloured kinds are the best choice as a foliage edging. In a small raised vegetable bed, growing lettuce is a very efficient use of space, and by regular sowing you can easily achieve a constant supply of tasty, fresh salad leaves for your salads (see also page 180). The choice of types and varieties you can grow is huge – see pages 134–5.

GROWING LETTUCE

Early in the year, lettuces grow best in a sunny but sheltered spot. In the summer, they will tolerate light shade, and may bolt prematurely in full sun. In a vegetable plot, try to grow them in a different part of the plot each year or incorporate them into a crop rotation (see pages 36–7) in case soil pests or diseases start to build up.

A neutral soil with plenty of organic matter is best, so grow them with the cabbage family (see pages 83–9). They can be used to fill in between slow-growing winter crops – for example, Brussels sprouts, sprouting broccoli, winter cauliflower – during the summer.

In pots or containers, lettuce will thrive in a multipurpose compost, provided it is kept constantly moist. Allowing the compost to dry out will encourage the plants to bolt. A 15–20-cm pot is large enough to grow a lettuce to maturity, provided it is kept well watered and fed weekly with a high-nitrogen fertiliser. In larger containers allow about 23cm between plants, or grow closer together for a crop of loose leaves.

When planting lettuces in

'Cocarde' in a container

a border, treat them just like bedding plants but work a small amount of a

balanced fertiliser into the soil before planting and water well if the soil is dry.

Calendar

OUTDOOR LETTUCE

FEBRUARY

Make the earliest sowing under cover. Sow two or three seeds together, about 1.5cm deep, in small pots or modular seed trays (those with 40 cells are best). Lettuce germinates at low temperatures so an unheated greenhouse or windowsill in a cool room will suffice.

MARCH

Plant out the earliest sowing under cloches, which should be put in place a week or two before to help warm up the soil. Water the soil if it is dry. Space plants 30cm apart each way. Some small varieties such as 'Little Gem' can be grown 23cm apart, and for large firm heads of crisphead varieties increase the spacing to 38cm.

Sow seed in small pots for containers, borders and vegetable plots. Rather than sowing lots of the same variety, try sowing a few pots of several varieties. Keep the pots or trays somewhere cool and sheltered.

In a vegetable plot you can also sow directly into a well-raked seedbed. Make seed drills about 1.5cm deep and 30cm apart. Sow seed thinly and thin out in stages to leave one seedling every 30cm.

APRIL–JULY

Keep sowing further batches at fortnightly intervals to maintain a constant supply throughout the summer. Plants raised in pots can be planted out as soon as they have four true leaves.

In a raised bed, sow or plant short rows across the bed at fortnightly intervals to produce a continuous supply. Four or five lettuces a fortnight should be plenty. The same applies to containers. Try to make sure that when

lettuces are harvested, you have more young plants to replace them.

Remove cloches from the earliest sowing in April. These should be ready from May to June, depending on the type. From June onwards you should be rewarded with a steady supply of lettuces throughout the summer. As the summer progresses, later sowings will catch up with earlier ones.

Lettuce, especially butterhead types, may fail to germinate in high summer when the temperature is over 20°C. To overcome this, sow in the late afternoon, so that the critical stage of germination occurs in the cool of evening.

AUGUST

A final sowing can be worthwhile for an autumn crop. Use a variety that is resistant to downy mildew, a disease that strikes in cool, damp weather.

Alternatively, sow a loose-leaved variety and pick leaves as required, rather than hearted lettuce.

You could also plant a hardy winter lettuce, which will produce loose leaves the following spring, or hearts in May.

SEPTEMBER–OCTOBER

In colder areas, cover autumn crops with cloches. In all areas, cover winter lettuces with cloches.

Sow seed thinly

Thin out if necessary

Planting lettuce

Cover early crops

HARVESTING

Harvest lettuces in the early morning, when the leaves are turgid, and store in a plastic bag in the fridge to keep them cool and moist. To check that hearted lettuce is ready, lay the back of your hand on top and press gently – it should feel firm.

Harvesting 'Lollo' lettuces

Varieties

BUTTERHEAD

These are less popular than they used to be, mainly because they do not keep well, but this is not a problem if you grow your own rather than rely on shop-bought lettuce. The leaves are rounder, softer and thinner than those on the more popular crispheads, and the hearts are looser and yellow. They are better later in the season, and some varieties are resistant to downy mildew. They mature in 9–12 weeks.

The leaves brown quickly if cut or shredded, so either use the leaves whole or tear them with your fingers. Butterheads are at their best as a base for a mixed salad, for lettuce soup or for wrapping fish or meat for steaming. **'Avondefiance'** and **'Musette'** are large varieties with some resistance to downy mildew and root aphid.

'Tom Thumb' is a very old miniature butterhead. Its taste was somewhat disappointing in a *Gardening Which?* trial but it is still useful for small gardens.

'Lollo Rossa'

Butterhead 'Dolly'

Crisphead 'Set'

CRISPHEAD

This is the largest type of lettuce, with pale, crinkled outer leaves and firm, white hearts. In the shops they are sold as 'icebergs', with the outer leaves removed. They need plenty of space and take 11–13 weeks to mature.

Crispheads shred well, and complement stronger-flavoured ingredients in sandwiches. The green outer leaves can also be used in salads. The heart should be white, solid and crunchy. It will keep for a week in the fridge if wrapped in clingfilm. **'Saladin'** and **'Set'** are two reliable crisphead lettuces that scored highly in the *Gardening Which?* taste tests. Both were mild, with a slightly sweet flavour and a crunchy texture.

COS OR ROMAINE

These are large lettuces with tall, pointed hearts. The leaves are long and crinkled with a thick midrib. They are the best-tasting lettuces if well grown, but are slow to mature, taking 11–13 weeks. This is an advantage as it means they are slow to bolt.

They have a long shelf-life when harvested. Discard the tough, bitter midribs of the outer leaves. Tear up the leaves for mixed salads. They are ideal in a Caesar salad and for supporting spicy ingredients, or on their own as a salad with a dressing.

Mixture of hearted and loose-leaved lettuces

'Little Gem'

'Frisby'

'Red Salad Bowl'

variety that is still hard to beat. It is a small cos that can be grown with closer spacing than normal. It matures two weeks faster than other cos and is perfect used as an early crop or as a catch crop between slower-growing vegetables.

LOOSE-LEAVED

These have loose heads of divided or crinkled leaves. They take 10–14 weeks to mature but stand for up to four weeks before bolting. They are still attractive when they bolt and make a novel border plant. Red varieties need space to develop their full colour, which may also be more intense in colder weather.

Loose-leaved varieties can be very bitter and are often used as an attractive garnish rather than as the bulk of a salad. To make them less bitter, grow them fast with a plentiful supply of water. The Lollos are the most attractive but are fairly tasteless and they dislike the hottest part of summer.

The leaves hold dirt, so rinse them thoroughly before serving. Pick individual leaves about 10cm long instead of mature heads for garnish. You can start picking them when the plants are about four weeks old. They are also used as cut-and-come-again crops (see page 180).

'Cocarde' is an interesting, oak-leaved lettuce with green

and brown leaves. But it looks better than it tastes.

'Frisby' is a compact variety with a tight head of green, frizzy leaves that can be used in summer or over winter.

'Lollo Rossa' is an Italian variety grown for its very attractive, frilly leaves. Several newer versions with darker or more intense colours are now available. A pretty choice for the ornamental garden, although the taste is often disappointing. 'Lollo Bionda' is a pale-green version.

'Salad Bowl' is a reliable old variety with long, indented leaves. There are red and green versions.

BABY LETTUCE

'Mini Green' is a miniature crisphead, which will grow as close as 13cm apart to produce tiny, crisp hearts. 'Blush' is similar but the outer leaves are flushed with pink, making it more ornamental.

Small traditional varieties such as 'Little Gem' and 'Tom Thumb' can also be grown close together as baby lettuce.

WINTER LETTUCE

'Arctic King' and 'Valdor' are very hardy butterhead types, which are sown in autumn and harvested in spring. 'Frisby' can also be treated this way.

'Winter Density' is a hardy cos type bred for autumn sowing. It is slightly larger than 'Little Gem'.

They are less successful in sandwiches and go slimy when cut.

'Corsair' forms neat-looking plants with an excellent sweet flavour, although they are rather chewy.

'Pinokkio' is another sweet-tasting lettuce with the bonus of having some resistance

to downy mildew.

'Sherwood' is a new cos that was highly rated in a *Gardening Which?* taste test for its sweet, fresh flavour and crisp texture. It is a large variety, not the most attractive, but with good downy mildew resistance.

'Little Gem' is a very old

HOW TO PREVENT PROBLEMS

The main pests that affect lettuces are **cutworms** and other soil grubs, **slugs**, **snails** and **greenfly** (lettuce aphids).

Cutworms sever the stems of young plants at ground level and are rarely visible. **Slugs and snails** nibble irregular holes in the leaves at night and are often detectable by the telltale slime trails the next day. You can use soil insecticides or slug pellets to destroy slugs, snails and cutworms. However, a better strategy is to start plants off in small pots or modular trays and plant them out when they are large enough to survive. Lettuces in containers are unlikely to be attacked by cutworms, although slugs and snails can be a nuisance, often travelling some distance from their daytime retreats. Try a couple of night-time forays with a torch to collect and destroy them.

Lettuce aphids will attack plants in containers as well as in the garden. Check the undersides of the leaves occasionally, and if numbers start to build up and natural predators such as ladybirds and hoverfly larvae cannot keep up, you may have to spray. Use a natural insecticide such as soft soap or pyrethrum.

Downy mildew is a disease that occurs particularly in cool, wet summers and on greenhouse lettuce. Leaves become mottled yellow with a white downy mould on the undersides. Remove and destroy badly affected plants and avoid wetting the leaves.

Tip burn is caused by poor movement of calcium within the plant and shows as watery edges to the inner leaves, which turn brown and rot. Keep the plants well watered in hot, dry weather to prevent this problem.

Tip burn

Downy mildew

HOW TO GROW BABY LETTUCE

Harvesting 'Mini Green'

Unlike some other vegetables, lettuces will not necessarily be small-hearted if grown closer together. You are more likely to end up with a mass of leaves. If this is what you want, see pages 180–3 for the range of salad leaves available.

'Mini Green'

If you want small lettuce hearts, choose one of the naturally small varieties on page 135 and space them just 13–15cm apart. These are a good choice for growing in pots, window boxes or mini-vegetable beds. Each plant should make a heart about 7.5cm across, which is ideal for a salad for two.

Calendar

GREENHOUSE LETTUCE

If you have a greenhouse, you can carry on growing lettuce throughout the winter. This is an economical way of keeping the greenhouse borders occupied when the tomatoes are finished. And if you do not have any borders, try growing them in pots or used growing bags (see below).

You will need to keep the greenhouse frost-free. Insulate it with bubble polythene and use a greenhouse heater to keep the temperature above freezing – set the thermostat on an electric heater to 3°C to be sure. Use a maximum–minimum thermometer to monitor the temperature (see pages 54–5).

AUGUST

Use a quick-maturing greenhouse variety and sow in small pots for a December harvest.

SEPTEMBER

Make a second sowing to be sure of getting lettuces after Christmas.

Plant the earlier sowing as soon as there is space in the greenhouse border or pot on into larger pots.

OCTOBER–NOVEMBER

Make a third sowing to crop in April, before the first outdoor lettuces are ready. Plant out the September sowing as soon as space permits.

DECEMBER–SPRING

Water greenhouse lettuces so the soil or compost is always moist but apply carefully to avoid wetting the leaves.

Open the vents on mild days to prevent fungal diseases such as downy mildew and grey mould.

Cut the plants as soon as they have developed a reasonable heart.

Varieties

You can try hardy outdoor varieties in the greenhouse, or one of the varieties especially bred to cope with low temperatures and low light levels.

'Kwiek' is a butterhead variety that is fast to mature and has a strong flavour.

'Kellys' is a crisphead variety, slow to make a firm heart but has a good quality and flavour.

'Winter Density' is an older cos, also suitable for an unheated greenhouse.

HOW TO REUSE GROWING BAGS

Pull out the tomato plants with as much of the thicker root as possible. Fluff up the bags to loosen the compost and increase the depth. If there are not adequate drainage holes near the base of the bag, make some more. If you have been using tomato feed, you will need to flush the excess salts out of the growing bag by flooding with water a couple of times. Add a little balanced fertiliser, then you are ready for a second crop of lettuce. The same procedure applies to large pots of compost previously used for tomatoes.

MARROW

To grow proper marrows, it is best to select a specific variety rather than just leave courgettes to get bigger. Unlike courgettes, you have a choice of bush or trailing varieties. Bush varieties can take up a lot of space, so they are more manageable on a vegetable plot. Trailing varieties are easier to fit into an ornamental garden, as they can be trained up a trellis, pergola or wigwam. The latter can look impressive in autumn with the fruits hanging down. 'Vegetable Spaghetti' is an interesting novelty in the kitchen. If you find marrows bland, consider winter squash, which are just as easy to grow. See pages 168–9.

Varieties

'Badger Cross' is a modern hybrid variety that produces uniform, good-quality, striped fruits. It is a bush plant, resistant to mosaic virus.

'Tiger Cross' is fairly similar. 'Early Gem', an old dual-purpose variety, will produce a reasonable crop of courgettes and also give well-shaped, all-green marrows if left to grow large. 'Long Green Striped' is the trailing variety for characteristic big, striped fruits.

'Long Green Trailing' is a trailing variety with long, all-green fruit.

'Table Dainty' bears small, striped fruits on trailing plants that can be trained up supports.

The unusual small, pale-yellow fruits of 'Vegetable Spaghetti' are cooked like other marrows. However, the flesh comes out in strings, like a low-calorie spaghetti – hence the name. Not particularly tasty, but an interesting talking point. It is a trailing plant, although there is a new variety called 'Tivoli' with a more bush-like habit.

For varieties bred specifically for growing as courgettes, see pages 108–9.

'Badger Cross'

'Table Dainty'

'Vegetable Spaghetti'

Calendar

MAY

Marrows are very sensitive to frost so it is not worth sowing or planting them outside until all risk of frost has passed. Sow the seed in pots in a greenhouse or on a warm windowsill for planting out in June.

Sow the large flat seeds on edge into 7-cm pots and cover with compost. This will help to prevent rotting and allow the seedling to push the seed out of the compost. Keep the pots somewhere with plenty of light and a minimum temperature of 18°C.

Keep the young plants well watered and if you cannot plant them out within four weeks, pot them on into bigger pots.

Gradually harden off the young plants, putting them outside on warm days and under cover on cooler nights.

JUNE

Even in the coldest areas, it should be safe to plant out by mid-June. On a vegetable plot, marrows can follow an early or overwintered crop after it has been harvested.

Unless the soil is already rich in organic matter, prepare a planting hole. Dig a hole up to 30cm in diameter and 30cm deep. Refill with a mixture of soil and well-rotted manure or garden compost, leaving a low mound to plant into. This will encourage rain to drain away from the base of the plant, and help to prevent stem rot.

Allow an area at least 1m in diameter for bush types. Trailing types can be trained up a fence, trellis or other structure. But make sure that they get enough water and nutrition in a crowded border.

Water sparingly at first, aiming to keep the soil moist. Do not overwater, or you will encourage too much leaf.

The easiest way to prevent competition from weeds, conserve moisture and provide a steady supply of nutrients, is to mulch the area with lots of well-rotted manure or garden compost. Leave a small gap around the base of the stem to prevent rotting.

On a vegetable plot, you could plant through a permeable plastic mulch instead.

JULY

Once flowering starts, soak the soil once a week in dry weather. Feed plants, especially those in well-planted borders, with a dilute tomato feed.

Train climbing plants by tying the shoots loosely to supports and prevent wayward shoots trying to take over the border. Bush types can be left.

When fruits start to develop, keep them off the ground, for example, by pushing a tile under them. Plants trained as climbers may be damaged by the weight of large fruits. Provide some support, using net bags or mini-hammocks made from plastic netting.

Marrow as a climber

Ripe marrows

HARVESTING

Pick fruits for summer use when they reach about 25–30cm long. This will encourage more fruits to form. Most varieties continue cropping until the first frost. For winter storage, leave the fruits to ripen and develop their full colour. Striped varieties will turn green-and-yellow and harden.

Gather the mature fruits before the first severe frost. Often the first mild frost of the autumn will cause the foliage to collapse and make harvesting easier. Do not leave it too late, or the fruits will be harmed too.

Store only sound, fully-ripened fruits with hard skins. They should keep for up to four months, given suitable conditions. Stand them in a single layer, not touching, on wooden trays. Better still, hang them individually in nets to allow air to circulate around them. Store in a well-ventilated, cool (but frost-free) shed or outbuilding. Check occasionally for any signs of rotting.

ONIONS

This must be one of the easiest vegetables to grow, especially if you start from sets. Each small set will grow into a full-sized onion during the summer. On a vegetable plot, onion plants need very little attention and can be left to mature and dry off for winter storage. It should be possible to store home-grown onions until the following spring. Onions will grow and produce a worthwhile crop in large containers, too. There is now a good choice of varieties from sets. For even greater choice, try growing onions from seed, though this does take a little more effort.

HOW TO PREVENT PROBLEMS

White rot is the most serious disease of onions. It is a very persistent disease, and remains in the soil for up to 18 years. The leaves turn yellow prematurely and wilt. A white, fluffy mould with minute black spots grows on the bulbs. It spreads rapidly, so destroy all infected plants. As there is no chemical treatment, the only solution is to grow onions and related crops on a new site in subsequent years. Take care not to spread soil from infected areas on footwear and tools.

Downy mildew is another disease that affects the leaves. Pale oval areas, which later turn brown or purple, appear. Eventually, the leaves die back from the tips. This disease is likely to be worse in cool, wet seasons, when the leaves remain damp for long periods. If bulbs are affected, they become soft and will not store. Destroy all affected plants and spray the remainder with Dithane 945.

The best way to prevent both these diseases is to rotate onions and related crops. Grow them on a fresh piece of the vegetable plot each year, on a three- or four-year cycle (see page 37).

HOW TO GROW ONION FROM SEED

If it is so easy to grow onions from sets, why bother with seed? Apart from the greater choice of varieties, seed also works out much cheaper if you want a lot of onions.

Sow the seed thinly into trays of multipurpose compost in late February or early March. The seed will germinate quickly at a temperature of 10–15°C. When the plants, which resemble grass, are large enough to handle, transplant them into pots or modular trays. Harden them off gradually until they are ready to plant out in late March to April. You can also sow the seed directly into the soil from February (under cloches) to April. Sow into seed drills 1cm deep and 15cm apart. Thin the seedlings to 2.5–5cm apart.

Multi-seeding works well with onions. Sow about 6–8 seeds together into 7-cm pots or modular trays, and do not thin the seedlings out. Plant out the whole potful together. Plant the clumps about 15cm apart each way. As the bulbs grow they will push each other apart to produce clumps of small, round onions.

Multi-seeded onion seedlings

Calendar

When you buy a bag of onion sets, you are buying immature onions that were raised from seed the previous summer. Because they are sown at a very high density, they do not reach sufficient size to bolt (produce a tall, erect flowering shoot) or produce flowers in the second season – they just carry on growing instead. Under normal conditions, onions are biennial, producing a bulb in the first year and flowering the second season. Sets are a convenient way of cutting out the seedling stage. Some varieties are more prone to bolting in their second year.

FEBRUARY

As soon as the soil is workable and not too wet, you can plant onion sets. In cold areas or on heavy soil, delay until mid-March or even April. Sow onion seed indoors.

MARCH–APRIL

Prepare the ground by digging the soil to loosen it. Soil that is too compact or firm will cause the onion roots to push the sets out as they grow. The ideal site is a piece of well-cultivated, weed-free ground that has been manured in previous years but not recently. Onions benefit from a little balanced fertiliser – i.e. up to 35g a sq m of growmore or similar – but do not add fresh manure before planting.

Push the sets gently into the soil so the tips are level with the surface. Birds will pull them out given the chance, so cover them with garden fleece or a cloche. The spacing will, to some extent, determine the final size of the bulbs. For lots of small bulbs, about 5cm in diameter, plant the sets 2.5cm apart in rows 15cm apart. This spacing allows room to get a hoe between the rows. This is important as onions cannot compete with weeds, so you will need to hoe or weed by hand. As the onions grow, the bulbs will push each other apart. For larger bulbs (up to 10cm across), increase the spacing to 10cm within the rows.

To plant sets in containers, push them into the compost 7.5–10cm apart each way. If you have left-over sets, plant them almost touching in a 15-cm pot and cut the shoots as spring onions.

MAY–JULY

Hoe between the rows, and if necessary hand-weed between the plants. You can buy special short-handled onion hoes that allow you to bend or kneel down to hoe. Even when fully grown, onions cannot shade out other plants so they are very sensitive to weed competition.

In most years, onions do not need additional watering.

AUGUST–SEPTEMBER

The foliage will start to yellow and fall over naturally. Let nature take its course – if you bend them over too early, the leaves can get damaged and let in diseases. Lift the bulbs with a fork to break the roots and leave them on the surface to ripen fully in the sun. In a wet summer, cover them with cloches or move them to a greenhouse bench to complete their ripening.

You can sow Japanese onions early in September in the north, later in the south.

OCTOBER

Lift the spring crop for storing. You can plant autumn sets now for an early crop next summer.

Planting sets

Drying off ripe onions

Multi-seeded onions

Varieties

SPRING SETS

The sets of certain varieties are heat-treated by suppliers to kill the flower embryo and so prevent bolting. Treated sets tend to be more expensive than untreated sets but generally store better.

'British Bulldog', **'Centurion'** and **'Turbo'** are reliable untreated varieties that produced high yields in the *Gardening Which?* trial, but did not store so well.

'Dobies All Rounder' was among the best performers of the untreated sets for early sowing. It also stored the longest.

'Golden Ball' and **'Orion'** are heat-treated sets for an April sowing. Both performed well and stored better than untreated onions.

'Red Baron' is the best of the red-skinned onions. In the trial, it gave the best yield, very few plants bolted and the bulbs stored well into spring.

SPRING-SOWN ONIONS

'Albion' is one of the few white-skinned onions.

'Balstora' and **'Red Baron'** are both available as seed.

'Bedfordshire Champion' is an older variety that produces large, well-shaped onions which store successfully. It is a favourite with people who grow onions for shows.

'Hygro' is similar to **'Balstora'** and is another

'Red Baron' (red), 'Albion' (white), 'Bedfordshire Champion'

'Balstora'

'Turbo'

'Red Baron'

variety that keeps well.

'Kelsae' is one of several varieties used to produce giant onions for exhibiting.

'Owa' is an unusual, elongated variety only

available as seed, with a mild flavour (but not worth storing).

'Shakespeare' is a mini-onion variety bred in Warwickshire. Grown at

close spacing, it produces lots of small, brown-skinned bulbs that can be pickled (see page 145) or used in stir-fries and casseroles. One for the mini-vegetable bed.

'Owa'

HARVESTING

If some plants have bolted, the bulbs are still edible, but use these as soon as possible as they will not store well. Store sound onions in a cool, dry, airy place through the winter. If you do not wish to plait onions into the traditional strings, you can tie them in tights or store them in net sacks. You can also spread bulbs in a single layer in shallow trays. Inspect them regularly and throw out any that show signs of mould, rotting or softening.

AUTUMN SETS

Autumn sets are even easier. These are mostly varieties bred in the UK. Plant them just as you would spring sets, but in October or November. Take the usual precautions to stop birds pulling them out of the ground. They too will mature by the following June or July. **'Radar'** is a reliable, yellow-skinned autumn variety.

AUTUMN-SOWN ONIONS

Autumn-sown onions, originally known as 'Japanese' onions, are hardy enough to stand over winter from an autumn sowing. They are ready to harvest in June, and bridge the gap between the last of the stored onions and the first of the spring-sown or planted crop. They are sown

Onions from seed

in August either directly into the soil or in modular trays, and are planted out in September. The plants need to be 15–20cm tall by October to survive the winter. In January or February give them a dusting of a high-nitrogen fertiliser. They should be ready to harvest in June or July. Aim to use

Autumn-sown onions

them up through the summer (they do not store as well as spring-sown onions).

'Senshyu Semi Globe Yellow' is a yellow-skinned Japanese variety.

SALAD ONIONS

Salad onions, often called spring onions, are immature onions that are used raw in salads or as a garnish. Their small size also makes them ideal for stir-fries.

You can get a worthwhile crop of salad onions from the smallest space, be it a container, small raised bed or border. They are ready to harvest in 10–12 weeks, so you can sow every fortnight in spring for a continuous supply all through the summer. Some extra-hardy varieties will overwinter, which means that you can pull your own salad onions the following spring.

Varieties

SALAD ONIONS

'White Lisbon' is one of the oldest varieties and still the most popular. It has a pronounced bulb and a short white shaft.

'Ishikura' is a Japanese bunching onion with long white stems, but no bulb.

'Guardsman' is a modern, bulb-less variety which is a cross between a traditional spring onion and a Japanese bunching onion. Once ready, it remains in peak condition for a long time and is claimed to be resistant to white rot.

'Ishikura'

'White Lisbon Winter Hardy' is an extra-hardy strain which can be sown in autumn and harvested the following spring.

'Redmate' is worth trying for something different.

It produces bright-red spring onions and, if left, will go on to produce small onions.

PICKLING ONIONS

'Brown Pickling SY300' is a brown variety. **'Paris Silverskin'** has white bulbs.

'Redmate'

Calendar

FEBRUARY

Make the first sowing under cloches.

MARCH–JULY

Start to sow outdoors from mid-March. Make several sowings, either in pots of multipurpose compost or in patches in the border. In a vegetable plot or raised bed, sow short rows or bands, once a fortnight for a summer-long supply.

In pots, scatter seeds roughly 2–3cm apart, and cover with about 1.5cm of compost. In the garden, sow in rows 10cm apart and thin the seedlings to 2.5cm apart. Alternatively, sow in bands. With a draw hoe, take out a shallow drill (about 1.5cm deep and 8–10cm wide). Scatter the seed thinly so that you end up with a plant every 2–3cm, allowing about 30cm between adjacent bands. The ideal density is 320 plants per square metre, or 30 to a 30-cm square. You should get away with about 30 in a 30cm-diameter pot.

For tender, succulent salad onions, water weekly in dry weather to keep the plants growing rapidly.

AUGUST–SEPTEMBER

For an early crop the following spring, sow a hardy winter variety now.

> **HARVESTING**
>
> Pull bunches of plants as soon as the stems are 1cm thick. Some varieties will have a distinct bulb at the base, others will not.

Spring onions growing

Harvesting 'Ishikura'

PICKLING ONIONS

These are simply onions sown very thickly to produce lots of small bulbs. It is best to use one of the special varieties (see left). Sow the seed thinly in broad drills 15cm apart, and aim for a plant every 2cm each way. For perfect pickling-sized onions you should aim for 100 plants per square metre. When the tops have died off and the bulbs are fully ripened, lift them for pickling.

Pickling onions

PERENNIAL ONIONS

Welsh onions

Despite their name, these onions probably reached Europe via Russia. They are perennials and, once established, produce large clumps like chives. The hollow leaves can be chopped and used as a substitute for salad onions in the spring, and the small bulbs can be used as onions. There are white and red forms, both of which can be grown from seed. The plants produce white flower heads in summer, which attract bees. Established clumps can be divided up and individual bulbs transplanted.

Egyptian Tree Onions

A curiosity for the border, perhaps? This hardy perennial onion produces small bulbs, the size of a cocktail onion, in the 60–90cm flowering shoots. If left, these will bend over and plant themselves in the autumn. Pick the aerial bulbs in September and lift the small underground bulbs through the winter. Replant a couple of bulbs for next year.

ORIENTAL GREENS

Despite the popularity of Chinese food, oriental greens are not widely grown in the UK. This is unfortunate, as they are a quick, easy crop, and decorative enough for a small garden.

There are two main points to consider when growing these vegetables. First, they have a tendency to bolt if sown too early, but this is easily prevented by choosing improved varieties (see page 148) or by sowing later in the summer than European cabbages. A second potential problem is that oriental greens are prey to all the pests and diseases that affect other members of the cabbage family (see pages 86–7). So it is worth using a crop cover.

Like European cabbages, oriental greens require a very fertile, moisture-retentive soil, with a high nitrogen content. This is particularly important if you are using them as a follow-on crop from mid-summer onwards, to enrich the soil.

HOW TO PREVENT PROBLEMS

Slugs and **snails** relish the young tender leaves of oriental greens. If necessary, use slug pellets sparingly when you plant the young plants out. Barriers made from 10cm sections of plastic bottles pushed into the soil around new transplants will protect them from surface slugs. Plants in raised beds and pots can be surrounded by physical barriers (see pages 40–1).

Most of the other common pests – **cabbage aphid, flea beetle** and **cabbage root fly** can be kept off the crop by a covering of fine mesh or garden fleece.

Plants in borders or containers are vulnerable to **cabbage white butterflies**. Inspect plants regularly, rub out eggs and remove small caterpillars before they do any damage. Oriental greens are also vulnerable to **clubroot** (see page 86–7).

CUT-AND-COME-AGAIN

Mustard as a cut-and-come-again crop

All types of oriental greens respond well to the cut-and-come-again treatment (see pages 180–3).

Sow them directly into the soil, do not thin out or transplant and keep them well watered. When the young plants reach a height of 10cm, cut them with scissors, leaving a 2-cm stump. This should regrow producing a further flush of tender young leaves.

Calendar

MARCH–MAY

Sow all types of oriental greens for a crop of loose leaves (see also Salad leaves, pages 180–1). (Chinese cabbages have rough seed leaves, which are not as good to eat as when they are larger.) The leaves can be cut at any stage, either as seedlings or as immature plants. Spring-sown plants are likely to bolt if left too long, though the flower shoots are also edible before the flowers open.

JUNE

Most oriental greens are a useful follow-on crop after broad beans or peas have finished. Chinese cabbage will bolt if transplanted from a seedbed, so these and other kinds of oriental greens can be sown directly into their final position and thinned out later. However, it is more efficient to start the seed off in 7-cm pots, ready to follow an early crop. Keep them in partial shade and watch out for pests.

JULY

Keep the seedlings well watered until a space is ready in the vegetable plot, ornamental border or containers.

Earlier crops of peas or beans can be cut off at soil level and their roots left to nourish the greens. If you are not following on from a crop of peas or beans, then fork plenty of well-rotted manure or garden compost into the soil before planting. Give the soil a thorough soaking if it is dry, and scatter a generous amount of balanced fertiliser.

Chinese cabbage and larger types of oriental greens need a spacing of 30–38cm each way to produce heads. Pak choi can be planted as close as 23cm apart. Direct-sown crops can be thinned to the spacings above, or to a closer spacing of 10–15cm apart for a crop of loose greens.

Cover the crop with insect-proof netting or be prepared to hand-pick or spray pests (see left).

Further sowings can be made throughout July, although they will need to be kept moist.

Water the plants well and, if possible, apply a mulch of well-rotted organic matter to help keep the roots moist.

AUGUST

Make a final sowing of Chinese cabbage for an autumn crop. Mature heads from the earliest sowing should be ready to harvest.

SEPTEMBER

Chinese cabbage and pak choi are not very frost-hardy, so cover later sowings with cloches or garden fleece. A late sowing in a greenhouse or polythene tunnel, which can be kept frost-free, should provide fresh greens all winter.

Komatsuna, mizuna, mustard 'Green in Snow' and rosette pak choi or 'Tat Soi' are the hardiest and may survive outdoors in mild areas.

Young pak choi

Mature pak choi

Young 'Tat Soi'

HARVESTING

Cut Chinese cabbage heads, leaving a stump – this should produce a flush of new leaves. Mature heads and older leaves are best steamed or used in stir-fries. Younger leaves, immature plants and seedlings of all oriental greens can be used as alternative salad ingredients (see pages 180–3).

Varieties

The names used in seed catalogues can be confusing, so here is a brief guide to varieties under the following headings: Chinese cabbage, pak choi, mustards and mizuna.

CHINESE CABBAGE

These are either tall and cylindrical or barrel-shaped. The barrel-shaped ones are best suited to the UK climate. They have a mild flavour and crunchy texture and can be used as a substitute for iceberg lettuce. Loose-leaved varieties are sometimes available.

'Kasumi' was the best barrel-shaped variety in the last *Gardening Which?* trial. It had heavy, dense, mid-green hearts with very little internal leaf stalk. It did not bolt.

'Early Jade Pagoda' is a cylindrical variety which produced heavy heads up to 27cm tall. It will bolt if sown before June.

'Ruffles' is an unusual variety with large heads of pale, fluffy, internal leaves.

PAK CHOI

Even though these do not make dense hearts, the fleshy, mild-flavoured leaf

Mizuna

stalks are edible. Upright varieties with either white or green stalks are the most commonly available.

'Pueblo' is a new variety that is claimed not to bolt from sowings as early as April.

Green pak choi tended to bolt easily in trial – but

a new F1 hybrid called **'Mei Quing Choi',** which was not in the trial, is claimed to bolt less readily.

'Joi Choi' was by far the best pak choi variety in the trial. It was uniform in appearance, with contrasting dark-green leaves and white stalks; it did not bolt.

'Joi Choi'

'Kasumi'

OKRA

To grow this successfully outdoors in the UK is something of a challenge, although you should succeed in a greenhouse or polythene tunnel.

Start the seed in a heated propagator in March and provide the same conditions as for aubergine (see page 68–9). Grow on in large pots or in the greenhouse border. The pointed green pods should be picked when they reach about 7cm long.

Okra pods

'Tat Soi'

Red mustard

'Tat Soi' is a small green rosette type and did not bolt in the *Gardening Which?* trial. It is hardier than most pak choi.

MUSTARDS

These have a hotter flavour than Chinese cabbage and pak choi and are best stir-fried. The seedlings are milder, and used in salads.

'Green in Snow' ran to seed readily in the trial. It is less likely to bolt from a July sowing. It can be grown as a seedling crop.

'Giant Red' has attractive red leaves but also bolted readily. This variety is worth considering as a colourful and spicy salad leaf.

Komatsuna (or **spinach mustard**) is very hardy and has a flavour halfway between Chinese cabbage and mustard. You are most likely to find unnamed komatsuna, although one called **'Tendergreen'**, produced large dark leaves in the *Gardening Which?* trial.

JAPANESE GREENS

Mizuna produces frilly rosettes of mild leaves.

Mibuna have strap-shaped leaves. Both will overwinter if given some protection and can be used for winter salads.

'Green Spray' (mibuna) has sprays of long, narrow leaves and is winter hardy.

'Youzen' (mizuna) was a great success in the trial. The plants were uniform, and the finely divided leaves were very attractive. It did not bolt and is definitely worth considering for salad crop (see pages 180–3) or as a late filler in an ornamental border.

OTHER ORIENTAL GREENS

Celtuce or **Chinese stem lettuce** is a type of lettuce with a tender edible stem. It is no relation of celery, but the stems have a mild flavour and crunchy texture. It is best as a summer-to-autumn crop. Harvest it when the stems are 30cm tall and 2.5cm thick.

Chinese broccoli or **Chinese kale** is grown mainly for its edible flowering shoots. It can be sown throughout the summer and crops after about two months.

Chop suey greens or **shungiku** is a type of chrysanthemum which will flower very quickly. If it is sown little and often and picked young, its leaves add a piquancy to salads or can be cooked as spinach. It becomes very bitter when it starts to bolt.

Celtuce

Chop suey greens

PARSNIP

Once thought of as just a winter standby, parsnips are now available from summer onwards as a baby vegetable. In a small garden or even in containers it is possible to grow a quick crop of small parsnips. With more space, parsnip is an easy winter crop – you simply leave it in the ground until you want it.

You can also try some other, more unusual, root crops such as Hamburg parsley, salsify and scorzonera. These are easy to grow and worth trying as novelties.

Parsnips do best on deeply dug, fertile soil with a pH of about 6.5 (just on the acid side). Ideally they should follow a previous crop that has been well-manured rather than have the manure added now. Fork in a small amount of a general fertiliser. Long-rooted types hate stony, heavy or compacted soil, so try a shorter-rooted variety like 'Avonresister'.

HOW TO PREVENT PROBLEMS

Parsnips are sometimes attacked by the **carrot fly**. (see page 97). To combat this, grow parsnips with carrots and surround both crops with a carrot fly barrier or cover with garden fleece.

Parsnip canker used to be a serious problem. All modern varieties and some of the old ones are resistant to parsnip canker, so you are unlikely to encounter it.

HOW TO GROW GIANT PARSNIPS

You may have seen these at garden shows. If you want to have a go, you have to cheat. To increase the depth of fine, stone-free soil, you need a container, such as a plastic dustbin, with the bottom cut out. Loosen the underlying soil as deeply as you can. Then fill the container with good sandy or loamy soil. You can add well-rotted garden compost, but not fresh manure – some gardeners

use a crowbar to make several long, tapered holes and fill these with fine soil. Sow two seeds, about 30cm apart. Keep the container well-watered and feed with a liquid fertiliser later in the summer to keep the plants growing strongly. In the autumn, carefully ease out the root, trying to keep the fine tap root intact. If grown well, giant parsnips should not be woody and will be edible.

TIP

Parsnip seed loses its viability rapidly. Always buy fresh seed each year – do not save surplus seed. Once the packet has been opened, re-seal it and store it in a cool, dry place if you intend to make further sowings of, for example, baby parsnips.

Calendar

MARCH

Postpone sowing until April unless the site is particularly favourable. What you can do this month is dig the ground deeply to loosen the compacted soil. Like carrots, parsnips need a deep, well-worked soil.

Sow the seed directly into the ground – starting the seed off in pots usually results in forked roots. Parsnip seed is slow and erratic to germinate, so there is no real advantage in starting too soon, as early sowings into cold, wet ground are likely to be disappointing.

APRIL

In the vegetable plot, sow into seed drills 1cm deep and 30cm apart. The seed is attached to a light membrane and is easily blown about. Sow a couple of seeds at 15-cm intervals, to limit the amount of thinning later. If more than one plant comes up at each position, thin out all but the strongest. You can now buy seed tapes in which the seed has been pre-spaced and sandwiched between thin paper ribbons. All you do is lay the tape down in the seed drill.

The seedlings are slow to appear, so sow a quick-growing crop such as radish in the same drill, as a marker. The radishes will be out of the way before the parsnips need the space. For baby parsnips, space the rows 15cm apart and aim for one plant every 5cm.

MAY–JUNE

As they are slow-growing, parsnips cannot compete with weeds early in the season. Hoe between the rows regularly to keep weeds under control. Further sowings can be made through the summer for a succession of baby parsnips. Water well until the young plants are established.

JULY–AUGUST

Parsnips growing in the ground do not need regular watering, but make sure that the soil does not dry out in very hot weather. If necessary, water to re-moisten the soil to a good depth. Heavy watering or rain following a drought, however, will cause the roots to split.

Baby parsnips in beds and pots will need watering. Harvest when the top of the root is between 2.5cm and 5cm wide. Use a hand fork to ease them out.

SEPTEMBER

Continue to harvest baby parsnips. The largest roots of winter parsnips can also be lifted before the tops have died off. Although frost is said to enhance the flavour, you can lift them before the first frosts if you wish.

OCTOBER

Once the tops have died down, the roots can be lifted for storing under cover. They can also be left where they are and will keep in good condition until spring. In very cold areas, cover the row with straw to stop the ground freezing solid.

HARVESTING

The flavour of the roots is likely to be better if they are left in the ground until needed. However, once the ground has frozen they are hard to harvest, so you may prefer to lift them beforehand and store the roots indoors in boxes of sand. Use a garden fork to ease the roots out of the ground.

Aim to finish digging them up by late winter, before they start to re-grow. Parsnips, like carrots, are biennials and will throw up flowering shoots in the spring.

Seed tape

Sowing seed

Parsnip growing

Varieties

PARSNIP

'Avonresister' was the first variety bred for resistance to parsnip canker. The short, wide-shouldered roots can be grown close together and cope better with shallow soils than most varieties. It is still widely available, but has

'Gladiator'

'Lancer'

Salsify, scorzonera and Hamburg parsley

been more or less superseded by more recent varieties.

'Gladiator' is the first F1 hybrid parsnip, resistant to canker and with smooth, tapered roots. It is fast-growing and the best choice for small gardens.

'Lancer', **'Arrow'** and **'Javelin'** have thin, tapered roots, ideal for close spacing and the best choice for baby vegetables.

'Tender and True' is an old variety with some resistance to parsnip canker. The heavy roots are said to have a full flavour.

Calendar

HAMBURG PARSLEY, SALSIFY AND SCORZONERA

MARCH–MAY

All three crops can be grown in the same way as parsnips and prefer similar soil conditions. Sow the seed directly into seed drills 1cm deep from March to May. Hamburg parsley needs more space, so keep the rows 30cm apart and thin the plants to 20cm. Salsify and scorzonera can be closer, with 15cm between rows and 10cm between plants. Salsify seed has poor viability – sow several per position.

JUNE–SEPTEMBER

Hoe regularly to keep weeds down. None of these crops needs watering in a typical summer. Being a perennial, scorzonera can be sown in the autumn to crop the following autumn.

OCTOBER–NOVEMBER

Roots should be ready for lifting or storing as required.

HARVESTING

All three crops can either be left in the ground until they are needed, or lifted from October onwards and stored in boxes of sand. Brush clean under running water, peel and boil briefly.

Scorzonera can be cooked unpeeled, then run under the cold tap to remove the skin. Once cut, surfaces will discolour, so cook quickly or rub them with cut lemon. Hamburg parsley is an ingredient of bortsch and the roots can be roasted like parsnips. Salsify and scorzonera can be boiled in vegetable stock, and the thicker roots roasted.

If left to grow, the young leaves of salsify can be blanched the following spring rather like chicory. The young flower shoots are said to taste like asparagus.

Hamburg parsley

Salsify

Scorzonera

Hamburg parsley is a type of parsley bred for its edible parsnip-like roots. The leaves are coarser than normal parsley, but are fine for flavouring soups and stews. **'Berliner'** is the only named variety you are likely to find. It has fewer leaves but bigger roots than the unnamed version.

Salsify is a biennial, so it will flower in the second season. It has blue flowers and long, thin white roots with an oyster-like flavour, hence its common name 'vegetable oyster'.

Several varieties exist, such as **'Giant'** and **'Mammoth Sandwich Island'**. All are essentially similar.

Scorzonera is a perennial, so if the roots are not big enough to eat after one season, you can leave it to grow. It has wider leaves than salsify, yellow flowers and long, thin, black roots. The young leaves of both can be used in salads. **'Russian Giant'** is the best of the named varieties.

PEAS

Fresh garden peas are a treat compared to the ubiquitous frozen type. Do not be put off by the thought of having to shell them – you can eat mangetout and snap peas pod and all.

Peas can be grown in several ways: taller varieties can be trained up a wigwam, trellis or against a fence. Dwarf ones can be grown in a container or even a hanging basket.

Peas thrive on deep, well-drained soil with plenty of organic matter. On poor soil, it is worth preparing a trench over winter and filling it with a mixture of soil and well-rotted organic matter. Since peas manufacture their own nitrogen fertiliser from the air through the nodules on their roots, they need no feeding. And the roots left in the ground after harvest will benefit the next crop.

Taller varieties are likely to crop over a longer period than the shorter varieties from a single sowing. However, by making several sowings of the shorter varieties throughout the summer, you can prolong cropping. An alternative is to make one sowing of an early and a maincrop variety.

HOW TO PREVENT PROBLEMS

Pea moth grub

Pea and bean weevils nibble semicircular notches out of young leaves in spring. They rarely cause any serious harm and control is not usually needed.

Pea moth, on the other hand, usually goes unnoticed until you start shelling the peas. One or more of the peas has been burrowed into by a small white grub, and the grub, plus its faeces, is usually still inside the pod. The simplest way to avoid this pest, which lays eggs on pea flowers during June and July, is to concentrate on early sowings, which flower in May and early June. Late sowings which will flower after July may also escape. Another approach is to grow a mangetout variety and pick before the peas have developed.

Spraying with a contact insecticide such as permethrin is an option. This should be done when the first flowers start to form, and again after ten days.

Gaps in rows of peas could be due to **mice or other rodents**. Set traps, or start peas off in pots (see 'How to pre-sow peas', page 157) or sow extra seed to allow for filling gaps later. Other methods that have been suggested include soaking seed in paraffin, and covering seed drills with spiky leaves.

Calendar

FEBRUARY

In mild areas, it is worth making an early sowing under cloches or garden fleece. Take precautions against mice (see page 154). In colder areas, start peas off in small pots or modular trays in the greenhouse or coldframe.

MARCH

Sow tall peas for the ornamental border in pots under cover. Sow a couple of seeds per 7-cm pot and do not worry if more than one comes up.

Make the first outdoor sowings in milder areas. Peas are normally sown in wide (10cm) drills about 2.5–5cm deep. Sow seed thinly, aiming for one every 5cm each way. If you prefer, sow single rows with seeds 5cm apart or triple rows with seeds 12cm apart. Allow 60cm between adjacent rows or bands, slightly more for taller varieties.

All but the very dwarf varieties will need support of some kind. Tall varieties will need very solid supports. Twiggy branches called pea sticks are the traditional solution – simply push them into the rows. If you cannot get these, use lengths of pea and bean netting securely tied to posts. It is always easier to put the supports in place before or shortly after the seedlings emerge.

APRIL

Plant tall varieties in the border, about 12cm apart, alongside their supports. Make outdoor sowings in colder areas, cover with garden fleece if severe weather is forecast. Peas will germinate at 4°C, but nearer 10°C is preferable. Try growing a crop in a container. Aim for 8 plants to a 10-litre pot, sowing a few more seed to allow for failures.

Push a couple of twiggy sticks into the pot for support.

MAY

The earliest crop should be ready. Pick frequently, removing all the pods that are ready. Leaving pods on the plants for too long will shorten the cropping season.

JUNE

Peas that are in flower now are at risk from pea moth (see page 154) but peas sown now should escape damage.

If the soil is very dry, a good soaking when the plants are in full flower and the first pods are starting to form will increase the yield.

JULY

Later crops are still at risk from pea moth. It may be worth a very late sowing in milder areas: use an early variety.

AUGUST–SEPTEMBER

Keep picking over later sowings regularly. When the crop is finished, cut the tops off the plants at ground level and leave the roots with their nodules to fertilise the next crop.

OCTOBER–NOVEMBER

Now is the time to sow the hardiest varieties for a very early crop the following spring. These plants are guaranteed to be free of pea moth.

Spare borders in the greenhouse can be used for an overwintering crop of mangetout peas – they will be well out of the way when you need the space for tomatoes.

Planting pot-raised plants

Pea sticks

Peas for shelling

HARVESTING

Pick mangetout regularly when they reach 5–7.5cm. Pick garden peas when the pods are plump and the peas inside are full-sized but still tender. See page 156 for more on the different types.

Varieties

Garden peas and mangetout are the two main types of pea. It is worth growing more than one type, as both have something to offer.

Garden peas are grown for the tender young peas, which are allowed to reach full size. The pods are discarded.

With **mangetout peas**, the pods are eaten whole (*mange tout* in French means 'eat everything'). The pods are picked while they are still young and tender, and before the peas inside have developed fully. You may come across different types of mangetout. For example, snap peas with their plump, fleshy pods that often 'snap' when bent. These pods are very sweet and are eaten when the peas inside are almost full size. Picking time is crucial; if left too long on the plant, these pods may become stringy. Sugar peas have flat pods and are eaten before the peas inside start to show. These are best picked before the pods reach full size.

All types include both dwarf varieties (which are better suited to the open vegetable plot) and tall varieties (which can be trained up supports in the ornamental garden).

GARDEN PEAS

Early varieties

'Feltham First' and **'Meteor'** are hardy varieties, sometimes referred to as round seeded. They can be sown early in the spring for the earliest crop, or sown in the autumn to overwinter for an even earlier crop.

'Kelvedon Wonder' is an old, but reliable, wrinkle-seeded variety. It is quick-maturing, producing an early crop from a spring sowing. It is dwarf and requires only minimal support.

'Early Onward' and **'Hurst Greenshaft'** will crop about a fortnight after **'Kelvedon Wonder'**. Both grow to 60cm or more and will require support.

'Waverex' produces pods containing very small, sweet peas known as petits pois. This is one of the best varieties for freezing.

Maincrop varieties

'Onward' is a popular older variety. The plants, up to 90cm tall, will require support. It will crop about 14 weeks after sowing.

'Markana' is one of the newer semi-leafless varieties. It has fewer leaves than normal varieties, but more tendrils. This may explain the claim made that it is self-supporting. In practice, some support may be needed

Tall varieties

'Alderman' is one of a few very old, tall peas still widely available. The plants reach 1.8m or more and need

'Purple Podded'

Sugar pea

'Onward'

strong supports. It has white flowers and will crop over a long period if picked over regularly.

'Purple Podded' pea is one of many heritage varieties that are no longer sold but can be obtained from seed libraries.

This one is unusual in

'Oregon Sugar Pod'

'Purple Podded' in flower

having purple flowers followed by purple pods. The peas, rather disappointingly, are still light green and taste like any other variety.

MANGETOUT PEAS

'Carouby de Maussane' is a very old variety – highly rated for its ornamental value. The plants grow 1.5m or more in height and are covered in purple flowers that can easily be mistaken for a sweet pea. The pods are flat and light green and best picked frequently when they are 5–8cm long. The plants will crop for several weeks if picked over regularly.

'Oregon Sugar Pod' is a shorter variety that grows no more than 1m tall and bears

sweet, flat pods. It can also be sown in the autumn for an early spring crop. **'Sugar Dwarf Sweet Green'** is another dwarf variety (about 90cm) with an early crop of very sweet pods.

'Sugar Bon' and the newer **'Sugar Gem'** are very dwarf (about 60cm) snap peas. **'Sugar Snap'** is a heavier-cropping, but much taller snap pea variety, reaching 1.5m or more.

Sowing into a length of guttering

HOW TO PRE-SOW PEAS

Take some sections of plastic guttering about 1m long and block the ends. Half fill with multipurpose compost or decent topsoil from a garden border. Sow pea seeds evenly about 5cm apart each way and cover with more compost. Keep the 'rows' well watered and protect from mice.

When the pea seedlings have emerged, scoop out a shallow trough in the vegetable plot, wide and deep enough to take the section of guttering. Remove the ends of each gutter section and carefully slide the compost with the seedlings into the trough.

Sliding the row of peas out

PEPPERS *and* CHILLIES

If you are successful with tomatoes, try growing peppers, too. You can grow different shapes and colours of sweet pepper, and also try one of the hundreds of varieties of hot chilli peppers – used to add heat to curries and other exotic dishes.

Both sweet peppers and chillies can be trained easily into neat, bushy plants and yield enough ripe fruits to more than pay for a prime site in a container on the patio. Chilli plants are particularly decorative, and just one plant should keep even the keenest chilli-eater supplied all winter. In a greenhouse, both types will grow happily with the tomatoes.

You should find young plants for sale in garden centres, but for considerable saving, and the greatest choice of variety, grow your own from seed.

HOW TO PREVENT PROBLEMS

Peppers in a greenhouse may be attacked by all the pests that affect tomatoes: aphids, whitefly and spider mites.

Aphids can infect the plants with a virus as well as weakening them by feeding on the sap. The sugary substance the aphids excrete will make the leaves sticky and will encourage a black, sooty mould. Check regularly for aphids, especially on the undersides of the leaves and, if necessary, spray with an insecticide based on pyrethrum or soft soap.

Whitefly can spoil the appearance of the plants and, if left to build up in large numbers, can weaken them too. Spray with pyrethrum and repeat at fortnightly

intervals to catch flies that hatch from the impervious larvae or scales. Biological controls are available for both aphids and whitefly and are worth considering if either pest is a serious problem under glass. The secret with biological control is to maintain a constant temperature of about 20°C and to introduce the control before the pest has built up large numbers.

Spider mites are hard to see with the naked eye. It is worth inspecting the undersides of the leaves regularly for the characteristic flecking and webbing. Maintaining a damp atmosphere by pouring water on the greenhouse floor will help to prevent spider mites building up to damaging

levels. If they do appear, the most effective solution is the biological control agent *phytoseiulus*. Buy these as you spot the first spider mites, maintain a constant temperature as near to 20°C as possible, and the larger predatory mites will deal with the problem for you.

Outdoors, biological control is less likely to work because temperatures fluctuate too much. So instead use a non-persistent insecticide spray based on pyrethrum or soft soap solution.

Sweet peppers may suffer from **blossom end rot** – a discoloration at the end of the fruit (see page 198). This condition can be prevented by regular watering throughout the hottest period.

Calendar

MARCH

Sow two seeds to a 9-cm pot. You will need a heated propagator or at least a warm windowsill, where you can maintain a constant temperature of 20°C.

APRIL

Gradually wean the seedlings, reducing the temperature to a minimum of 14°C at night. If both seeds germinate, remove the weaker one.

MAY

As the plants begin to fill their small pots, pot them on into 2-litre pots of multipurpose compost (or growing bag compost).

JUNE

Pot the plants on into 5-litre pots. This final pot should be sufficient to produce neat, manageable plants. When the plants reach about 20cm high, pinch out the growing tip with your finger and thumb to encourage them to branch and bush out. Vigorous varieties may require further pinching to keep them bushy. This method worked well in the *Gardening Which?* trial. Sweet peppers can also be planted directly into a greenhouse border or growing bags and trained as cordons in the same way as tomatoes (see page 201).

Remove the first fruit that forms, to encourage branching and further fruits to develop.

JULY–AUGUST

Sweet peppers may need some support once the fruits start to swell, but chillies should look after themselves. During this period you may need to water the plants twice a day on hot days. After the first flowers start to form, feed regularly with a tomato fertiliser, according to the manufacturer's instructions. It is also worth moving the plants out of a greenhouse to a sunny position outside.

SEPTEMBER

Peppers are sensitive to frost. If the fruits are still developing, move outdoor plants under cover at night.

HARVESTING

Pick peppers and chillies when they are ripe but while the skin is still smooth – avoid those with wrinkled skins. Fruits store well and will keep for up to ten days in the fridge. Wash cut fruit, and remove the seeds with a knife before eating.

Surplus chillies can be stored by drying or freezing. In tropical countries, ripe chillies are dried in the sun, but in the UK climate, it is much harder to dry them completely. The long, slim types with thin walls are best for drying. It is also possible to dry chillies in an oven on the lowest setting for 24 hours or more.

By far the easiest way to store chillies for winter use is to freeze them. The chemical capsaicin, which is responsible for the heat, is present in the flesh but is concentrated in the seeds and the membrane surrounding them. Removing the seeds and core will reduce the heat.

WARNING

Be careful when handling or harvesting chillies, and wash your hands before eating or touching your eyes. Some varieties, even those grown in the UK, can be extremely hot. If you eat one that is too hot, milk or yoghurt are the best antidotes.

Pricking out

Chilli in a container

Varieties

SWEET PEPPERS

Most varieties produce the familiar bell peppers that are sold in the supermarket, but more unusual shapes and colours are available from specialist seed companies.

'New Ace' is a typical 'bell' pepper with chunky, flat-bottomed fruits that start off green and ripen to bright red. In the *Gardening Which?* trial it gave the best yield, of eight ripe fruits per plant and a couple of green ones.

'Redskin' has normal-sized, red bell peppers on compact plants, so it is perfect for patio pots.

'Gypsy' was the favourite sweet variety in the trial. The pointed fruit starts off a pale yellow-green and ripens through orange to red, making it a colourful choice for a patio. The fruits are fleshy and sweet.

'Chocolate Beauty'

'Gypsy'

'Luteus'

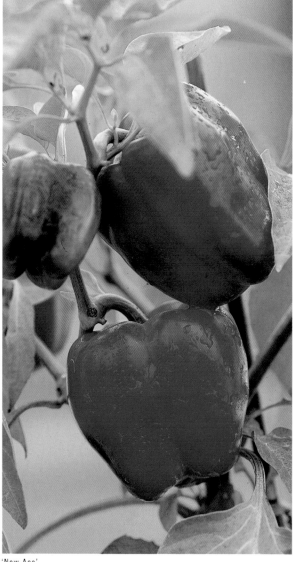

'New Ace'

'Chocolate Beauty' and **'Sweet Chocolate'** are bell peppers, but with unusual dark-brown fruits.

'Luteus' was the best yellow bell pepper in the trial, with a decent yield of bright-yellow fruits.

'Mavras' is another unusual colour, with the fruits starting off dark purple but eventually ripening to red.

CHILLIES

The heat of a chilli pepper is measured in Scoville units, with the hottest 'Habañero' type measuring 300,000. A simpler rule of thumb is the smaller the fruit, the hotter it is likely to be.

'Hungarian Wax' (also known as **'Hot Banana'**) has large carrot-shaped fruits that start off yellow. It can be

'Mavras'

'Hungarian Wax'

'Early Jalapeño'

sweet and mild in the summer, but if left to ripen it turns red and the flavour intensifies. It is easy to grow, starts cropping early and is one of the mildest of the hot peppers. It came out top in the trial.

'Numex Twilight' is an ornamental variety with lots of tiny, very hot fruits that change colour from purple to orange.

'Habañero' is reputedly the hottest chilli variety, although the round, wrinkled, orange fruits look fairly harmless.

'Cayenne' and **'Hot Mexican'** bear similar-looking long, thin fruits, which ripen to bright red.

'Serrano'

'Early Jalapeño' and **'Serrano'** both have short, blunt-ended fruits that are fairly hot. They can be eaten green or left to ripen to red.

'Apache' has small, pointed fruits that ripen to red and are medium hot. The plants are naturally small so are ideal for pots.

'Numex Twilight'

POTATOES

You do not need an allotment to grow potatoes. All you need is a decent-sized container (at least ten litres) to grow a crop of tasty new potatoes in the smallest garden. You can even grow several container crops throughout the year, including, if you so wish, new potatoes for Christmas dinner.

If you want a conventional crop of potatoes grown in the ground, turn to pages 166–7.

HOW TO START SEED POTATOES

Lay the tubers out in trays, with the 'rose' end – the one with the greatest concentration of eyes – uppermost. Place the trays in a cool, dry place with good light but not direct sunlight. After a few weeks, sprouts will start to grow.

This process, known as chitting, helps to start the tubers into growth and gains a few precious weeks while the soil is too cold for them to grow outdoors. Rub off all but the four strongest sprouts at the rose end.

Chitting potato tubers

HOW TO GET A SECOND CROP

You can make a second planting of early tubers in summer for an autumn crop of new potatoes. Specially treated tubers are available by mail-order for planting in July, but these are expensive. The first crop of earlies (planted in spring) will not usually sprout in time for a second planting the same year. So, here is a way you can cheat.

When you plant your early potatoes in spring, keep some tubers back.

Spread them out in a tray and leave them somewhere cool and dry but with good light. They will develop short, fat, green sprouts. Keep a watch for aphids,

which may introduce viruses. If necessary, cover the tubers with garden fleece to keep aphids off.

In early June, pot each tuber into a 15-cm pot and keep it well watered in a sheltered spot outside. The tubers, though shrivelled, will burst into growth.

From late June onwards, when you have space in containers or in the vegetable plot, dig a hole large enough to take the potato plant. Bury the base of the shoots, too.

The tubers should be ready in October or November and can be left in situ for use at Christmas.

Planting a second potato crop

Calendar

POTATOES IN CONTAINERS

FEBRUARY

Seed potatoes (tubers for planting) are often sold in 3-kg bags. If you need just a couple of tubers, look for garden centres that sell loose ones by weight and ask if they will sell you single tubers. Failing that, you could ask a gardening friend for a couple of spare tubers. You can grow any variety in a container, but an early variety is best because it crops quicker and has less top growth.

MARCH

In mild areas, or if you have a frost-free greenhouse or other place that is light and frost-free, plant your tubers (see left). If you cannot guarantee to keep the plants frost-free, plant next month.

APRIL

Prepare your container. This can be a large pot or tub with a capacity of at least ten litres. A plastic dustbin works well, too. Make some large drainage holes in the bottom if there aren't any. Line the bottom with a layer of stones or broken polystyrene to help drainage. Half-fill the container with compost. You could use multipurpose compost, the contents of a growing bag or garden compost. To save money, you could mix the compost with garden topsoil.

Plant the sprouted tuber with a trowel, so that it is covered with compost. One tuber to a 10–15-litre pot, or two to a dustbin, is plenty. As the plants grow, keep adding more compost to just cover the tips. If frost is forecast, cover the pot with garden

fleece or bring it indoors.

MAY

It should be safe to leave the potatoes outdoors in milder areas, but in colder parts continue to watch out for frosts. Keep the containers moist, but not too wet. Keep adding compost until it almost reaches the rim of the container.

JUNE–JULY

Water regularly and feed a couple of times with a balanced fertiliser.

If you have saved tubers from the spring, plant them in containers now for a late crop of new potatoes. You can re-use the container after harvesting the first crop. Refresh the compost by replacing about half with fresh compost and add a handful of balanced fertiliser.

SEPTEMBER–DECEMBER

When frost is predicted, cover second crops of early potatoes with garden fleece, or pull the container under cover. If you want new potatoes for Christmas, simply leave the tubers in the container after the tops have died back and keep them somewhere frost-free.

HARVESTING

When the plants start to flower, tubers will be starting to form. Push your hand into the compost and feel for tubers. When you can feel several the size of a hen's egg, pull them out but leave the plant to produce more. When the top dies down, tip the compost out and collect the tubers.

Planting tubers in pots

A good crop

Potatoes on the patio

Potato blight

Blackleg disease

Spraying to prevent blight

HOW TO PREVENT PROBLEMS

Generally, potatoes are an easy crop, though there are a number of potential problems. Most can be prevented by a few simple precautions.

Always buy certified seed potatoes. Look for the words 'Elite' or 'AA' grade on the bag. Do not save your own tubers.

Follow a three- or preferably four-year crop rotation. In other words, do not grow potatoes on the same piece of land more than once every four years (see pages 36–7).

Work in plenty of organic matter on dry soil to retain moisture and help prevent scab and spraing.

Control aphids, which can spread viruses, as soon as you see them.

Earth up the plants to help prevent blight (if it occurs) affecting the tubers. To prevent scab, do not lime the soil the previous winter.

You may come across the following problems in some years.

Blackleg is a bacterial disease that causes the leaves to roll and wilt, and the stems to blacken. It usually occurs early in the season and in dry weather. Destroy any affected plants.

Blight is a serious disease of potatoes. It starts as small brown spots or blotches on the leaves from June onwards, especially in warm, wet spells. Plants may die gradually, and neighbouring potatoes and tomatoes can be infected. Spores washing into the soil will affect tubers, which will rot. Earthing up will help prevent this happening. A more drastic alternative is to cut off affected foliage to prevent spores infecting the tubers. Blight can be prevented by spraying with a copper-based fungicide (Bordeaux Mixture is acceptable to organic gardeners) or Dithane 945, before symptoms first appear. Repeat this treatment every two weeks.

Eelworms are minute worm-like creatures which attack the roots of potatoes. The first signs are weak plants that start to wilt. Reddish-brown cysts the size of a pin-head can be seen on the roots. Eelworm is very persistent. Destroy all traces of the affected crop and do not grow potatoes on that area for eight years.

Scab is caused by a fungus and is worse in light and limy soils. Plenty of organic matter, and watering during a hot summer, will help. Affected tubers can be eaten after peeling.

Slugs can be a major problem on heavy and wet soil. Early varieties may be less affected, and early lifting of maincrops may help to reduce damage. If all else fails, scatter slugs pellets as you earth up, or water with a slug killer based on aluminium sulphate.

Spraing is caused by a virus spread by small worms in the soil. The tubers appear normal until cut open, when brown marks are seen in the flesh. It is worse on dry, sandy soils. Destroy affected tubers and practise crop rotation.

Viruses cause the leaves to curl up or become mottled or crinkled. The plants are stunted though the tubers are not affected. Viruses are spread by aphids or are present on the seed potatoes. Always buy certified seed potatoes (see above) and spray aphids with pyrethrum or soft soap if they appear.

Volunteer potatoes is the name given to tubers left in the ground at harvest that start to grow the following spring. If you follow a crop rotation, they will inevitably come up under newly-sown crops and are then difficult to remove. It is therefore worth spending time removing every tuber, however small, at harvest time.

Calendar

POTATOES IN THE GROUND

If you have a vegetable plot, you can grow the whole range of potato types, including maincrops to store through the winter. The basic method of growing potatoes is described below, but some alternatives are given on page 166.

Trenching and adding well-rotted organic matter will help to retain moisture on light soil. Take out a trench about 25cm deep and 30cm wide, piling the soil to one side. Add a generous layer of organic matter and plant the tubers into this. Refill the trench and leave any surplus soil for earthing up later.

JANUARY–FEBRUARY

Unpack seed potatoes straight away and start them into growth (see page 162).

Meanwhile, prepare the ground if you did not do so before Christmas. Dig the area deeply to loosen it and if you have well-rotted manure available, work this in at the same time. You can leave the surface fairly rough. On light soils it can be worthwhile preparing a trench (see above) but this is not essential on most soils.

MARCH

Plant early varieties in milder areas, but wait until early April in colder areas.

APRIL

Plant earlies in colder areas and follow with second earlies and maincrops by the end of the month.

Scatter a little balanced fertiliser over the area. Plant tubers about 15cm deep and about 40cm apart. Allow 75cm between rows of maincrops and 45cm between rows of early varieties.

When the first shoots appear above the surface, start to draw earth from between the rows over the centre of the row, to cover the shoots. Earthing up encourages underground shoots and hence more tubers. It also prevents tubers pushing above the surface and turning green, and protects young shoots from frost. Aim for a flat, round-topped ridge about 30cm across and 25cm high.

MAY

Cover the foliage, if frost is predicted, with garden fleece, cloches, straw or sacking. The foliage is easily blackened or killed by frost and the yield will be reduced.

JUNE–JULY

Early potatoes will benefit from a thorough soaking each week in dry weather and when the tubers are swelling.

Do not water maincrops until later in the summer when the tubers are forming – you will only encourage leaves. Maincrop varieties can be given a scattering of general fertiliser along the row. Watch for the first symptoms of blight and aphids, which can infect the plants with virus (see page 164).

AUGUST

When flowers start to appear, give maincrop potatoes a thorough soaking in dry weather.

SEPTEMBER–OCTOBER

Lift maincrop potatoes. Delaying beyond this time gives the slugs a chance to damage them, and the weather may deteriorate. Choose a day when the soil is fairly dry.

Planting chitted tubers

Potatoes on a raised bed

Earthing up

Harvest time

ALTERNATIVE GROWING METHODS

Black polythene is an easier alternative to earthing up. Plant the tubers and then cover the whole area with thick black polythene sheeting. When the shoots start to push up the polythene, cut a cross-shaped slit and carefully pull them through. When mature, the tubers should be on the soil surface, under the polythene.

Planting 'on the flat' is an alternative to growing in raised beds. Plant the tubers deeply with a trowel or potato planter but do not earth up the plants. If tubers do start to push to the surface, cover them with a mulch of compost.

Starting in pots works as well with potatoes as with dahlia tubers. Plant each tuber in a 15-cm pot and grow on somewhere frost-free. Dig a planting hole about 5cm deeper than the pot and drop the plant in. Draw spare soil up around the plant.

The no-dig method involves covering the tubers with a 10-cm layer of old straw or hay to exclude light. First spread a 2.5-cm layer of well-rotted manure or garden compost. Sit the tubers on top and cover them with the straw. Finally, cover the straw with a layer of grass clippings. Keep adding more grass throughout the season. To harvest, simply peel off the mulch.

Planting under black polythene

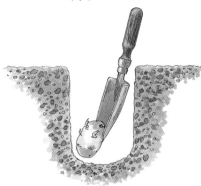

Planting 'on the flat'

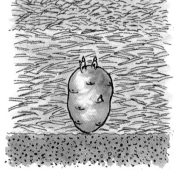

No-dig method

Starting in pots

'Accent'

'King Edward'

'Desirée'

'Nadine'

'Pink Fir Apple'

'Roseval'

HARVESTING

Start digging early potatoes as soon as there are decent-sized tubers. Try pushing your hand under a plant and feel for egg-sized tubers. An alternative is to lift a plant gently with a fork. If the tubers are still immature, replant it and give it a good soaking.

Start digging second earlies as soon as the tubers are large enough. They can also be lifted for storage later. Use them before you start on the maincrops.

With maincrops, leave the plants to die down completely. To avoid spearing tubers with the fork, push it in about 30cm from the dead top and push under the plant. Lift the potatoes on a dry day. Spread them out in a dark shed for a day or two to dry off completely. Sort out any that have been damaged by slugs or the fork and use them immediately. Store sound, dry tubers in hessian or double paper sacks until spring, when they shrivel and start to sprout.

good all-rounder, particularly for chips or frying.

'Pink Fir Apple' is an interesting late-maturing potato. It has unusual, long, knobbly tubers, flushed with pink. They are valued as a salad potato, and are tasty with a waxy texture. They keep well into the winter. Scrub these and cook in their skins, then peel by hand.

'Romano' and **'Santé'** have some resistance to blight.

P U M P K I N *and* S Q U A S H

Pumpkins are a familiar sight at Halloween, hollowed out and carved into lanterns, but their flesh can be disappointingly lacking in flavour. Some smaller varieties of pumpkin, however, are an excellent choice for eating.

When it comes to winter squashes, a huge range of shapes and sizes is available. Most are vigorous, trailing plants, which need a lot of space, though those with smaller fruits can be trained up trellis and arches. Unlike pumpkins, winter squashes will store well into the New Year. Some are very decorative, and most have a rich, nutty or buttery taste, ideal for hearty winter soups and stews.

Calendar

Pumpkins and winter squashes are very sensitive to frost and need a long, hot summer to ripen fully. Grow them exactly as you would marrows (see page 138). Once established, they are very easy going. They will crop even in a dry year, though a couple of really thorough soakings when the fruits are swelling will increase the crop.

APRIL
Sow the seed at a background temperature of 18–22°C. Follow the advice for growing marrows.

MAY–JUNE
Plant outside into a well-prepared planting hole after all danger of frost has passed. Allow at least a square metre per plant.

JULY–SEPTEMBER
If shoots stray out of their allotted area, curl them round the centre of the plant. Plants trained to grow up supports should scramble on their own, but you may need to support the heavier fruits to prevent damage to the stems. If the weather is very dry, give a couple of generous soaks of water once the fruits have started to swell.

SEPTEMBER
Cut and remove the full-sized fruit – the first frost will kill the foliage overnight.

HARVESTING
Allow fruits to develop their full colour and ripen in the sun. If necessary, lift them and put them in a sunny spot to complete their ripening. Bring the fully ripe fruits indoors before the first frosts of autumn.

Pumpkins do not store well, so aim to use them before Christmas. Winter squashes store better, and some will remain in good condition well into the following spring. Store both in a cool, dry, light spot.

Winter squashes have dense, usually orange flesh that can be roasted, baked or puréed.

Varieties

PUMPKIN

'Atlantic Giant' is the biggest variety of all, and current holder of the world record, but it is not one for eating.

'Baby Bear' and **'Becky'** are small-fruited pumpkins, better for eating than some of their larger cousins. Both grow to about 10–15cm across.

'Halloween' (**'Sunny'**) is a medium-sized fruit which is ideal for carving into lanterns. The flesh is edible but rather bland.

WINTER SQUASH

'Buttercup' and **'Sweet Mama'** bear medium-sized, dark-green fruits weighing about 1.5kg. The flesh is bright orange, dense, sweet and buttery. In a *Gardening Which?* trial these did not store as well as others, so they are best eaten before Christmas.

'Butternut' produces fawn, club-shaped fruits. The seed cavity is small and confined to the bulbous tip, which means the proportion of edible flesh is larger than in other varieties and it can be easily sliced.

'Crown Prince' produced three huge, steel-grey fruits per plant in the last *Gardening Which?* trial; each weighed nearly 4kg. The fruits will store well into the spring. The flesh is dense, orange and creamy textured, with a sweet, nutty flavour. It is excellent for soups.

'Red Kuri' goes under several names, including **'Onion Squash'** and **'Uchiki Kuri'**. The bright-orange, onion-shaped fruits are a useful size, just over 1kg, and this was one of the tastiest in the last trial.

'Sweet Dumpling' produces lots of small green-and-white flecked fruits. The flesh is sweet and firm, rather like that of a sweet potato. They are ideal for halving and baking. This is a suitable variety for training up a trellis or arch.

NOVELTIES

A huge range of North American, European and Asian varieties is now available through specialist catalogues.

'Jack Be Little' are tiny, orange pumpkins, just 10cm in diameter. They can be halved and roasted, but also make interesting decorations.

'Turk's Turban' is a bizarre winter squash, and one of the most decorative. The fruits store well and can be used as decorations throughout the winter as well as roasted as a vegetable.

'Becky'

'Sweet Dumpling'

'Red Kuri'

'Crown Prince'

Ornamental gourds are useful ornamental climbers, but inedible. They are available in a huge range of shapes and colours. Once fully ripe and dry, they can be varnished for use as table decorations. The fruits are quite small, and borne on rampant vines.

R A D I S H *Summer*

Summer radishes are very easy to grow and will fit into the smallest garden, or even a patio container or window box. They are quick, too, taking only 4 to 6 weeks from sowing to harvest. By sowing small amounts in succession through the summer, you can have a constant supply of radishes for adding colour and spice to salads, or as a garnish.

If you have more space, consider radish pods as an unusual border plant, or the more exotic winter radishes (see pages 172–3).

H O W   T O   P R E V E N T   P R O B L E M S

Summer radishes are in the ground for so little time that they rarely suffer problems. However, **flea beetles** will pepper the young leaves with small holes. Normally, rapidly growing plants will grow out of danger. If damage is severe, dust the plants with derris.

Grow radish with related crops (any member of the cabbage family) and rotate them around the vegetable plot on a three- or four-year cycle (see pages 36–7). Because flea beetles tend to hibernate in the soil under a previous crop, covering radishes with garden fleece should stop them attacking new sowings in a different area.

Winter radishes are especially prone to **clubroot** and **cabbage root fly** which will both produce swollen and distorted roots (see pages 86–7).

Flea beetle damage

R A D I S H   P O D S

If you let any radish bolt, it will produce a large, sparse head of small white or purplish flowers. Leave it, and an impressive crop of hollow green pods will form. These are crunchy and slightly hot. They make an unusual edible addition to an ornamental border and will continue cropping for some time if picked regularly. Support the flower stems with sticks to prevent the plant falling over.

Radish pods

Calendar

FEBRUARY

Make the first couple of sowings under cloches.

MARCH–AUGUST

Sow small amounts of seed in pots, a small patch in a border or short rows on the vegetable plot at regular intervals. Bear in mind that a 1-m row will yield about a kilo of radishes; a 30-cm pot about ten bunches.

Sow the seed thinly in a seed drill 1cm deep and 10–15cm apart. Allow room to get a hoe between the rows for weeding. Aim for a seed about every 2.5cm, but do not bother to thin out the seedlings – the round roots will push each other apart as they grow.

In pots or a window box, scatter the seed on the surface of the compost, aiming for a seed every 2.5–5cm apart each way, then cover with another 1cm of compost.

For mild-flavoured, crunchy roots, radishes need to grow rapidly without a check to their growth. Lack of water will make them woody and hot, so in dry spells water weekly. Aim to wet the soil thoroughly rather than just sprinkle the surface.

SEPTEMBER

In milder areas, a final sowing is still worthwhile. Cover late sowings in colder areas with cloches. You could also use up spare seed in a vacant greenhouse border over winter.

HARVESTING

Pull radishes as soon as they reach about 2cm across. Much larger than 3cm, and they will start to become tough. Radishes grown rapidly, with plenty of water, should be mild and crunchy.

Varieties

'Cherry Belle' and 'Sparkler' are the familiar round, red-skinned varieties.

'French Breakfast' is a cylindrical variety with characteristic white tip.

'Long White Icicle' produces long, white carrot-shaped roots, which should be pulled before they exceed 15cm long.

'Pink Beauty' has unusual round pinkish-red roots.

For radish pods

'München Bier' is the variety most often used for pod production. It is, strictly speaking, a winter radish, but when sown in the summer, will rapidly flower at the expense of producing a root.

'French Breakfast' and 'White French Breakfast'

Winter radishes are not often grown in the UK, though they are popular in the Far East as a winter vegetable. They can grow very large, and although some milder varieties are eaten raw as a salad vegetable, others are very hot. The long white moolis now available in the supermarket are a type of winter radish.

Like other oriental vegetables, winter radishes are a useful follow-on crop after an earlier vegetable has been harvested, because they are best sown from July onwards.

Varieties

'**April Cross**' is a mooli type that can produce huge, long white roots. These do not store well, but are crisp, juicy and mild-flavoured, though rather bland when cooked.

'**Black Spanish Long**' is an old variety with black-skinned roots that grow to about 20cm long. It is very hot when eaten raw, but less bland than others when cooked.

'**Black Spanish Round**' is a round version of 'Black Spanish Long' with similar qualities. Both can be stored for months.

'**Cherokee**' grows to the size of a cricket ball, but tastes like a summer radish. The skin is bright red, the flesh white.

'**Mantanghong**' is the reverse of 'Cherokee'. The white skin conceals a red flesh, though the colour can vary. It grows to about the same size, and, like 'Cherokee' also stores well. The mild, nutty flavour adds interest and variety to a salad.

Left to right: 'Black Spanish Round', 'Cherokee' and 'Mantanghong', 'April Cross', 'Black Spanish Long'

Calendar

JULY

Sow winter radishes in summer, after the longest day, or they will run to seed. Sow the seed directly into open ground in seed drills 1cm deep and 25cm apart. If the soil is dry, water the drill thoroughly before sowing.

AUGUST–SEPTEMBER

Thin the seedlings to 15cm apart, to give them plenty of room to produce large roots. They will need little attention during the summer and autumn.

OCTOBER

Roots should be large enough to harvest when they have developed the shape and skin colour characteristic of the variety. Before this, they are likely to be hotter-flavoured and will not store.

NOVEMBER

The roots can be left in the ground, but may be damaged by frost or slugs. Cover the rows with a layer of straw. Once mature, the roots can also be lifted and stored indoors.

Harvesting moolis

HARVESTING

Cut off the leaves to within 5cm of the root; removing the leaves prevents the stored roots drying out. Stand the roots upright in a box and pack damp sand round them. Leave the tops exposed to the air to prevent rotting. In a cool but frost-free place they will keep for months.

The fiery flavour is usually close to the skin, so the depth of peeling will affect their taste. Cooking also reduces the strength of the flavour, and cooked winter radish will be milder, as well as more tender. Hot varieties such as 'Black Spanish' can be overpoweringly hot raw, but are tastier when cooked. Milder radishes, while better raw, can become bland when cooked.

Use winter radish grated raw in salads, marinated in vinegar or soy sauce or instead of onion in hamburgers. Use them diced as a substitute for turnip in stews and casseroles or roast with the Sunday joint in place of parsnips.

HORSERADISH

This is not related to other radishes, but is a hardy perennial with hot-flavoured roots. Even if you eat a lot of horseradish, be aware that this plant can become very rampant. Plant a 15-cm section of root about 15cm deep in well-manured soil. It may be advisable to plant inside a pot sunk into the ground, to prevent the roots spreading.

In October, lift the plant and remove every piece of root (do not put it on the compost heap). Save one decent piece of root to replant in spring. Store the rest in damp sand until needed. Scrub the young roots and grate them for use as a garnish or mix with vinegar and milk or thick cream to make a sauce. There are no named varieties.

Horseradish root

RHUBARB

Rhubarb must be one of the easiest vegetables to grow. Being a long-lived perennial plant, it needs little attention and, whether you get round to forcing or not, it offers the first 'fruit' of the year. Most people inherit a clump, often tucked away at the bottom of the vegetable plot or beside the compost heap.

With its huge leaves and bright-red leaf stalks, rhubarb also makes a spectacular addition to a herbaceous border. The flowers are stunning, although flowering will weaken the clump. Regular harvesting of the young leaf stalks will keep the clump trim. It is a very easy crop to propagate; just cut off small sections of the clump and replant in the autumn. You can improve the quality of the stalks by blanching, or force it indoors for an earlier crop.

SEAKALE

This is an unusual perennial vegetable, which grows naturally on sea shores. Grown and forced in much the same way as rhubarb, it is also attractive enough for a place in the ornamental border. Grow it in an open, unshaded spot and well-drained, preferably sandy soil, with plenty of organic matter.

Blanch by placing a forcing pot or a large (30-cm diameter) upturned flower pot over the crown in January to exclude light. Cut the succulent white stems that grow underneath when they are about 10cm long. Stop cutting by May to allow the plants to recover.

Cook seakale lightly, like asparagus, to avoid destroying its subtle flavour. The young flower heads can also be eaten. But cut off any flower heads in the summer if you want to force the plant next year.

In a border you could leave some plants to flower – seakale is related to the ornamental *Crambe*.

Plants are raised from seed or from root cuttings; or as 'thongs' from mail-order suppliers. Seed is slow to germinate, so start it off in pots in a coldframe in the spring or autumn. **'Lily White'** is the variety most often offered as seed.

Blanched seakale

Seakale

Calendar

Rhubarb prefers a sunny position and moist but not waterlogged soil.

MARCH

Early rhubarb varieties left uncovered should be ready to pull.

In late March feed established clumps with a general fertiliser to increase the size of next year's crop. Mulch around the clump with well-rotted manure if you did not do this in the autumn.

Rhubarb can also be raised from seed. Germinate the seed in pots at about 10°C in March and plant outside when the plants are large enough.

APRIL–MAY

Harvest the sticks regularly.

JUNE

Boost leaf growth by scattering a handful of a nitrogen fertiliser (e.g. sulphate of ammonia or dried blood).

JULY

Stop harvesting. Allow the plants to build up their strength for next year.

NOVEMBER

Established clumps should be thinned about every five years. Dig around the crown and trim it back to four or five good buds. You can slice off sections of crown with a sharp spade, each with a couple of buds, to make new plants.

The best time to plant new crowns is November or December, into well-manured ground. The top bud should be just below the surface. You can also plant in the spring. Whenever you plant, do not harvest until the second summer.

DECEMBER

For an early crop of blanched rhubarb in February, cover the dormant clumps to exclude light. If your budget does not run to a terracotta forcing pot, a large flower pot or an upturned dustbin will be perfectly adequate.

HARVESTING

Young stalks are the most tender and tasty. Always pull rather than cut them. The leaves are poisonous and should be cut off, though they can be composted. The reddish leaf stalks contain low levels of these poisons and should not be eaten raw.

Rhubarb plant

Rhubarb seedling

Blanched rhubarb

Varieties

It is worth seeking out some of the gourmet varieties such as **'Red Prolific'** or **'Valentine'** for their superior taste and appearance. These do not disintegrate when cooked. Gourmet varieties are not widely available, so you will need to find a specialist supplier.

For a rhubarb to grow in a border, look for a compact variety (one that spreads to 75cm) with bright-red stems. For example, **'Cawood Delight'** (a late variety) or, for an early variety, choose either **'Champagne'** or **'Early Victoria'**.

To raise rhubarb from seed, you will need **'Glaskin's Perpetual'** as it bulks up quickly.

HOW TO FORCE RHUBARB

Dig the roots up in the autumn after the leaves have died back and leave them exposed for a fortnight. Wait until the temperature has dropped below 10°C. Pack the roots into pots or boxes filled with moist compost or light soil and store them somewhere dark and cool but frost-free – for example, in a garden shed, or black-out the area under a greenhouse bench with black polythene. The sticks should be ready to pull in about five weeks time.

Forced plants can be replanted in the garden, but give them a couple of years to recover before forcing them again.

R U N N E R   B E A N S

Runner beans are one of the most popular garden vegetables. A couple of plants will supply enough beans for a family over the summer, even if no other crops are grown. They are both decorative and versatile and can fit into any garden: in the ornamental border, as a temporary summer screen or as a container crop.

The ideal site for runner beans is sunny and sheltered from strong winds. They are even worth trying in partial shade. The soil should be well supplied with organic material and kept moist. Grow them up trellis screens, over arches or against a sunny fence. When growing them on a vegetable plot, choose a position where they will not be casting shade over other vegetables. In an ornamental border, leave room for access, since you may need to pick every other day.

You can even grow runner beans as a bush if you prefer (see page 178).

HOW TO PREVENT PROBLEMS

Runner beans are usually trouble-free but you might get the following problems.
Blackfly can build up rapidly later in the summer and in severe cases can stunt the plants and reduce the crop. Natural enemies such as ladybirds should keep them under control. If not, spray with an insecticide based on soft soap or pyrethrum. Do this in the evening to avoid harming bees.
Halo blight is the only disease you are likely to come across. This shows as

dark spots on the leaves, surrounded by a paler halo. Pull out and destroy any affected plants as soon as you spot them. Do not save seed for next year as this disease is carried in the seeds.
Flowers sometimes fail to produce pods. Cool spells may discourage pollinating insects, or high night-time temperatures or drought could cause the embryo beans to abort. Water the soil on hot, dry evenings. Do not bother spraying the flowers – it will not help.

Good soil preparation is the key. Dig a trench 60-75cm wide and 30cm deep in autumn. Fork over the bottom, and, if possible, work in some well-rotted manure. Fill the trench over winter with old bedding plants, cabbage stalks, kitchen waste, shredded newspapers and partially rotted garden compost, mixed with the topsoil.

If you did not dig a bean trench, work plenty of organic matter into the soil before planting.

Calendar

MARCH

It is worth putting the supports (see page 179) in place now, to save time later. To utilise the space between bean double rows, or in the middle of wigwams, sow a catch crop of lettuce, spinach or even early peas. These should be out of the way by the time the beans need the space.

APRIL

In milder areas, sow the beans in pots. Sow two seeds to a 12-cm pot. Keep the pots at a constant 10–12°C. If both germinate, do not separate them later, but plant both together. Grow them on at a minimum temperature of 7°C until they are 15–20cm tall.

MAY

Gradually harden the young plants off, ready for planting out later in the month in milder areas. You could also sow the seed directly into the soil or in containers after the danger of late frost has passed. Sow 2cm deep when the soil is 10°C.

Sow or plant two or three plants to a 10-litre pot. Push a tripod of 1.8m canes into the pot or stand next to a trellis.

On the vegetable plot or ornamental border, scatter a little general-purpose fertiliser about two weeks before planting out. Water the ground a day or two before sowing if the soil is dry. Sow or plant two seeds to each support at 15cm intervals. You may need to protect the young plants from slugs (see pages 38–41).

In colder areas, sow seeds in pots this month for planting out in early June.

JUNE

Sow directly or plant out in colder areas. In exposed areas, protect young plants from cold winds until they are well established.

Mulch around the plants with well-rotted manure, compost or grass cuttings to help retain moisture and suppress weeds.

If the first shoots flop on to the ground, wind them anti-clockwise round the support and tie them in. Eventually, the plants will cling on by themselves.

JULY

Water regularly in dry weather. Give a generous soaking – 10 litres of water a sq m once a week. Watering encourages flowering and increases the size of the pods. However, spraying the flowers to aid setting is a waste of time.

When the plants reach the top of their supports, pinch out their growing tips, to encourage the formation of side shoots. Watch for blackfly and spray if necessary.

The first beans should be ready for harvesting in mild, sheltered areas.

AUGUST–SEPTEMBER

Pick the beans regularly when they reach about 17–18cm long. If you let them grow too large they will become tough and stringy, and cropping will fall off. Pick every bean, even if you cannot eat or freeze them all, to prolong cropping into late summer. Before you go on holiday, pick all the beans, even the tiniest ones, and the flowers, to ensure a continuing crop when you return.

Sowing in pots

Planting out

Save seed for next year

HARVESTING

You can pick pods as small as you like, but the bigger they are, the better developed the flavour. However, if you leave them too long they will become stringy and the seeds will start to swell. In a *Gardening Which?* trial, 17–18cm was found to be the optimum length for tender, flavourful beans. The bean should snap cleanly, without any string.

Varieties

'Desirée' is a stringless variety, full of flavour with white flowers and white seeds.

'Enorma' is an older, high–yielding variety with red flowers. It is tasty, but the pods may become stringy unless picked frequently.

'Painted Lady' is a heritage variety with bicoloured red-and-white flowers. An attractive choice for the ornamental garden, it only has average flavour and a lower yield than modern varieties.

'Red Rum' is a variety with average flavour. It is claimed to set pods early in the season and is resistant to halo blight.

'White Lady', a new, white-flowered variety, gives a high yield of well-flavoured pods.

'White Emergo' is an older variety that came top for appearance and flavour in a *Gardening Which?* taste test.

DWARF

'Hammond's Dwarf Scarlet' and **'Pickwick'** are both red-flowered, dwarf varieties.

'Hestia' has attractive red-and-white bicoloured flowers and is useful for containers, but the flavour may be disappointing.

'White Emergo'

'Red Rum'

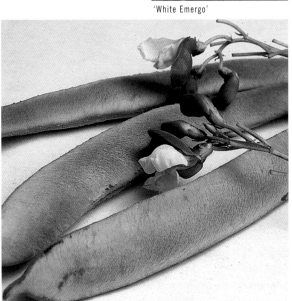

'Painted Lady'

'Hestia'

HOW TO SUPPORT RUNNER BEANS

There are many options when it comes to supporting runner beans. Choose a method that suits where you plan to grow them.

In a small garden or in a mixed border, a simple wigwam of beanpoles (coppiced hazel is ideal if you can get it) or bamboo canes is best [1]. Make the base at least 60cm diameter or square and space supports 15cm apart. Tie them securely at the top – or use a plastic wigwam grip. You can substitute intermediate sticks with twine or string. Wigwams should be at least 1.8m tall, so you will need 2m canes.

To grow beans up a fence, trellis, arch or pergola you can use bean netting.

In sheltered gardens, a single row of canes or poles should be adequate [2]. You could also erect a couple of stout posts and stretch string supports or pea and bean netting from it.

A summer screen of runner beans

Whatever method you choose, space plants 15cm apart or pairs of plants 30cm apart. A variation on this theme is to angle the canes, supporting them halfway up with a cross member, so that the beans hang down clear of the supports [3].

In exposed gardens, double rows are more secure. Space the bases of the rows 60cm apart and brace the supports together, crossing either near the top [4] or at the half-way point [5]. Strengthen the structure further by tying canes or poles horizontally where the uprights cross.

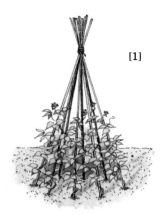

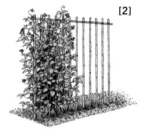

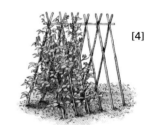

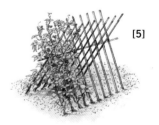

HOW TO GROW DWARF RUNNER BEANS

You can grow any runner bean variety as a bush, like dwarf French beans. Sow them 15cm apart in rows 60cm apart. Pinch off the growing tip when each plant reaches 30cm. Keep removing any climbing shoots regularly and soon you will have dwarf bushes that should start cropping a fortnight earlier than normal. **'Kelvedon Marvel'** and **'Scarlet Emperor'** are the best varieties to try.

A few true dwarf varieties are also available. They do not produce climbing shoots. These are worth growing if you have a very exposed garden, want to grow beans in containers or want to grow under cloches for an early crop. However, the yield is disappointing compared to climbing beans, and the pods trail on the soil.

SALAD LEAVES

These days, salad means so much more than just lettuce and cucumber. Continental salad leaves, hot oriental leaves, herbs – in fact, almost any edible leaf is now acceptable as a salad ingredient. And because you can harvest the leaves of all these plants as soon as they are large enough to pick, you can grow them in the smallest of spaces – even without a garden. Cut-and-come-again salad leaves (see below) are ideal for a window box, patio container or the smallest raised bed.

By following the instructions given here, you can have a constant supply of fresh salad leaves to rival those you can buy in the supermarket. They will not only be fresher but can be grown organically, too. Apart from lettuce (to grow mature, hearted lettuces see pages 132–7), you can grow a whole range of leafy plants to vary the mix each time you pick an instant salad.

CUT-AND-COME-AGAIN SALAD

This technique relies on the fact that many leafy salad plants will regrow from the stump left when the leaves are cut. You could opt for a packet of mixed leaf salad seeds or create your own mix (see pages 182–3 for ideas).

The aim is to harvest small quantities of leaves, either as whole immature plants or as individual leaves over a period of a couple of weeks. You should get at least two pickings and possibly up to four from one sowing.

Sow the seed in bands or in single rows, 10cm apart. In both cases, aim for roughly 1–2cm between seeds.

When the seedlings reach an average height of about 10cm, cut the whole lot with a pair of scissors about 2cm above the compost or soil, leaving the cut stump.

Apply a high-nitrogen liquid feed and keep the plants well watered.

Within three or four weeks, a flush of new leaves will grow from the cut stumps. These can be cut as before, and so on.

Watch out for weeds, such as nettles, growing alongside the salad plants.

Cut the leaves with scissors

Calendar

To grow salad leaves in a container, choose one with a diameter of at least 30cm. Scatter the seed thinly and cover with about 1cm of compost. In the garden you could create a dedicated 'salad bar' (see pages 20–1) or earmark a section of a raised vegetable bed for salad leaves. In this case, each time you sow you have the choice of sowing either short rows 10–15cm apart or small patches of individual ingredients. If you opt for a mixture, sow thinly in bands 10cm wide or broadcast in patches. Leave about 1–2cm between seedlings.

FEBRUARY

The first batch of salad leaves in containers can be started off under cover. Start the seed in small pots or modules in the greenhouse or on a windowsill for planting outside when conditions are more favourable.

Outside, use cloches to cover seed sown directly in the ground or sow in containers and cover them with garden fleece. You will need a site in full sun for early sowings, although a semi-shaded site will be better in mid-summer. If you grow them in the ground, the soil should be fertile and moisture-retentive. To improve the soil, work in plenty of organic matter at the start of the season. Add a scattering of balanced fertiliser. The ideal site should be free of annual weeds. If this is impossible, sow in straight rows, so that you can identify the crop easily when you weed. In containers, use multipurpose compost.

MARCH–JULY

Sow small amounts at regular intervals. Either sow at two- or three-week intervals and accept that the later sowings will start to catch up with the earlier ones, or wait until one sowing has germinated or reached a certain stage before sowing the next batch. This should help to spread them out over the season.

Whether they are growing in garden soil or in containers, water regularly to keep the seedlings growing strongly without a check to their growth. Watch for slugs, snails and aphids (see below).

AUGUST

It is worth making a final sowing of hardy salad plants, such as winter lettuce, Chinese cabbage and other oriental greens, chicory, corn salad, endive, kale and rocket to harvest in the autumn.

Pick young leaves

Raised 'salad bar'

Mix and match ingredients

HARVESTING

For really fresh salad, pick it at the last minute, wash thoroughly and shake dry. Pick immature plants or individual leaves as required. Always pick the larger leaves from the outside to keep the plants small and encourage young, tender leaves in the centres.

HOW TO PREVENT PROBLEMS

Keep a watch for **slugs and snails**. If you prefer not to use slug pellets, hand-pick the pests by torchlight on damp nights to reduce numbers, or use a barrier (see page 41). Protect pots with bands of copper tape.

Aphids are the other major pest. Spray with pyrethrum or soft soap based insecticide. If you prefer not to spray, nip out any badly infested plants or rub off individual aphids as seen.

Flea beetles may nibble members of the cabbage family, such as rocket, kale and oriental greens, but generally do little damage.

Varieties

SALAD LEAF

Creating a salad

Lettuce is the basis of any traditional salad. **'Little Gem'** or another cos type such as **'Pinokkio'** or **'Sherwood'** (see pages 132–7) is the obvious choice for flavour. These are crunchy and sweet and also respond well to cutting when small.

'**Green Salad Bowl**' and **'Frisby'** are loose-leaved varieties for adding bulk to a salad.

Spinach (see pages 186–9) has a mild, buttery taste. It is best in spring or autumn, as plants tend to bolt in mid-summer. For summer sowings, leaf beet (perpetual spinach) is more reliable but slightly coarser tasting.

Corn salad is mild, juicy and crunchy and is especially useful over winter as a substitute for lettuce.

Chinese cabbage comes into its own for autumn salads. Sow it from July onwards. **Pak choi** and **mizuna** are other mild-flavoured oriental greens which are more amenable to early summer sowings (see pages 148–9).

Cos and loose-leaved lettuces

Mizuna

Endive

Kale 'Red Russian'

More flavours

Sugarloaf chicory and **curly endive** can both be very bitter, so do not overdo it. Young leaves are sweeter and less bitter than older ones.

Oriental mustards such as the hot '**Green-in-the-Snow**' or the red-leaved but milder-flavoured **'Red Giant'** add a kick.

Mustard (actually rape) and **cress**, normally grown indoors, can be sown outdoors and harvested as a seedling crop.

Salad rocket adds a bite to a salad, but the plant has an annoying habit of going to seed very quickly, especially in hot weather. Sow little and often and pick frequently.

Kale 'Black Tuscany'

American land cress is a substitute for watercress that will tolerate dry soil and cold weather. Pick the leaves young before the plants start to bolt.

Nasturtium leaves also have a peppery flavour

Mixed lettuce in a container

Misticanza

and if you let the plants grow, the flowers can be scattered in salads, too (see pages 218–9).

Annual herbs can be added to the salad bed for cutting as immature leaves, for example:

Cilantro or **leaf coriander** has a fresh, exotic flavour,

and **sorrel** has a sharp lemon flavour (see pages 216–7).

Chervil has a subtle aniseed flavour (see page 208).

Par-cel or **leaf celery** has the authentic flavour of celery without the effort of growing the real thing.

Basil can add a Mediterranean or oriental touch, depending on the variety (see pages 206–7).

Onion Along with salad onions (see pages 144–5), chives and garlic chives are both easy to grow from seed. Garlic chives have a subtle garlic flavour. If you leave them uncut, the white flowers of garlic chives and the purple flowers of chives can be used as a garnish, too (see pages 208–9).

More colour
Plenty of red lettuce varieties are now available, some with very intense colours. A couple of leaves of frilly **'Lollo Rossa'** adds colour. Fortunately, the plants will keep growing while you pick individual leaves. **'Red Salad Bowl'** is another option. Young **beetroot leaves** can be added to salads. Better still, grow the bright red **Ruby chard**. **'Charlotte'** is a new variety with intense red stems and purple leaves.

Swiss or **Silver chard** has green leaves with white midribs, and **'Bright Lights'** has a vibrant mix of white, yellow, red, pink and

orange midribs and stalks.

Radicchio or red chicory can be very bitter. Simply pick the leaves when they are still small and tender before they start to turn bitter. The colour is more intense in the spring and autumn.

Kale is another interesting addition, with a subtle cabbage flavour. New **'Redbor'** has bright-red, curly leaves; the leaves of **'Black Tuscany'** are puckered and dark blue-green; and **'Ragged Jack'** has a reddish tinge.

Mixed leaves
You can buy seed packets of mixed lettuce or a mixture of edible leaves, which usually includes lettuce, endive and chicory, along with other

Par-cel

flavours. These are called **'Saladini'**, **'Mesclun' or misticanza**. You can also mix your own leaves to suit your taste using any of the ingredients above.

WATERCRESS
You might think you need a stream to grow watercress, but in fact you can grow it quite easily in a container. Place this somewhere in partial shade, and where you can water it easily. Sow the seed thinly and cover with about 1cm of compost. Water regularly to keep the compost moist at all times.

The leaves may not grow as lush as

Watercress

those available in supermarkets, but they will taste just as good. Pick the leaves and stems frequently to stop the plants running to seed.

SHALLOTS

What vegetable could possibly be easier to grow? You push one bulb into the soil in spring and by midsummer it has multiplied into a dozen or so. With more flavour and less pungency than onions, shallots are also a versatile ingredient in the kitchen, delicious roasted or in casseroles. As they are expensive in the supermarket, they must be worth the space in any garden. Although they do not qualify as an attractive border vegetable, try pushing a few into an ornamental border early in the season. They will be harvested and out of the way of summer flowers by July.

Shallots are an unfussy vegetable. They will do well on any reasonably well-drained, fertile soil and prefer a neutral pH. They need only a little general fertiliser and in most years will not need to be watered.

The easiest way to grow shallots is from sets (small single bulbs). Varieties of shallot are now available as seed (see right).

Varieties

SHALLOTS FROM SETS
'**Delicato**' was the best-looking of the red varieties in a *Gardening Which?* trial, with a high yield of large, flat bulbs. It stored well, too.
'**Pikant**' and '**Red Sun**' are other red-skinned shallot varieties that gave a high yield and stored well.
'**Santé**' is supposed to be planted after the middle of April to avoid bolting, though this was not a problem in the last trial. It is worth

considering if you want a reddish-brown shallot. '**Topper**' gave high yields of medium-sized, yellow-skinned shallots and stored well in the last trial.

SHALLOTS FROM SEED
There is little to choose between '**Creation**', a yellow-skinned variety, and '**Matador**', a red-skinned variety.

'Topper'

'Pikant'

'Creation'

Calendar

MARCH

If the soil is still cold and wet, delay planting until April. Prepare the site by forking over to loosen the soil. Work in a little general fertiliser, unless the area has been manured for a previous crop. Do not add organic matter when growing shallots.

Push the individual bulbs into the soil so that the tips are just covered. Birds may pull them out if they are visible. Give them more space than onion sets, 15cm apart in rows 30cm apart should be fine. You could space them 23cm apart each way in a raised bed, but allow enough space for hoeing between the plants later.

APRIL

Aim to complete planting by early April. Shallots cannot compete with vigorous weeds, so hand weed between plants and hoe between the rows regularly, taking care not to damage the plants.

MAY–JUNE

Keep weeds under control. Shallots do not normally need watering, but in a very dry summer, a soaking when the bulb is swelling and dividing increases the yield.

JULY

As soon as the top starts to dry off, lift the clump of bulbs out of the soil to expose it to the sun. Leave the bulbs to dry and ripen in the sun. But cover them with cloches or bring them indoors to complete drying in wet weather.

AUGUST

Lift and store bulbs when fully ripe.

HARVESTING

Fully-ripened shallots should store well into the following winter and early spring. Spread them out in a single layer on wooden trays or wire racks, and keep them in a cool, dry place. If you keep them beyond New Year, check occasionally for signs of rotting.

Shallots growing

Shallots growing

HOW TO GROW SHALLOTS FROM SEED

Shallot seed is a fairly recent innovation. Bearing in mind the cost of shallot sets, growing from seed can be worthwhile if you want a large crop.

The seed is very similar to onion seed. You can sow directly into the ground, or start in pots.

If you decide to start them in pots, consider the following multi-seeded technique. Sow about six or eight seeds together in a 7-cm pot in February or early March. The seed will germinate at temperatures as low as 10°C. Do not thin out the seedlings. Gradually harden them off until they are ready to plant out in early April. Plant the clump of seedlings together, about 23–30cm apart, with a trowel. As they grow, the small bulbs will push each other apart, and the end result will be a clump of large bulbs, just like starting from sets.

Alternatively, sow the seeds thinly in seed drills 1.5cm deep and 30cm apart. Thin the seedlings out and you will get a single bulb per seed, like a small onion. Varying the final spacing will dictate the size, so if you want large shallots, give them plenty of room.

You could also harvest them immature, as an alternative to spring onions.

Shallot sets and seedlings

SPINACH *and* CHARD

True spinach is an annual, green leafy plant. Better known as a cooked vegetable, the young leaves, or baby spinach, are also used raw in salads.

Leaf beet, or perpetual spinach, is much easier to grow than true spinach. The related chards have larger, often brightly coloured, leaf stalks that make striking ornamental plants for containers or borders. Further afield, most parts of the world have different crops cooked as a spinach, many of which you can try in your garden.

As it is an annual, true spinach will bolt or run to seed in the first season. Some varieties claim to be resistant to bolting, but in a *Gardening Which?* trial, all varieties sown in March had run to seed by June. True spinach is best sown in succession through the summer and cut when small, before it starts to bolt.

Leaf beets, including the coloured-stemmed chards, are biennials and are less likely to bolt in the first summer. They are best sown once in spring and the leaves harvested regularly.

HARVESTING

True spinach is usually cut when it reaches a certain size and will not regrow. Pick when leaves are 5–10cm for eating raw in salads. For cooking, let it grow to 15–20cm. You need to collect a large amount of leaves, as they condense hugely in the cooking process. Wash the leaves thoroughly, pack them into a pan without adding water, cover and cook over a low heat until they have softened.

Leaf beet grows very fast, producing large leaves. Pick the outer leaves regularly when they reach 10–15cm, allowing the central leaves to continue growing. You can also cut the whole head about 2cm above soil level. The plant should re-sprout. Leaf beet will continue growing all summer and can be picked over regularly. Older, larger leaves can be cooked,

but remember to strip out the tough midribs first.

Chard leaves can be picked very small for salads or cooked like leaf beet. The leaf stalks are also edible. They can be cooked with the leaves when small. Larger stalks are best separated from the leaf and steamed or boiled as a separate dish. The coloured-stemmed types are particularly appealing.

Calendar

FEBRUARY

Make the first sowing of **true spinach.** Sow short rows or small patches at a time once every three weeks to ensure a continuous crop. It is easiest to sow directly into a well-prepared seedbed. Rake in some balanced fertiliser and water if the soil is dry. Sow thinly into seed drills 1cm deep and 30cm apart.

Start the first couple of sowings under cloches in cold areas. Spinach is a useful catch crop (see pages 48–9).

MARCH – APRIL

Continue to sow small amounts of true spinach at intervals. Thin the seedlings from earlier sowings to about 10–15cm apart. These can be used in salads.

Make one sowing of **leaf beet.** You can start the seed off in 7-cm pots for planting out later, or sow directly into the vegetable plot. Sow into seed drills 1.5cm deep and 30cm apart. Thin the seedlings later so they are 30cm apart.

Chard may bolt prematurely in the first summer if sown too early, so wait until April. You can sow directly into containers, aiming for about six plants in a 10-litre pot, or grow individual plants in a 4-litre pot. Each seed will produce a clump of seedlings which can be thinned out later. For a border it may be easier to start the seed off in 7-cm pots and to transplant them later, as you would bedding plants. Allow roughly a 30-cm diameter space for each plant so they can show off their true colours.

MAY

The earliest sowings of true spinach should be ready for cutting about 10–12 weeks from sowing. It is worth continuing to sow through May, but after that, the weather is likely to be too hot and the soil too dry, and plants will bolt readily.

JUNE – JULY

Water spinach by giving the soil a thorough soak once a week to prevent plants from bolting. Keep picking over regularly; this also applies to the young leaves of leaf beet and chard.

Leaf beet and chard which has been picked over regularly will benefit from a scattering of high-nitrogen fertiliser to boost further leaf production.

AUGUST

Sow a variety of winter-hardy true spinach for an early crop next spring.

You can make a second sowing of leaf beet for picking in winter. This late sowing should continue cropping well into the following summer before bolting. Spring-sown leaf beet and chard should also survive over winter and will provide a couple of pickings in spring and early summer before bolting.

SEPTEMBER – NOVEMBER

Keep cutting true spinach and picking over leaf beets. In cold areas, protect true spinach with cloches.

Young leaf beet

Thinning seedlings

Harvesting leaf beet

HOW   TO   PREVENT   PROBLEMS

True spinach and leaf beet are generally trouble-free, though they may be attacked by aphids or downy mildew.

Aphids congregate on the undersides of the leaves. Spray these thoroughly with a solution containing pyrethrum or soft soap.

Downy mildew appears as a white, furry growth on the undersides of leaves. It is common in cold, wet spells. Remove affected leaves and thin out to increase air circulation.

Varieties

True spinach is often claimed to have the better flavour, and this may be the case when it is eaten raw as a salad ingredient. However, in a trial by *Gardening Which?* members, cooked leaf beet was preferred to true spinach by most people, and they found it much easier to grow.

Like beetroot, the 'seeds' of leaf beet and chard are, in fact, corky capsules containing up to six seeds (see page 73). Each will produce a small clump of seedlings, which can be thinned out or teased apart later. Spinach seed is smaller and each produces a single seedling.

TRUE SPINACH

There are many named varieties, which were all fairly similar in a small-scale trial by *Gardening Which?* **'Giant Winter'** is a hardy variety that will overwinter from an autumn sowing. **'Medania'** is a summer variety with some resistance to downy mildew.

Most spinach contains high levels of oxalic acid, except for **'Monnopa'**.

Leaf beet   True spinach

Chard 'Bright Lights'

LEAF BEET

This is the most high-yielding of the plants grown for spinach and will keep on producing new leaves if picked over regularly. The leaves can become very large, but if you strip out the midribs they will cook down to a tasty spinach. Unlike true spinach, leaf beet is a biennial and will not usually bolt until the second year.

Despite all leaf beet's virtues, there are no named varieties and no breeding has been done to improve this leafy relative of the beetroot.

Strawberry spinach

CHARD

This group contains the most decorative members of the beet family. You can grow them for their edible and often highly coloured stalks, as well as for their spinach-like leaves.

'Bright Lights' is a mixture of seven coloured stalks, from red through orange and yellow to white. The leaves are green and make an acceptable spinach. It is suitable for the ornamental border or the patio.

'Charlotte' is an improvement on the old

red **'Rhubarb chard'**, with bright-red stalks and leaves. One for imaginative bedding schemes.

'Swiss' or **'Silver'** chard has green leaves and ghostly white stalks.

ALTERNATIVE SPINACH

Good King Henry is a native perennial, sometimes called 'poor man's asparagus' because the shoots can be forced in

Swiss chard

the spring. The young leaves can be cooked as spinach.

Malabar spinach or **basella** is a climbing plant that is best grown in a greenhouse or polythene tunnel and can serve as a conservatory plant. Pick individual leaves and shoot tips, but leave at least one tip to continue growing.

New Zealand spinach is a native of the Pacific Rim, and very tolerant of drought. It is best treated as a half-hardy annual. Sow in pots under glass in April and plant out after the last frost, or sow directly in late May or June. The crop is likely to be disappointing compared to other spinach plants, but plants will continue to produce leaves even when they have flowered. Pick individual small leaves and shoot tips regularly.

Strawberry spinach is a novelty with small leaves and unusual red fruits, which superficially resemble wild strawberries. The fruits are edible with a slightly sweet, sesame-seed flavour; the leaves are buttery. It is a relative of the notorious weed, fat hen.

Vegetable amaranth or **callaloo** is an attractive plant with red, green and white-leaved forms. If left to flower, it resembles 'love-lies-bleeding'. Pick leaves and shoots regularly. It will do best in a hot summer.

New Zealand spinach

SWEDES, TURNIPS
and KOHL RABI

 Summer turnips Kohl rabi Swedes Winter turnips

You may think winter turnips and swedes only have a place in the traditional allotment. But many smaller turnip varieties take as little as eight weeks from sowing to eating, so they make excellent catch crops.

Kohl rabi is a continental relative of the turnip and is a decorative substitute worth considering in even the smallest garden.

The larger varieties of turnips and all the swedes (originally an abbreviation for Swedish turnip, after their origin) are slow-growing and produce large roots that can be stored for winter use. The smaller, summer turnips and kohl rabi, which produce an edible swollen stem above ground, rather than a root, are grown as summer crops. The calendar for winter turnips and swedes is on page 193.

CATCH CROPS

Summer turnips and kohl rabi are useful catch crops. Because they are related to the larger and slow-growing members of the cabbage family, they are usually grown in the same crop-rotation group. Use them to fill space from February to June before winter crops such as sprouting broccoli or winter cauliflowers are planted out.

Sow them in May between Brussels sprout plants. These will not need all their allotted space until later in the summer, by which time the catch crop is ready to be harvested.

Grow them after an early crop of broad beans or early peas have been cleared, so they benefit from the nitrogen left by the previous crop.

Purple kohl rabi

Calendar

SUMMER TURNIPS AND KOHL RABI

Both crops need a moist, fertile soil, but will tolerate light shade during the summer. They also do best on a slightly alkaline soil. Because it forms globes above rather than below ground, kohl rabi is better able to cope with heavy soil than turnips.

FEBRUARY

An early sowing of turnips can be made under cloches. In colder areas or for growing outside, wait until March.

MARCH

It should be safe to sow turnips directly outside, but leave kohl rabi until the end of the month. Both crops can be grown close together to produce lots of small baby roots. They can be sown little and often through the summer.

Prepare the soil by forking and raking to create a seedbed. Work in a reasonable amount of balanced fertiliser and water the soil a couple of days before sowing if it is dry.

Make seed drills 1.5cm deep and 15cm apart. Sow the seed thinly, to avoid having to thin out later. If the soil is dry, water the bottom of the seed drill before sowing.

Both crops can be used as a catch crop (see left) and can be multi-seeded in pots (see page 73).

Both will succeed in containers, provided the compost is kept moist. Scatter the seed thinly and cover with about 1.5cm of compost. Thin the seedlings to roughly 7.5–10cm apart. In an ornamental border, kohl rabi (particularly one of the purple varieties) is the best choice. Sow small patches and thin out later, or start the seed off in pots for transplanting later.

APRIL

Sow another batch and thin out the earlier sowings to give roughly one plant every 10cm for larger roots, or 3cm for baby roots. You do not need to be too thorough, as the roots will push apart as they grow.

MAY–JULY

For tender roots, the plants should grow rapidly without any check to their growth. This means that in dry spells they should be watered regularly – give a generous soak once a week to wet the soil thoroughly. Watch out for flea beetle, which can seriously damage the young leaves. If necessary, dust or spray with derris.

The first roots should be ready in early May. Start to pull them as soon as they reach golf-ball size.

Sow further batches at fortnightly intervals if you want to extend the harvest into autumn.

AUGUST–SEPTEMBER

Continue to pull the later sowings as soon as they reach either golf-ball or just before tennis-ball size.

Multi-seeded turnips

Baby turnips

HARVESTING

Both turnips and kohl rabi are best harvested before they reach tennis-ball size. Trim off the long root and outer leaves of kohl rabi, leaving the swollen stem with just a small tuft of immature leaves. Small roots (about golf-ball size) need to be peeled thinly and can be eaten raw – grated in a salad, for example.

Kohl rabi has a milder flavour, usually described as nutty, whereas raw turnip can be too strong for some tastes. Larger roots may have a fibrous layer under the skin, which should be peeled off before cooking.

Varieties

KOHL RABI

'**Cindy**', '**Kongo**' and '**Trero**' are green varieties that produced a high yield after ten weeks in a *Gardening Which?* trial.

'**Logo**' is the best green variety for growing as a baby vegetable, and is harvested when golf-ball size.

'**Purple Danube**', like other purple-skinned varieties, is

Kohl rabi 'Logo'

Kohl rabi 'Purple Danube'

Swede 'Marian'

Turnip 'Tokyo Cross'

said to be more winter hardy. It is also a very attractive plant for the ornamental border or for growing in containers.

SWEDE

'**Marian**' is the best variety, giving high yields of red-skinned roots. It is one of the few members of the cabbage family with in-built resistance to clubroot and mildew.

TURNIP (Summer)

'**Arcoat**' is a newer summer variety with slightly flattened, red-topped white roots. It is a good choice as a baby vegetable.

'**Snowball**' is a fast-growing, round summer variety with white skin and flesh. A useful catch crop.

Turnip 'Golden Ball'

'**Tokyo Cross**' is a very fast-growing white summer variety, best sown from June onwards to prevent it bolting.

TURNIP (Winter)

'**Golden Ball**' is a reliable maincrop variety with yellow skin and flesh. It stores well.

Calendar

WINTER TURNIPS

Maincrop varieties of turnip are much slower growing, and swedes are slower still. Both are left to mature for storing through the winter. They are not particularly fussy but, like all members of the cabbage family, do best in a slightly alkaline soil. If necessary, apply lime during the winter. They do not need organic matter but, ideally, should follow a crop manured the previous year. If not, they will need a balanced fertiliser.

Grow them in the same crop-rotation group as other cabbage family members.

MAY–JUNE

Make a single sowing of swede for winter use. Make seed drills 2cm deep and 35–40cm apart. Sow very thinly to avoid having to thin out later.

Both crops can be started in pots or modules. If space in the vegetable plot will not be available until late July, this is a good option. It also saves thinning.

AND SWEDES

JULY–AUGUST

Maincrop turnips are usually sown later. Space the rows 30cm apart. Thin both crops early to avoid damaging the roots. If necessary, thin out in stages to leave 15cm between turnips and 23cm between swedes. They do not need regular watering, but make sure the soil does not dry out completely or they will become tough and woody.

SEPTEMBER–OCTOBER

Both crops should be ready for lifting with a fork. They can be left in situ until the New Year, or lifted and stored.

Harvested swedes

HARVESTING

Start to lift the roots of both crops as soon as they are large enough – you do not have to wait until they reach full size. The roots can also be stored for use later in the winter. Twist off the leaves and store the roots in boxes filled with sand. Keep them in a cool but frost-free place until required. Swede is generally regarded as sweeter and milder in flavour than turnip.

HOW TO PREVENT PROBLEMS

Although swede, turnip and kohl rabi can be attacked by all the usual cabbage family pests – flea beetle, cabbage aphid, whitefly and cabbage caterpillars – the most troublesome is the **cabbage root fly** (see pages 86–7).

The grubs of this small fly burrow into the roots and cause nodules to form. These nodules are unsightly and make the roots vulnerable to disease.

Superficially, roots attacked by cabbage root fly look similar to those affected by clubroot disease.

Kohl rabi is less severely affected by cabbage root fly than turnips and swedes. Some varieties of swede have an in-built resistance to clubroot. Liming the soil will also help prevent damage.

HOW TO GROW TURNIP TOPS

The leaves of turnips (turnip tops) can be used as spring greens. Like spring cabbage, these are a valuable, fresh green vegetable early in the year.

Sow a winter variety in August or September or a summer variety as early in the spring as possible.

In either case, cut the first crop of leaves when the seedlings are about 15cm high. Leave a stump about 2.5cm high and keep the plants well watered. Several further crops of leaves can be cut until the plants eventually run to seed.

Turnip tops

SWEETCORN

Nothing beats the taste of fresh sweetcorn, so if you have space in your garden it is well worth growing your own. And you need no longer endure chewy, starchy cobs; modern varieties are sweet and tender. You do not need a huge vegetable plot – a group of nine plants per square metre should produce at least nine cobs. Or you could grow them in a row as an exotic-looking screen in front of a sunny fence.

Sweetcorn needs a favourable position, in full sun, as it is tender and needs a long growing season. A sheltered site will protect the tall plants from being blown over or damaged by heavy rain. Any reasonable soil will do but avoid extremely wet or dry. The roots go deep into the soil, so dig the area over well and add plenty of well-rotted organic matter.

It is a myth that sweetcorn cannot be grown north of a line from the Bristol Channel to the Wash. Trials over several seasons at Harlow Carr Botanic Gardens in Harrogate found that most varieties produced a reasonable crop so long as they were started off under glass by April.

HOW TO SOW DIRECTLY

If you prefer to sow directly into the soil, you need to start early, to get a long enough growing season. The best way to succeed is by sowing under a clear polythene sheet.

First, create a series of troughs and ridges. Scoop out trenches about 5cm deep with a draw hoe, 30 or 35cm apart. Pile the soil into ridges about 5cm high. Sow the seed about 2cm deep into the bottom of the troughs. Stretch the clear polythene over the ridges and secure the edges by burying them. The sweetcorn seedlings will grow in the protected environment under the polythene. When the leaves touch the polythene, make a small slit and pull them through to continue growing.

HOW TO SAVE SPACE

Sweetcorn is deep-rooting, so it is feasible to grow a catch crop such as lettuce, spinach or garden peas between young plants. In South America, maize is often grown with squashes and beans. Try dwarf French beans or a trailing squash among the sweetcorn.

Another trick is to combine sweetcorn with an early crop of broad beans. Plant pot-raised sweetcorn between rows of broad beans in early June. The sweetcorn will benefit from the shelter and from the nitrogen stored in the beans' roots. Cut the broad beans at soil level after cropping.

In an ornamental border, plant trailing nasturtiums and allow them to scramble among the sweetcorn, or edge the bed with pot marigolds, or any other annual flowers that take your fancy.

Calendar

APRIL

In the mildest areas, sweetcorn can be sown directly in the soil, but it is better to sow in pots to get a head start. Sow one seed per 7-cm pot. Use tall pots if possible to avoid disturbing the main root when you plant out later. Germinate the seed somewhere warm. Sweetcorn needs a minimum temperature of 15°C, but the higher the temperature, the faster it will grow. Sometimes the seed is treated with a fungicide and coloured pink or blue. Do not leave such seeds lying around if you have young children.

MAY

If the ground is not already rich in organic matter, fork in a little balanced fertiliser before planting.

Gradually get plants used to outdoor conditions by standing them outside on warm days and bringing them indoors on cold nights. Delay planting out until all danger of frost has passed (in most years this means from the middle of the month in the South or in mild areas. In the North or in cold areas, wait until June). Cover the plants with cloches or garden fleece to protect the young plants from late frosts and cold winds.

Because sweetcorn is a member of the grass family and is wind-pollinated, it is usually grown in blocks, rather than straight rows. Growing in blocks of at least nine plants (three by three) should ensure that pollen from the male flowers at the top of the plant reaches the female tassels that produce the kernels. Poor germination will lead to poorly filled, gappy cobs.

Place the plants 35cm apart to give you roughly two cobs per plant. With a spacing of 30cm each, you may get only one cob per plant.

To cut down on weeding later, you can plant sweetcorn through a sheet mulch. One that allows rain through is best (see page 39).

JUNE

Plant out in colder areas after the last frost date. Weed between young plants if necessary.

JULY

When flowering begins and the grains are swelling, give plants a thorough soak once or twice rather than just wetting the soil surface. On warm, windless days, give plants a gentle nudge to release the pollen from the taller male flowers.

AUGUST

In windy areas, use a hoe to heap earth around the stems to stop the plants blowing over as the cobs start to ripen.

SEPTEMBER

Keep harvesting but stop once the grains are doughy when pressed with your nail. This is a sign that the cobs are overripe.

OCTOBER

Pull up the harvested plants and put the remains on the compost heap.

HARVESTING

Harvest when the tassels on the cobs start to shrivel. Peel back the leafy sheaf and gently press your thumbnail into a grain. If the cob is ready, a creamy liquid will squirt out. If the liquid is watery, leave the cob a few days and test it again. Once picked, use as soon as possible. Sweetcorn is usually boiled and served with butter and seasoning but it is also delicious cooked in its husk, either under the grill or on a barbecue.

Young plants in pots

Planting out

The growing crop

Testing for ripeness

Varieties

Normal sweetcorn varieties are sweet when mature and have that distinct sweetcorn taste, but you must eat them really fresh as the sugar rapidly turns to starch soon after the cobs are picked.

Modern varieties either have the same amount of sugar as the normal varieties but take longer to go starchy (sugar-enhanced varieties) or they are sweeter right from the start (super-sweet varieties). The sugar-enhanced ones are easy to grow but fall down slightly on taste. The super-sweets are early to mature but as the grains have less starch in them they are more delicate and harder to germinate in a cold spring. You can easily get round this by starting super-sweets off in pots.

Varieties listed in gardeners' seed catalogues change from year to year, usually reflecting which varieties commercial growers are after, so choose a type that appeals to you and see what varieties are offered. If you decide to grow more than one type, especially the super-sweet or bicoloured varieties, grow them in separate parts of the garden. Stray pollen carries over large distances and the cobs will be a mixture of conventional and sweet or bicoloured grains.

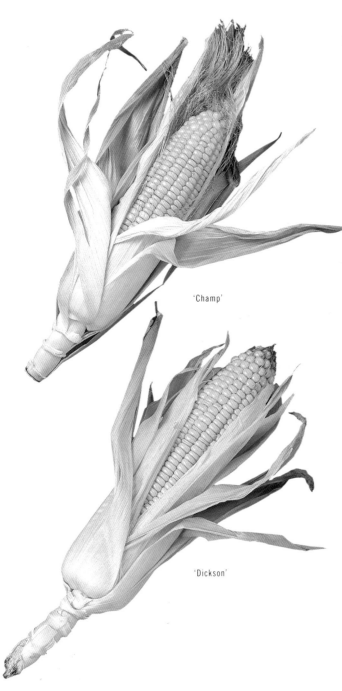

'Champp'

'Dickson'

NORMAL SWEETCORN

'Jubilee' and 'Sundance' are both easy to get started in a cold spring but slow to mature. Of the two, 'Sundance' is a better choice for northern gardens.

SUGAR-ENHANCED

'Champ' is a reliable, early-maturing variety, worth trying even in colder areas. 'Incredible' and 'Butterscotch' produce bigger cobs but are slower to mature, so are more suited to milder areas.

SUPER-SWEET VARIETIES

'Dickson' is one of the best, though it can be difficult to germinate. 'Challenger', 'Conquest' and 'Early Xtra Sweet' are others worth trying.

NOVELTIES

'Ambrosia' and 'Honey Bantam' are bicoloured varieties with white grains scattered amongst the yellow ones. In the Eastern USA, sweetcorn varieties are traditionally bicoloured to distinguish them from maize, which farmers used to pass off as sweetcorn.

'Minor' and 'Mini Pop' produce the crisp but rather tasteless baby corn used in stir fries. They are tall varieties that produce half a dozen short cobs per plant. These are picked when they reach about 6–8cm and before they start to turn woody. Some trial and error is necessary to get them at just the right stage. The cobs require no fertilisation so the plants do not need to be grown in blocks and can be planted closer together

'Red Strawberry' has small, round bright-red cobs. This is a popcorn variety rather than a sweetcorn. To make popcorn, the cobs need to be well dried (you can do this indoors in an airing cupboard) but also ripe, so this is worth a try only in favourable sites.

Multi-coloured varieties, or **Indian corn**, are worth growing as decorative border plants. They are edible but taste floury. The plants may be green or flushed with red or purple. The cobs contain different-coloured grains, including red, purple, brown and black as well as yellow and white.

Multicoloured Indian corn

HOW TO PREVENT PROBLEMS

Mice may nibble the seed, particularly when it is sown straight into the ground. Set mousetraps or cover seeds with upturned jam jars.

Slugs may also attack the seedlings. Use slug pellets or a slug-proof barrier (see pages 38–9).

Both these problems can be minimised by raising the seeds in pots and planting out the young plants.

The only other major pest is the **frit fly.** The maggots damage the growing point and cause the plant to wilt and die in May or June. Plants are immune once they have five or six leaves. To prevent the problem raise seedlings in pots, transplant later than normal and grow under a crop cover.

Uneven cobs, the result of some grains not being fertilised, can be prevented by planting in blocks and by tapping the stems to disperse the pollen.

Smut is a fungal disease that can infect sweetcorn. Large green or white swellings form on the developing cobs. Destroy these before they burst and spread their spores. As a precaution, grow sweetcorn on a new site next year.

Boron deficiency shows up as undeveloped cobs, dead growing tips and white-striped foliage. To prevent, apply borax at 3g a sq m when planting.

'Ambrosia'

TOMATOES *Indoor*

If you have a greenhouse, this is the obvious place to grow tomatoes. You can give them a longer season and are likely to get bigger crops than if you grow them outdoors. You can cut out the seed stage and buy young plants from a garden centre later in the spring, but raising your own plants from seed is easy and you'll have a much larger choice of varieties.

In the past, gardeners have tended to be rather conservative in their choice of tomato varieties. But modern hybrids, developed for commercial growers, have been joined in recent years by a huge number of heritage varieties from all over the world. These include varieties with green, white, brown, orange, yellow and striped fruits as well as the conventional red. They can be anything from currant-sized to giant beefsteaks.

HOW TO PREVENT PROBLEMS

By providing the following ideal conditions, you should experience few problems with your tomatoes.

Water frequently in very hot spells.

Feed regularly with a high-potash tomato fertiliser – one containing magnesium is best.

Ventilate the greenhouse in the hottest part of the summer.

Prevent wide fluctuations in temperature, especially at night, early in the summer.

Maintain a moist atmosphere by damping down the greenhouse floor. Problems you may still encounter are:

Greenback – yellow patches on the shoulder of the fruit – is caused by heat injury from direct sunlight, very high temperatures or insufficient potash.

Older varieties are more susceptible.

Blossom end rot – a sunken dark patch on the fruit – is caused by inadequate watering early in the fruits' development. Later trusses should not be affected.

Flowers dropping without setting fruits or **undersized fruits** can be due to dry air or dryness at the roots.

Uneven ripening can also be due to insufficient potash, lack of moisture or excessive heat.

PESTS AND DISEASES

Many soil rots can affect tomato plants. By rotating crops around the greenhouse borders and thoroughly cleaning the greenhouse at the end of the season, you can help prevent trouble. If all else fails, switch to growing in containers.

Aphids, spider mites and whitefly

Blossom end rot

can all attack tomato leaves. See page 158 for control measures.

Potato blight can also attack tomatoes, especially outdoors. See page 164 for prevention.

'Cherry Belle'

'Shirley'

Varieties

CHERRY TOMATOES

'Cherry Belle' is a new red cherry variety that has done well in *Gardening Which?* trials.

'Gardener's Delight', although an old variety, has done consistently well in trials over the years. It produces a high yield of sweet, tasty little fruits.

'Nectar' is the first of a new type of 'vine ripening' varieties. This means that the first fruits on each truss to ripen will remain in tip-top condition while later fruits ripen. However, seed is very expensive.

'Sungold' usually does well in taste tests. The orange tomatoes are very sweet and fruity.

'Santa' is a small, plum-shaped variety grown as

'Sungold'

'Nectar'

a cordon. The tomatoes are firm and tart.

STANDARD-SIZED TOMATOES

'Shirley' F1 has consistently proved itself over the years, with high yields of tasty fruit.

'Yellow Perfection' is the best standard-sized yellow-fruited variety, worth trying for a change.

BEEFSTEAK TOMATOES

'Dombito' was the best in the last *Gardening Which?* trial.

PLUM TOMATOES

'Inca' and **'Roma Improved'** produce huge yields of tasty fruit, and can be grown under glass in colder areas.

NOVELTIES

The list of varieties available, especially through specialist mail-order

suppliers, is now huge. If you have room, make a point of trying a couple of heritage varieties each year. Although the yield may be disappointing by modern standards and the beefsteak varieties may look unattractive, you may find a personal favourite, and unusual tomatoes can add interest to summer salads.

Calendar

INDOOR TOMATOES

FEBRUARY

If you are prepared to provide some background heat in the greenhouse later in the spring, start sowing now. Plants will be ready to plant out about eight weeks from sowing.

MARCH

All seeds sown usually germinate, and as seed of modern hybrids can be very expensive, decide how many plants you want and sow just enough. Surplus seed can be saved and should remain viable for up to five years if stored somewhere cool and dry. An airtight jar containing a bag of silica gel, and kept in the fridge, is ideal.

Scatter the seed thinly into a small pot containing moist multipurpose compost and cover with another 1cm of compost. Place the pot in a propagator set to a minimum of 15°C, but preferably nearer 21°C. Germination takes 7–10 days; less at the higher temperature. If you do not have a propagator, cover the pot with polythene or cling film and put it in a warm place until the seedlings appear. Move them somewhere warm and light, e.g. a sunny windowsill.

When the seedlings are large enough to handle, carefully separate them, holding the tip of the seed leaf, not the stem. Pot them individually into 7- or 8-cm pots. Water and keep at 18°C for a couple of days, then lower the temperature to 15°C to produce short, stocky plants.

APRIL

Three or four weeks after pricking out, pot the plants into 10-cm pots. If the plants are tall and leggy, remove the lower leaves and plant them as deep as the new pot will allow. This will not harm the plant – in fact, the buried stem will quickly produce roots. Very leggy plants can be rescued by coiling the stem and burying it.

Gradually harden off the young plants. In a propagator, open the air vents progressively, then remove the top altogether. Finally, move them on to the greenhouse bench, providing background heat at night if necessary.

MAY

Plant into the open greenhouse. If you have soil borders, this is the best place to grow tomato plants. But do not grow tomatoes continuously in the same border because soil diseases gradually build up. Alternate tomatoes with non-related crops (e.g. cucumbers) each season. Work plenty of organic matter into the soil before planting to provide nutrients and retain moisture.

If you do not have borders, or have had poor results, use large pots filled with multipurpose compost or the contents of growing bags, rather than planting in the growing bags themselves. *Gardening Which?* trials have shown that it is easier to keep tomato plants watered if they are in pots rather than growing bags.

Plant one plant to a 10-litre pot or three plants to a standard growing bag. Using 15-litre pots or two plants to a growing bag will make watering easier in high summer.

Most greenhouse tomato varieties are tall plants with a main shoot that grows upwards for several metres. The best way to control them is to support the main stem and remove the side shoots. Tomato plants grown in this way are said to be grown as cordons. To grow as cordons, bury a length of soft string under the tomato plant and attach the other end to the greenhouse frame. Or, better still, grow each plant next to a garden cane tied to the top of the greenhouse. Allow about 45cm between plants.

JUNE

Tie the main stem loosely to the support as it grows. Pinch out any side shoots that form but take care not to damage the tiny clusters of yellow flowers.

JULY–AUGUST

Pick the fruit when it is fully ripe and has developed its full colour.

Water the plants frequently, which may mean twice a day in growing bags or pots on the warmest days. A trickle irrigation system will automate the process if you are not able to attend to the plants twice a day.

Feed plants regularly with tomato food, and ventilate the greenhouse on sunny days, by opening the door.

SEPTEMBER

Stop the plant in early September, by pinching out the growing tip of the lead shoot. This stops further trusses of fruit developing and allows the trusses already formed to ripen. Keep pinching out side shoots, and remove dead or yellowing leaves. Banana skins in the greenhouse will encourage ripening of green fruit.

OCTOBER

Pick unripe fruit, clear the plants and clean the greenhouse (see page 55).

Cordon plants

Pinch out all side shoots. Pinch out the growing tip when 6–8 trusses have formed, or in September.

HARVESTING

For the best flavour, leave the fruits to ripen fully on the plant. Note the difference in supermarket tomatoes, which are picked almost green and ripened off the plant. Excess tomatoes can be frozen whole or puréed for winter use. Green tomatoes can either be encouraged to ripen by putting them in a bag with some ripe tomatoes, or made into chutney.

SOME UNUSUAL TRAINING METHODS

The following three methods have been tested by *Gardening Which?* readers and are worth trying.

[1] Mini plants

Instead of throwing away the side shoots, push them into a pot of compost. They will root in a few days to produce a new plant. When a plant has produced one flower truss, pinch out the growing tip, just above the next leaf. The mini-plant will go on to produce one truss of fruit. Cuttings taken early in the season will give an early crop and take up little space, on a greenhouse bench for example.

[2] Double plants

Instead of pinching out the lowest side shoot, let it grow. Train it up a second cane parallel to the main stem. The extra stem should increase the yield by at least 50 per cent. Allowing a third stem to grow should double the yield from one plant.

[3] Horizontal plants

Take a tall plant, lay it along the ground and peg it down. Train four good side shoots up separate canes. Pinch out any further side shoots but allow fruiting trusses to develop on each stem. Meanwhile, the horizontal stem will root whenever it touches the soil to produce a vigorous multi-stemmed plant.

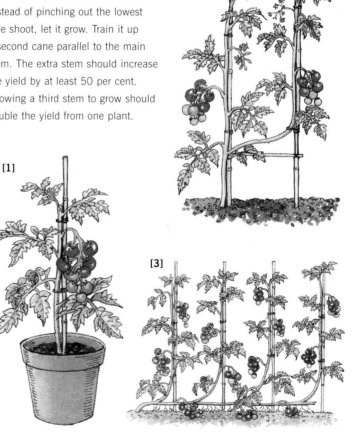

TOMATOES *Outdoor*

Any garden, however small, should have room for a couple of tomato plants. Compact varieties will grow in a container on the patio, in a window box or even in a hanging basket. Cordon tomatoes can be trained up a fence or trellis or grown on wigwams in the ornamental border. You have the choice of huge beefsteak, standard-sized or cherry tomatoes. Bush types need no training and include plum tomatoes.

If you have a greenhouse, your choice of varieties is even greater (see page 198).

Varieties

CHERRY TOMATOES
'Gardener's Delight' is a cordon variety that has done consistently well in *Gardening Which?* trials, producing plenty of sweet, tasty fruits.

'Red Alert' is a compact bush that produces a high yield of tasty cherry tomatoes.

'Tumbler' is a compact bush variety that will trail if planted in a pot or hanging basket. The cherry-sized fruits are produced early and the fruit is tasty. Considering its small size, it crops well.

'Incas'

STANDARD TOMATOES
'Tornado' is a bush variety that produces a large early crop and was the clear favourite for flavour in the last *Gardening Which?* trial.

'Harbinger' and 'Moneymaker' are reliable cordon varieties.

'Tornado'

LARGER TOMATOES
'Incas' and 'Roma Improved' are plum varieties with a bush habit. Both gave high yields in the last trial.

'Matador' is a cordon beefsteak variety that gave a high yield of tasty tomatoes.

'Gardener's Delight'

Calendar

OUTDOOR TOMATOES

Tomatoes are very sensitive to frost, but need as long a season as possible to produce a decent crop of ripe fruit. Start them off indoors or buy plants from the garden centre in May.

MARCH

Start the seed off indoors or in a greenhouse about eight or nine weeks before it is safe to plant outdoors in your area. In colder areas, wait until April.

Scatter the seeds thinly in a small pot containing moist multipurpose compost. Cover the seeds with 1cm of compost. Put the pot in a heated propagator, set to 18–21°C. If you do not have a propagator, cover the pot with cling film and put it in a warm place, such as an airing cupboard. Check occasionally and when the seedlings have emerged from the compost, usually in 10 days, bring the pot into a light place.

APRIL

Sow tomato seeds in colder areas. When the seedlings are large enough to handle, carefully tease them out of the original pot (holding the tip of the seed leaves, not the stem). Pot them individually into 8-cm pots. Make a hole in the compost and drop each seedling in so the seed leaves are level with the compost surface.

Water thoroughly and keep the seedlings at a constant 18°C for a couple of days. You can then reduce the temperature to 15°C. If you grow them on a windowsill, they may become a little leggy – turn them daily to ensure that they grow straight.

MAY

In milder parts of the UK, plant outside in containers or into prepared soil in late May. Use a container with a capacity of at least 15 litres for each plant. If you plant into the ground, first enrich the soil by digging in a generous amount of well-rotted manure or garden compost.

Cover plants with cloches to protect them from cold winds, until they are well established.

In colder areas or if the weather is not yet warm enough, re-pot young plants that you cannot plant outside into larger pots to prevent a check to growth.

JUNE

Plant outside in colder areas as soon as conditions are suitable. Covering the ground with clear polythene or cloches will help to warm up the soil first.

Planting through a black plastic mulch or mulching round the plants will help to suppress weeds and conserve moisture in the soil. Sink a large plastic bottle, with its bottom cut off, into the soil, to act as a water reservoir and help direct water to the roots (see page 47).

Bush varieties can be left to their own devices. Cordon varieties should be trained up a stout post up to 1.5m tall (see pages 200–1 for details on training).

JULY–SEPTEMBER

Water plants regularly and feed with a liquid tomato food.

Remove any dead leaves from the bottom of the plant to help the fruits ripen. Keep a look-out for signs of blight disease and aphids.

OCTOBER

Remove any full-sized fruit, before the plants are killed by the first frost.

Sowing seeds

Pricking out seedlings

Planting in a growing bag

HARVESTING

For the best possible flavour, leave the fruits to ripen fully on the plant. After picking keep them at room temperature rather than in the fridge.

GROWING YOUR OWN HERBS

Having your own supply of fresh herbs to accompany your home-grown vegetables and salads is an added bonus. We have picked out the easy ones that have most to offer in the kitchen, but there are hundreds of others to try as well.

Herbs are often sold in small pots, in which they look more or less the same size. However, once growing in the garden their individual habits soon show

Herbal teas are popular

Buy annual herbs...

...or grow from seed

A mixed container

themselves. There are short-lived ones such as basil and parsley which you will need to buy every year, rampant perennials such as mint that take over, and long-lived plants such as sweet bay and rosemary. So, rather than growing them all in a large container or in one raised bed, find out first which of the herbs you want to grow are annuals and which are more permanent. Place them around the garden according to the conditions they like and how they will fit in with your other plants. Annual herbs, especially those used in generous handfuls for cooking, are more economic to grow from seed. Many of the perennial herbs are worth buying as named varieties. These often need to be purchased as plants since they do not come true from seed, but you should need only one or two plants.

The majority of garden herbs are sun-lovers: the more sun they get, the more intense the flavour of their leaves. A sunny site invariably dries out in summer but most herbs cope better than many other plants with drought. There are a few exceptions: parsley and mint will do best in a moist site, for example, and often fail if grown alongside Mediterranean herbs.

All but a few herbs in this section (exceptions are borage and lovage) are ideal container plants. Containers need to be at least 15cm deep with drainage holes. Place them by the kitchen door, on a patio or on a windowsill to suit the needs of the cook.

As most herbs can be grown easily in containers or borders, and yield is not relevant when only small amounts are needed, we have not used the symbols given throughout the A–Z of Vegetables.

Herbs to raise from seed

Basil

Borage

Chervil

Chives

Coriander

Dill

Parsley

Herbs for the kitchen windowsill

Sow in late summer, bring indoors before the first frost.

Basil

Chervil

Parsley

Herbs for borders

Borage (M)

Chives (F)

Dill (B)

Fennel (B)

Lemon balm (M)

Lovage (B)

Marjoram (M)

Parsley (F, M)

Pot marigold (M)

Rosemary (B)

Sage (F, M)

Savory (F)

Thyme (F)

B   back of border

M   middle of border

F   front of border

BASIL *TENDER ANNUAL*

USES

Basil is best fresh but it can be frozen or made into pesto.

You can add fresh basil to many tomato and pasta dishes. It is well worth growing from seed and making several sowings.

GROWING GUIDE

Basil is very tender and blackens at the slightest hint of cold or frost. Slugs love the foliage. You will have most success by sowing late and keeping it in pots until the plants are a decent size. The purple-leaved varieties make colourful and eye-catching fillers for potagers and beds. If left to flower it produces pink flower spikes in summer.

MARCH

Towards the end of the month, sow in a greenhouse or on a sunny windowsill (3–4 seeds per 8-cm pot). The young seedlings are very sensitive to cold so move pots somewhere warmer at night. Take care not to overwater.

APRIL

Make the first sowing if not yet done and continue to sow little and often until the middle of summer.

MAY

When the young plants reach 15cm high, pinch out the shoots to encourage more leafy growth and a bushy shape. When buying basil plants, look for bushy plants with no sign of flowering. Start to harden off plants (see pages 56–7).

JUNE

Plants in pots can go outside once all danger of frost has passed – delay until the middle of the month if necessary. Protect from slugs (see pages 40–1).

Varieties of basil

JULY

Harvest plants. Pick young leaves from the top of the plant: you will need several pots on the go if you use a lot of fresh basil. After picking the leaves, feed the plant with balanced liquid feed and let it grow again. Keep other plants well watered and pick off flower buds.

AUGUST–SEPTEMBER

Make the last sowing so you will have basil into the autumn. Growth will be slower towards the end of the season.

VARIETIES

Sweet basil (sometimes sold as **'Sweet Genovese'**) is the variety with the classic taste. A *Gardening Which?* trial of 14 varieties revealed many interesting variations in aroma and appearance. **Greek basil** is the most compact and bushy with tiny leaves that do not need chopping before use. **'Green Ruffles'** combines classic taste with eye-catching leaf texture. Our favourite hot basil is **'Thai'**, which is strong and spicy but not bitter. Basils with unusual flavours worth trying are **'Cinnamon'**,

Pick individual leaves

reminiscent of aniseed sweets, and **'Mrs Burns' Lemon'**, a robust plant with a fresh lemon tang. For ornamental use, *Gardening Which?* recommends **'Purple Ruffles'** for its colour and crinkly leaves. The following are pretty in flower: **'Anise'** (green leaves with purple veins), **'Dark Opal'** (purple leaves) and **'Red Rubin'** (purple leaves). Seed companies often offer a mixture of half a dozen different basils; these can be grown together on a windowsill for a colourful green- and purple-leaved display.

BAY TREE *EVERGREEN SHRUB*

An unpruned bay tree can reach 2.4m but confined to a container and clipped it rarely exceeds 1m

USES

The leaves of the bay tree are a constituent of bouquet garni. They are also used, fresh or dry, to flavour sauces, soups and milky puddings. Rip the leaves just before adding to food to release the flavour.

GROWING GUIDE

The plants can be kept small if grown in containers, and are often clipped into formal shapes. Bay can be used as hedging, but not in cold regions, as these plants are only moderately hardy. Bay tolerates sun, shade and all soils except very wet ones. It must be sheltered from cold winds or the leaves turn brown. This plant often thrives in courtyards or front gardens.

MAY

Plant out new plants or bring container-grown plants out from their winter home. Protect from cold winds.

JUNE–JULY

Clip into shape if necessary.

AUGUST

Although leaves are available all year round, it is advisable to pick and dry some leaves now for winter cooking.

SEPTEMBER–OCTOBER

Protect the rootball of container-grown bay trees from freezing. Either move the plant under glass or lag the container with old hessian sacking or bubble insulation.

VARIETIES

The normal species, *Laurus nobilis*, is the one to go for. The only other variety is **'Aurea'** with yellow foliage, which looks a bit sickly.

CHERVIL *HARDY ANNUAL*

Chervil in flower

USES

The leaves can be used as garnish or as an ingredient of *fines herbes*, added to soups, egg and potato dishes. Pick the leaves just before use to preserve the delicate aniseed flavour.

GROWING GUIDE

Chervil is a relative of cow parsley but far less invasive, and its lacy foliage looks attractive as edging for a herb garden or border. It prefers moist soil and light shade. Sow little and often for a plentiful supply. Start picking the leaves early to delay flowering.

MARCH

Sow the seeds where you want them to grow (rather than transplanting them later). Chervil is slow to germinate. Thin out the seedlings so the plants are 20cm apart.

APRIL–SEPTEMBER

You can continue sowing each month if more chervil is needed. Sowings made in August–September will overwinter and provide early pickings next year. Water the plants in dry spells or they will bolt. Use a cloche or garden fleece to give some winter protection in cold areas.

VARIETIES

The species (*Anthriscus cerefolium*) is the one grown.

CHIVES _HERBACEOUS PERENNIAL_

USES

Chives are best appreciated fresh, their hollow stems snipped or chopped and used as a garnish or added at the last minute to dips and salads. The flowers can add colour to salads.

GROWING GUIDE

Chives are very easy to grow in sun or partial shade and in moist to dry soils. Either grow from seed or buy a plant and divide the clumps every couple of years. Chives are popular container plants, either in a mixed pot of leafy herbs or on their own. Keep the compost in the containers moist for fresher foliage. A row of chives planted along a bed or border gives a neat 25cm-high edging. If it gets a bit tatty during a drought, trim it down to the ground. Chives can sometimes suffer from the same diseases as onions and leeks (see pages 128–9, 140).

MARCH – APRIL

Sow the seed outdoors in groups of 3–4 seeds, 1.5cm deep. Thin out the seedlings to leave one plant every 15cm. For a row of chives to edge a border, take out a seed drill with a draw hoe.

JUNE

Keep the soil moist. Harvest as needed, and use sharp scissors to cut off handfuls of foliage 1cm or so from ground level.

JULY – SEPTEMBER

Sow in pots to provide fresh windowsill chives in autumn and winter. Or dig up a plant, cut down the leaves and pot up ready for winter use.

Chives are attractive in flower

OCTOBER

Lift and divide established plants.

VARIETIES

The normal species (_Allium schoenoprasum_), with its mauve flowers, is usually grown but you might be offered white-flowering versions. Named varieties include **'Forescate'**, which is more vigorous with bright-pink flowers. For leaves that taste like garlic as well as chives try garlic chives (see page 124).

Grow chives in pots and harvest in a rotation

CORIANDER *HARDY ANNUAL*

Despite its exotic flavour, coriander is hardy and can be sown directly into the soil in spring

USES

This herb is an essential addition to many Indian and Middle Eastern dishes. Leaves can be included in salads and used as garnish. You can use the leaves fresh, or freeze them. Seeds are used dry in baking.

GROWING GUIDE

A well-drained soil is essential, with sun or partial shade needed for leaves, but full sun for seeds. Coriander is best sown where you want it to grow as it does not transplant well. Sow little and often.

APRIL–MAY

Sow the seeds 0.5cm deep where you want the plants to grow. Thin out the resulting seedlings so the plants are spaced every 20–30cm.

JUNE

When the plants are 15cm high, cut the leaves; repeat this every month.

JULY–SEPTEMBER

For fresh herbs during autumn and winter, sow in pots for growing on the windowsill.

Seedheads can be gathered when ripe (usually between August and October). They are ready when the fruits begin to change colour and become aromatic.

VARIETIES

It is worth growing varieties or selections that have been bred specifically for leaf production or for seed production. **'Cilantro'** is a readily available selection that produces plenty of leaves. **'Leisure'** is another leafy type with large leaves and is slow to form seeds. **Moroccan coriander** will quickly run to seed.

DILL *HARDY ANNUAL*

The dry seeds of dill are used in baking and as a flavouring ingredients in dill pickles. The leaves and seeds are used in Nordic fish and potato dishes.

Dill in flower

GROWING GUIDE

Dill is a bushy plant with fine feathery foliage and, in mid- to late summer, tiny lime-yellow flowers. While it is not as easy to grow as fennel, it is worth trying in a warm, sunny site where the soil is well-drained. It is a waste of time to try growing dill on a cold, wet site.

MARCH–APRIL

Sow the seeds in the ground. Thin the seedlings out so the plants are spaced every 15cm.

JUNE

Water during dry spells to prevent the plants grown for leaves bolting. Pick the leaves well before the plant flowers.

JULY–AUGUST

Cut off the flowers to prevent self-sown seedlings establishing. Cut the seed heads as they ripen in summer if you want the seeds.

VARIETIES

It is worth growing varieties or selections that have been bred specifically for leaf production or for seed production. **'Dukat'** is mostly grown for its leaves, but seeds are produced as well. **'Fernleaf'** has dwarf plants, which are only 45cm high, with dark-green leaves. It is slow to bolt so it has a long cropping time. **'Mammoth'** quickly runs to seed. It has large decorative seed heads.

FENNEL *HERBACEOUS PERENNIAL*

Bronze fennel

USES

Fennel has a stronger aniseed flavour than dill and is used sparingly. Fresh leaves can be baked with fish, or added as a garnish. Dry seeds are sometimes used for baking, pickling, or as a stuffing for fish.

GROWING GUIDE

The herb fennel has the same feathery foliage as the vegetable Florence fennel, but not the bulb-like base (see pages 116–7). A larger plant (1.5m high) than dill but easier to grow, it is often placed in a sunny border or as a centrepiece to a herb garden. Do not grow fennel and dill near to each other as they will both produce inferior seedlings. Fennel likes a deep, moist but well-drained soil, so its long tap root has plenty of room.

MARCH

As only a single specimen is needed, you can buy a young plant in a pot rather than having to raise lots of plants from seed. Buy early since the plants soon suffer a check to their growth if kept in pots too long. Or get some seedlings from a friend who already has fennel. Allow the plant an area of 60 x 60cm.

JULY

Remove flowers before they shed seeds, to prevent self-seeding.

OCTOBER–NOVEMBER

Cut down top growth. Lift and divide plants every 3–4 years.

VARIETIES

Green fennel has rich feathery foliage, but the form with bronze-purple foliage is more unusual.

LEMON BALM *HERBACEOUS PERENNIAL*

Golden lemon balm

USES

The foliage has a strong lemon flavour when first picked but this fades quickly. Make herb tea by pouring boiling water over the leaves. Add leaves to chicken dishes or use in cakes and biscuits.

GROWING GUIDE

This bushy foliage plant is not fussy and grows well in sun or shade (although the yellow-leaved varieties are best in partial shade) in all but waterlogged soils. To maximise the refreshing aroma, position it where you will brush against the foliage.

MARCH

Sow seed in pots or buy young plants.

JUNE–SEPTEMBER

Yellow or variegated forms should have their flowers removed before they set seed or the green-leaved seedlings will take over.

OCTOBER

Cut down old foliage. Lift and divide established plants now, or in spring.

VARIETIES

Plants sold as **'Aurea'** may have either golden or variegated foliage – both are attractive. **'All Gold'** is all yellow.

LOVAGE *HERBACEOUS PERENNIAL*

Lovage

USES
Lovage has a distinct flavour, similar to celery, and is worth trying as seasoning in salt-free diets. All parts of the plant may be used in soups and stews. Young shoots can be blanched and eaten as a vegetable.

GROWING GUIDE
This rather coarse-looking foliage plant with shiny, dark-green leaves needs plenty of space and a deep, rich, moist soil. Sunny or partially shady sites are equally suitable. Unlike many herbs, this is a long-lived plant that can be left to grow into a big clump. If it gets too big, lift and divide in spring.

MARCH
Plant in spring, allowing for a height and spread of 1.5 x 1m. Remember to protect from slugs. Mulch well.

APRIL–AUGUST
Pick young leaves before the plant flowers – older leaves are coarse. Plants can be cut back hard and watered to stimulate more young leaves.

VARIETIES
The normal species (*Levisticum officinale*) is the one usually grown.

MARJORAM *HERBACEOUS PERENNIAL*

Marjoram in flower

Marjoram

USES
Also known as oregano, this herb adds an authentic touch to Mediterranean dishes containing tomato, cheese or fish. It is one of the few herbs worth drying.

GROWING GUIDE
Suited to a sunny, warm spot and a light soil that drains well, marjoram thrives on chalky soils and is loved by bees.

MARCH
Buy small plants in pots. Named varieties are not available as seed and even the species tends to germinate erratically. Established plants can have old stems cut back, if you did not get around to doing this last year.

SEPTEMBER–OCTOBER
Plants can be cut back almost to the ground after flowering has finished.

VARIETIES
Wild marjoram (**Origanum vulgare**) is hardy, so it can be grown as a perennial. Several garden-worthy forms are available: golden marjoram (*O. vulgare* **'Aureum'**) which creates a glowing carpet of golden foliage 30 x 30cm; compact marjoram (*O. vulgare* **'Compactum'**), only 15 x 30cm with golden-green foliage and pink flowers; and *O. vulgare* **'Country Cream'** with cream and green variegated leaves. Sweet marjoram (**O. majorana**) is grown as a half-hardy annual. Sow in pots under glass in early spring and plant out or sow directly into the ground in late spring. Thin plants to 20cm apart.

Golden marjoram

MINT *HERBACEOUS PERENNIAL*

Variegated ginger mint

Pineapple mint

Spearmint

USES

A sprig of young mint leaves makes a refreshing mint tea or garnish for new potatoes. Mint sauce or jelly goes well with roast lamb.

GROWING GUIDE

The secret of growing mint is to remember that it is not one of the typical Mediterranean herbs that like hot, sunny conditions, but a plant that likes moist soil and tolerates some shade.

All mint is invasive and spreads relentlessly via runners (creeping underground stems). Curtail it by growing in a large pot of soil-based compost sunk into the soil with 3–5cm of the rim above ground so the runners do not creep over. Mint can be grown this way for 2–3 years. After that, start afresh with new compost and a few healthy runners from the parent plant.

Self-seeding can be a problem and you will need to deal with this promptly by pulling up the seedlings by hand when you spot them.

MARCH

Buy small pots of mint, plant in pots sunk in the ground and keep well watered.

JUNE–JULY

Remove flowers to prevent seeding (plants do not come true from seed and once out of the pot will be very invasive).

MINT RUST

Small orange spots on leaves and stems is a sign of mint rust. This fungal disease can spread rapidly so remove and destroy any plants with these symptoms. Using a flame gun in autumn to sterilise the soil is an option. Rhizomes can be warmed in water to prevent re-infection. Immerse in a pan of water (41°C) for ten minutes, cool in cold water and plant. Start again with fresh plants on a new site.

OCTOBER

For a fresh supply of mint over the winter, dig up a pot of mint that has become congested. Tip it out of the pot, select some runners and cut them off the parent plant. Plant them in a pot and cover with 2–3cm of compost or soil. Water compost

Propagate mint from runners

and stand the pot in a cool greenhouse or porch.

VARIETIES

Many interesting mints are available, and starting a small collection can be fascinating. Below we list some of the most valuable culinary ones. **Spearmint** (*Mentha spicata*) is the familiar mint with long, pointed leaves and a refreshing taste. A variety called **'Brundall'** is claimed to be extra tasty. **'Moroccan'** is particularly fragrant and is used for mint tea. **Apple mint** (*M. suaveolens*) has rounded, woolly leaves, an apple scent and mild mint flavour, making it both decorative and valued by cooks. An attractive cream-and-green variegated version is sometimes sold as **pineapple mint** (*M. suaveolens* 'Variegata').

Ginger mint (*M. x gracilis* 'Variegata') is very eye-catching, with green-and-yellow variegation and red stems. It tolerates drier soils.

PARSLEY *HARDY BIENNIAL*

Flat-leaved parsley

USES

The intensely bright-green, curly parsley is widely used as a garnish but is also very tasty when chopped and added to sauces and soups. Flat-leaved parsley has a stronger flavour and is increasingly popular in salads.

GROWING GUIDE

Parsley prefers damp soil in partial shade. You can grow it in pots, but this means regular watering throughout the growing season.

Try parsley as a foliage plant for filling gaps in borders, or grow it among vegetables such as onions.

Parsley is a biennial but tends to be grown as an annual as the leaves are coarse in the second year. Growing from seed is worthwhile, even though it can be tricky to germinate, as parsley can be used in quantity. Always start the season with a fresh packet of seed.

You will need to protect plants against slugs (see pages 40–1) and carrot fly (see page 94).

FEBRUARY–MARCH

For the earliest parsley, sow in early spring at 15–18°C in a heated propagator or on a sunny windowsill.

APRIL–MAY

Sow parsley in pots or into the ground. It will germinate at a steady temperature of 15°C. To sow in pots, press seed 2–3cm down in compost. For a row of parsley, take out a seed drill and sow thickly in rows 25cm apart.

It is often suggested that pouring boiling water over parsley seed will get it to germinate quicker. *Gardening Which?* members took part in a trial that compared this method with normal sowing but found it to be a waste of time: untreated seed had higher germination.

Be prepared to wait up to two weeks for seed to germinate. Keep the soil moist.

JUNE–AUGUST

Sowing can continue.

OCTOBER

Parsley is hardy but to produce the best-quality foliage for the kitchen, it is best to cover crops with a cloche or move pots into a cold greenhouse.

VARIETIES

The standard curly parsley is **'Moss Curled'** but you may come across other named varieties. **'Curlina'** is compact with short stems, so useful for pots. Flat-leaved parsley is often sold as **'French parsley'** or **'Italian parsley'**.

Curly parsley

ROSEMARY *EVERGREEN SHRUB*

Hedge of clipped rosemary

USES

Rosemary retains its aroma and flavour well so is often used when roasting meat or for stuffings. The needle-like leaves can be chopped finely or used as sprigs that can be removed before the food is served. Rosemary can be dried, or fresh sprigs added to oil or vinegar.

GROWING GUIDE

This Mediterranean herb is slightly tender but usually thrives if grown in a sunny, sheltered spot in well-drained soil. It does well on chalk. In mild areas, rosemary can be grown as a hedge that is trimmed after flowering, but in most gardens it is to be found in a herb garden or border, or growing against a warm wall. A height and spread of 1.5 x 1m is typical but varieties may vary in habit.

MARCH

Plant in spring. It is worth forking in some grit to improve drainage if you have a clay or loam soil.

Old shrubs that are growing strongly can be cut back by half. Others should

have dead or straggly stems removed. Give plants some general fertiliser (or a rose fertiliser) if the soil is poor.

JUNE–JULY

Trim the plant into shape after it has flowered. Take semi-ripe cuttings if you want more plants or to insure against winter losses. Rosemary can be harvested from spring to early summer.

VARIETIES

The basic species, **Rosmarinus officinalis**, is the hardiest and forms a rounded-to-upright bush and is fine for cooking. You can pay more for a named variety that has a specific shape or more prominent flowers. **'Miss Jessopp's Upright'** is more vigorous and upright than the species. It will form a suitable shape for hedging or make a focal point in the herb bed. The **Prostratus Group** are spreading rosemaries 15cm high. They are suitable for a rock garden or the top of a wall. **'Severn Sea'**, at 1m high, is smaller than the species, with an arching habit and bright-blue flowers. It is not very hardy but a useful size for a container.

Take cuttings with a 'heel' from the parent plant

Cover and root somewhere cool but frost-free

SAGE *EVERGREEN SHRUB*

'Purpurescens'

'Icterina'

USES

Sage is a herb that retains its aroma and flavour so is often used when roasting meat and poultry or for stuffings and sausages (the leaves are sometimes blanched before cooking and then chopped finely). It is worth drying.

GROWING GUIDE

Sages are an attractive group of foliage plants that can be used in containers or borders. An individual plant will provide enough leaves for the kitchen, while the coloured-leaved sages are often planted in blocks or used as an edging along a path or border.

Sage needs a well-drained, fairly fertile soil in a sunny spot. If your soil is heavy, dig in some grit or opt to grow sage in containers. Sage will remain compact and attractive if pruned regularly; neglected old plants are best replaced.

MARCH

Cut back to 15–20cm above ground – this hard pruning each year prevents plants becoming leggy. Apply a balanced fertiliser if the soil is poor. Leaves can be harvested any time before flowering.

VARIETIES

Green sage (**Salvia officinalis**) is the one usually used for cooking, but varieties with more colourful foliage can be used too and are more garden-worthy.

'Icterina' is a yellow variegated form that needs sun, as it turns green in the shade. **'Purpurescens'** has purple foliage. **'Tricolor'** has leaves flecked with cream and pink. It is not as strong-growing as the others but an attractive subject for containers. **Pineapple sage** (**Salvia elegans**, or **Scarlet pineapple**) is tender and valued for its pineapple-scented leaves and red flower spikes.

SAVORY *HARDY ANNUAL*

Winter savory

USES

Savory adds flavour to dishes made with beans, cheese and eggs and is a substitute for salt and pepper. Summer savory can be used fresh or dried; winter savory is available fresh all year, and can be added to stuffings.

GROWING GUIDE

There are two types: the perennial winter species *Satureja montana* and the summer savory *S. hortensis* which is an annual. Both are worth growing as they take up little space (30 x 45cm). Dry summer savory after flowering.

Both types do well in problem sites like baking hot corners of poor, stony soil or chalk such as you might find at the foot of south-facing walls.

MARCH

Cut back established plants of winter savory to stop them sprawling.

APRIL–MAY

Sow seed in pots at 15°C, or directly in the ground. Thin plants so there is a plant every 20cm for winter savory and every 30cm for summer savory.

Pick leaves at any time once plants are 15cm high. After summer savory has flowered, cut the whole plant and hang it up to dry.

VARIETIES

Only the two species are grown.

SORREL *HERBACEOUS PERENNIAL*

Sorrel

USES
Sorrel has a sharp lemon flavour, and makes an unusual soup in its own right. It can be used as an ingredient in sauce for fish and as a substitute for spinach.

GROWING GUIDE
It is a very hardy perennial herb that can cope with shade and most types of soil. Sorrel looks like its distant relative dock, so is not particularly ornamental.

MARCH–JUNE
Sow thinly in rows 25–30cm apart. Thin plants out so there is 15–20cm between them.

Established plants can be harvested from spring onwards; young leaves are less bitter than older ones.

OCTOBER
Cut down the foliage when it suffers winter damage. Once plants are 3–4 years old it is worth lifting and dividing them, and re-planting healthy young sections.

VARIETIES
You are most likely to come across the large-leaved **French sorrel** (*Rumex acetosa*). But specialists may also offer **Buckler-leaved sorrel** (*R. scutatus*), a smaller plant only 25cm high with arrow-shaped leaves. Often grown as a groundcover plant, it tolerates drier conditions. **Sheep sorrel** (*R. acetosella*) is best avoided – it tastes bitter and is poisonous in large doses.

TARRAGON *HERBACEOUS PERENNIAL*

Tarragon

USES
The delicate aniseed flavour of tarragon complements chicken and fish. It is often used to make tarragon vinegar.

GROWING GUIDE
Tarragon is a very desirable perennial herb for use in the kitchen, although in the garden it makes only a modest clump of narrow leaves. It needs nurturing: a warm, sunny site and a well-drained soil are essential. Cold, wet soil can kill it off. It can tolerate summer drought, often coming to life again in the autumn.

MARCH
Plant on its own in a container or in a herb bed. It is fairly slow-growing and is easily taken over by more vigorous plants.

It takes a couple of years for a plant to form a sizeable clump, about 60 x 60cm, so you might want to buy several plants. After this it can be lifted and divided and the sections replanted.

Cut or pinch out the top third of the stems for use in the kitchen. This can be done throughout the growing season.

VARIETIES
The long, thin leaves of **French tarragon** (*Artemisia dracunculus*) have an aniseed flavour that is superior to the bitter, coarse **Russian tarragon** (*Artemisia dracunculoides*) – it is worth tasting a small leaf before buying if the plant label is ambiguous. French tarragon does not produce seed in the cool summers of the UK climate, so you need to buy it as a plant, while Russian tarragon is sharper, and seeds freely.

THYME *EVERGREEN SHRUB*

Container with a mixture of thymes

Lemon thyme

USES

Thyme leaves taste warm and spicy, and add a Mediterranean flavour to many dishes, from meat to cheese, eggs and pasta. The leaves are tiny and it is awkward to pick them off the woody stems. An alternative is to add a fresh sprig to a bottle of vinegar.

GROWING GUIDE

These small plants are versatile in the garden, whether as twiggy little bushes or carpeting mats. As well as aromatic foliage, the flowers provide a long-lasting summer display of pink or purple flowers.

A warm, sunny site on a well-drained soil is essential – thymes do very well on chalky soils, on walls or between paving cracks. They are best treated as short-term shrubby plants that need replacing every three years or so by taking cuttings.

MARCH

Plant thymes and fork in some grit to improve drainage or grow on a rock garden or in a container. Add a mulch to the mat-like ones to prevent mud splashing on to the leaves.

Leaves can be picked at any time – remove twiggy stems with secateurs and pick off the leaves in the kitchen.

JULY

Trim plants after flowering to keep them neat and bushy.

AUGUST

Trim plants if not done last month. Take semi-ripe cuttings.

VARIETIES

The **common thyme** (*Thymus vulgaris*), a native of the Mediterranean, is the one most associated with cooking. It has a rather straggly habit, although named varieties will provide neater and perhaps more garden-worthy plants (the named forms cannot be sown from seed). Variegated forms such as *T. vulgaris* **'Silver Posie'** are excellent and can be used for cooking, although

Common thyme in flower

they will not produce as much foliage as the plain green form. **Lemon thyme** (*T. x citriodorus*) is used to flavour fish dishes. Several named varieties exist, including a yellow-leaved one, *T. x citriodorus* **'Aureus'**.

EDIBLE FLOWERS

The following flowers are both ornamental and edible. Grow them alongside herbs and vegetables, or in containers or borders. As well as borage, pot marigold and nasturtium, other plants with edible flowers include: chives (see page 208), chicory, with its lovely pale-blue flowers (see pages 104–5) and thyme (see page 217). Courgette flowers (see page 109) are large, and delicious stuffed or dipped in batter, then made into fritters.

BORAGE

HARDY ANNUAL

NASTURTIUM

HARDY ANNUAL

These hairy buds and flowers are pretty and edible

USES

The flowers and leaves of borage have a cucumber flavour and are used in salads or floated on drinks such as Pimms.

GROWING GUIDE

Borage is easy to grow from seed in a sunny or lightly shaded site. Any well-drained soil – even if it is chalky or sandy – is suitable. Their brilliant blue, star-like flowers add colour but they self-seed prolifically. There is also a white-flowered version.

USES

The flowers and buds of nasturtium have a peppery taste, a bit like watercress, and were a clear favourite in a *Gardening Which?* taste test on edible flowers.

GROWING GUIDE

These cheerful, hardy annuals are quick and easy to grow. They add colour all round the garden, including in vegetable borders and containers. Trailing types can be trained up fences. They prefer

One of the tastiest edible flowers

full sun, and thrive on poor, dry soils.

Nasturtiums are a magnet for pests, including cabbage white caterpillars, blackfly, whitefly and slugs.

VARIETIES

In a *Gardening Which?* trial of 32 varieties, the following came top:
'Tip Top' has bright bold blooms on compact plants and is ideal for patios or containers. Its four single colours are: apricot with a red fleck, gold, mahogany with gold, and scarlet.
'Whirlybird' produces a carpet of colour in a bed or a trailing habit in containers. It is widely available, with seven single colours. Look out for **'Salmon Baby'** for its flower colour, dark-green foliage and compact habit. **'Empress of India'** is well over a century old and still impressive, with its rich orange-red flowers and dark blue-green foliage.

For a mixture of gold, scarlet, cream and carmine, opt for **'Alaska'**, which has green and cream foliage.

Try the climbing version of **'Jewel of Africa'**. It has gold, cream and yellow flowers with brown flecks.

POT MARIGOLD

HARDY ANNUAL

A colourful addition to green salads

USES

The golden-yellow or orange petals of the pot marigold add contrast to green salads and have a distinctive nutty taste.

VARIETIES

The original pot marigold, with its single, bright-orange flowers, is still available but has been joined by many new named varieties.

'Fiesta Gitana' has double flowers of orange, yellow and cream on compact plants only 30cm high.

'Indian Prince' has deep-orange semi-double flowers with mahogany-red on the reverse of the petals. It is 75cm high.

'Pink Surprise' has orange buds which open to pale apricot-pink semi-double flowers. It grows to 60cm high.

'Orange King' is 45cm high, with rich-orange double flowers.

Calendar

FEBRUARY–MARCH

Seeds of marigolds and nasturtiums can be sown in pots in a greenhouse or on a sunny windowsill. They will germinate at 15°C. Sow one or two seeds per 8-cm pot and push them 1cm down.

You can buy pots of seedlings. A single pot can yield 20–30 plants if you separate the seedlings and pot them up individually.

APRIL–MAY

Young plants raised under cover can be hardened off before being planted outside. When planting out pot-grown plants, leave 25–30cm between plants.

As the weather improves, you can sow seed outside, either in containers or into weed-free ground. Sowing seed in the ground is the best way to grow borage, but marigolds and nasturtiums can be sown directly too (see pages 50–1).

Nasturtium seeds can be pushed into the compost of hanging baskets and window boxes when planting them up with other plants.

JUNE–JULY

Harvest the flowers. After borage has flowered, collect the seeds and scatter them where you want the flowers to be the following year.

Remove pests or diseased plants by hand as soon as you see them. Problems seem to be worse later in the year, so aim to pick flowers for eating early on. If you do not want the plants to self-seed, pull them up as the flowers fade.

Nasturtium seeds can still be sown in pots in early June and planted out a month later to flower until late autumn.

AUGUST–SEPTEMBER

In mild areas, sow spare marigold seed in pots for earlier flowers the following year.

Pull up the plants as soon as they start to look tatty.

HARVESTING

Pick newly opened flowers early in the morning, just as the dew has dried. Avoid washing the flowers but check them over for insects. To keep them until the evening, place the stems in a glass of cold water or store them in a plastic bag in the fridge. When adding them to a mixed salad, mix in the dressing before you sprinkle with petals.

KEEPING SAFE

Not all flowers (or any part of a plant, for that matter) are safe to eat, so eat only those you know are edible. Use only plants you know have not been treated with chemicals.

JANUARY

Other jobs Buy vegetable seed, start to chit seed potatoes. Plan where to put your crops. Complete the greenhouse clean-up.

FEBRUARY

Sow from seed indoors Beetroot, broad beans, summer cabbage, calabrese, summer cauliflower, lettuce and onion. In milder areas sow outdoors under cloches early beetroot, carrots, lettuce, spring onion, peas, radishes, salad leaf, spinach, early turnip.

Other jobs Feed overwintered greens with nitrogen fertiliser; continue to chit potatoes. Put cloches in position to warm soil. Erect pea and bean supports to save time later; erect a carrot fly barrier.

MARCH

Sow in pots indoors, if not done last month Summer cabbage, summer cauliflower, calabrese, celery and celeriac, leeks, lettuce, onion. Also sow aubergine, peppers and tomatoes for greenhouse or for outdoors in milder areas.

Make first sowing outdoors (under cloches in colder areas) of early carrots, spring onion, peas, radishes, salad leaf, spinach and leaf beet, turnip if not done last month.

Plant Garlic, onion sets, shallots, early potatoes if soil is workable.

Pests and diseases Watch for slug damage, protect vulnerable plants.

Other jobs Complete winter digging on lighter soils. Apply loose mulches; cover soil with black plastic to plant through later.

JULY

Sow Spring cabbage in north or in cold areas, chicory and endive, oriental greens, winter radish.

Plant Brussels sprouts, sprouting broccoli, winter cauliflower, kale, leeks, oriental greens (if not done last month).

Keep sowing Beetroot, calabrese, carrots, summer cauliflower, fennel, kohl rabi, lettuce, spring onion, radishes, baby parsnips, salad leaf, spinach and leaf beet, turnip.

Pests and diseases Look out for blackfly on beans; spray if necessary. Keep spraying to protect potatoes and tomatoes from blight.

Other jobs Blanch endive. Dry off garlic, shallot and onions and store for winter use.

AUGUST

Sow Spring cabbage in milder parts, chicory and endive, greenhouse lettuce, autumn sown onions, spinach and leaf beet for winter.

Plant Any vegetables started off earlier in pots can be used to fill gaps in the garden or vegetable plot.

Keep sowing Make last sowing of calabrese, carrots, lettuce, spring onion, salad leaf, radishes.

Pests and diseases Cabbage white caterpillars, mealy cabbage aphid, cabbage whitefly – spray if necessary.

Other jobs Blanch endive. Pick courgettes and beans before going on holiday to prolong cropping.

SEPTEMBER

Sow Summer cauliflower for overwintering, greenhouse lettuce.

Plant Spring cabbage, chicory and endive, autumn onion from seed.

Other jobs Cover lettuce, oriental greens, spinach with cloches in cold areas. Store maincrop carrots.

APRIL

Sow Celery and celeriac, endive, kale. In milder areas sow French beans and sweetcorn indoors. Outdoors sow broad beans, kohl rabi, leeks, parsnips. Sow aubergine, peppers and outdoor tomatoes if not done already.

Plant All hardy vegetables sown indoors as soon as weather is suitable; garlic, onion sets and shallots if not done already; maincrop potatoes.

Keep sowing Beetroot, calabrese, early carrots, summer cauliflower, lettuce, spring onion, radishes, peas, salad leaf, spinach, turnips.

Pests and diseases Protect vulnerable plants from slugs and snails, flea beetle.

Other jobs Cover summer brassicas and carrots with crop covers to stop flying pests. Remove cloches from early crops – use instead to protect tender crops. Complete soil preparation as winter crops are cleared. Hoe to remove annual weeds.

MAY

Sow Brussels sprouts, sprouting broccoli, winter cabbage, autumn and winter cauliflower and kale in pots or seedbed. Sow maincrop beetroot and carrot, winter turnip and swede outdoors; courgette, outdoor cucumber, marrow, squash indoors and sweetcorn outdoors in milder areas, or in pots in colder areas.

Plant Vegetables started in pots last month, including celery, and greenhouse tomatoes in mild areas.

Keep sowing Calabrese, carrots, summer cauliflower, endive, fennel, dwarf beans, kohl rabi, lettuce, spring onion, baby parsnip, peas, radishes, salad leaf, spinach, turnip.

Pests and diseases Protect vulnerable plants from slugs and snails during damp spells, and flea beetle. Watch out for pea moth, pea aphid and blackfly.

Other jobs Cover potatoes and other vulnerable crops if frost is predicted.

JUNE

Sow Oriental greens, fennel, maincrop beetroot, turnip and swede if not done.

Plant Brussels sprouts, sprouting broccoli, winter cabbage, celery, autumn and winter cauliflower; leeks (if room); courgette, marrow, squash, outdoor cucumber, French beans, sweetcorn, outdoor tomato.

Keep sowing Calabrese, early carrot, summer cauliflower, endive, dwarf bean, kohl rabi, lettuce, spring onion, baby parsnip, radishes, salad leaf, turnip.

Pests and diseases Asparagus beetle, potato blight – spray as a precaution. Pinch out tips of broad bean plants to reduce blackfly damage.

Other jobs Hoe between rows of seedlings to get rid of annual weeds.

OCTOBER

Sow Broad beans, peas to overwinter.

Plant Garlic, autumn onion sets, spring cabbage in milder areas.

Other jobs Start to clear away plant debris. Lift and store marrow and winter squash before severe frosts; leave maincrop beetroot, carrots, parsnips, swede and turnip in the ground or lift and store; complete lifting onions and maincrop potatoes for storing.

NOVEMBER

Plant Garlic if not yet done.

Pests and diseases Protect overwintered cabbage from pigeons and rabbits with netting.

Other jobs Start a bean trench. Finish clearing crop remains and compost it. Start winter digging. Store Dutch white cabbage.

DECEMBER

Other jobs Try to complete winter digging on heavy soils. Check pH and if necessary lime acid soil where brassicas will grow.

	Spacing between rows	Spacing between plants	Sow in pots [1]	Plant outdoors	Sow direct	Frost protection [2]	Harvest	Sow in succession [3]
BEETROOT	15cm	2.5cm			Feb–Jul	Feb–Apr	May–Sep	✓
BROAD BEAN	45cm	13cm	Feb	Mar–Apr	Mar–Apr		Jun–Jul	
BROCCOLI, sprouting	60cm	60cm	Apr–May	Jun–Jul			Dec–May	
BRUSSELS SPROUTS	60cm	60cm	Mar–Apr	May–Jun			Sep–Mar	
CABBAGE, summer/autumn	45cm	45cm	Feb–Apr	Apr–May			Jul–Nov	
CABBAGE, winter	45cm	45cm	May	Jun			Nov–Feb	
CABBAGE, spring	30cm	30cm	Jul–Aug	Sep–Oct			Mar–May	
CALABRESE	30cm	15cm	Feb–Aug	Apr–Sep	Apr–Aug		Jul–Dec	✓
CARROT, early	15cm	2.5cm			Feb–Aug	Feb–Mar	Jun–Oct	✓
CARROT, maincrop	15cm	2.5cm			May		Sep–Dec	
CAULIFLOWER, summer/autumn	50cm	50cm	Feb–May	Mar–Jun	Mar–Jul		Jul–Nov	✓
CAULIFLOWER, winter	60cm	60cm	May	Jul			Apr–May	
CELERIAC	30cm	30cm	Feb–Mar	May			Sep–Oct	
CELERY, self-blanching	23cm	23cm	Mar–Apr	Apr–Jun			Aug–Oct	
CHICORY	25cm	25cm	Jul–Aug	Aug–Sep	Jul–Aug	Oct–Mar	Sep–Mar	
CHINESE CABBAGE	35cm	35cm	Jun–Jul	Jul–Aug	Jul–Aug	Oct–Nov	Sep–Nov	
COURGETTE	1m	1m	May	Jun		May	Jul–Oct	
CUCUMBER, outdoor	75cm	75cm	Apr	May–Jun		May	Aug–Oct	
ENDIVE, summer	30cm	30cm	Apr–Jun	May–Jul	Apr–Jun		Jul–Sep	
FLORENCE FENNEL	30cm	30cm			Jun–Jul		Sep–Oct	
FRENCH BEAN (dwarf)	30cm	7.5cm	Mar–Apr	May–Jun	Apr–Jul	Mar–May	Jul–Oct	✓
GARLIC	20cm	10cm		Oct–Nov			Jun–Jul	
KALE	45cm	45cm	Apr–May	Jul			Aug–Apr	
LEEK	30cm	15cm	Mar–Apr	Jun–Jul	Mar–Jun		Sep–Apr	
LETTUCE	30cm	30cm	Feb–Apr	Mar–May	Mar–Aug	Mar–Apr	May–Oct	✓

	Spacing between rows	Spacing between plants	Sow in pots [1]	Plant outdoors	Sow direct	Frost protection [2]	Harvest	Sow in succession [3]
MARROW	1m	1m	Apr–May	May–Jun		May	Aug–Oct	
ONION, from seed	15cm	10cm	Feb–Mar	Apr–May	Feb–Apr		Aug–Oct	
ONION, from sets	15cm	10cm		Mar–Apr			Aug–Oct	
ONION, overwinter sets	15cm	10cm		Oct			Jun–Jul	
ONION, salad	10cm	[4]			Feb–Aug		Jun–Oct	✓
PARSNIP	30cm	15cm			Mar–Apr		Oct–Apr	
PEA, garden/mangetout	60cm	5cm			Feb–Jul	Feb–Apr	Jul–Oct	✓
POTATO, early	45cm	40cm		Mar–Apr		Mar–May	Jul–Aug	
POTATO, maincrop	75cm	40cm		Apr–May			Aug–Oct	
PUMPKIN/SQUASH	1m	1m	Apr–May	May–Jun		May	Sep–Oct	
RADISH, summer	15cm	[4]			Feb–Sep	Feb–Apr	May–Oct	✓
RADISH, winter	25cm	15cm			Jul		Oct–Nov	
RUNNER BEAN	60cm	15cm	Apr	May–Jun	May–Jun	Apr–May	Aug–Oct	
SALAD LEAVES	10cm	[4]	Feb	Mar	Mar–Jul	Feb–Mar	May–Nov	
SHALLOT	30cm	15cm		Apr–May			Jul–Aug	
SPINACH, true	30cm	15cm			Feb–May	Feb–Mar	May–Aug	✓
LEAF BEET/CHARD	30cm	30cm			Mar–Apr		Jul–Oct	
SWEDE/WINTER TURNIP	40cm	23cm			May–Jun		Sep–Mar	
SWEETCORN	35cm	35cm	Apr–May	May–Jun		Apr–May	Aug–Oct	
TOMATO, outdoor	45cm	45cm	Mar–Apr	May–Jun		May	Aug–Oct	
TURNIP/KOHL RABI	15cm	10cm			Feb–Aug	Feb–Apr	May–Sep	✓

FOOTNOTES

[1] An alternative for leeks and brassicas is to sow in a seed bed and transplant the seedlings [2] Exact timing depends on the last frost in your area. Cover with garden fleece or cloches if frost is likely [3] Sow small amounts at regular intervals throughout this period [4] Sow thinly in bands (see relevant A–Z entry) **NB For perennial vegetables (artichokes, asparagus, rhubarb and seakale) and greenhouse crops (aubergines, cucumbers, peppers and tomatoes) see the relevant A–Z entry**

Which? Books are commissioned and researched by
Consumers' Association and published by
Which? Ltd, 2 Marylebone Road, London NW1 4DF
Email address: books@which.net

Distributed by The Penguin Group:
Penguin Books Ltd, 27 Wrights Lane, London W8 5TZ

The author and publishers would like to thank the following for their help in the preparation of
this book: Kate Hawkins, Mark Scott, Rachael Swann and Elaine Vigar

First edition 2001

Copyright © 2001 Which? Ltd

British Library Cataloguing in Publication Data
A catalogue record for this book is available from the British Library

ISBN 0 85202 834 2

For a full list of Which? books, please write to Which? Books, Castlemead, Gascoyne Way,
Hertford X, SG14 1LH or access our website at www.which.net

Cover and text design by Sarah Harmer
Cover photograph by Lynne Mack for *Gardening Which?*
Illustrations by Gill Tomblin

Gardening Which? magazine
You can find up-to-date information on all the latest plants, gardening products and techniques in
Gardening Which? magazine. It regularly carries out tests and trials of plant varieties and suppliers,
as well as gardening equipment and sundries such as composts and fertilisers. Each issue is
packed with ideas, practical advice and results of the magazine's independent evaluations

Plus
- Free expert advice
- Free factsheets. A range of 140 factsheets on every subject from pest and disease control
  to garden DIY
- OnHand telephone information service which gives instant access to up-to-date gardening
  advice, 24 hours a day
- Border Design Service gives you a full border planting plan and plant list
- Ten Tips for a Tenner offers professional design ideas for gardeners on a budget
- New English Garden Files provide you with a folder of personalised gardening advice, and
  money off our Border Design Service
- Soil Analysis Service gives you an accurate diagnosis of your soil type, with detailed advice on
  any action needed to improve it
- The opportunity to join GroundBreakers, our exclusive members' trials club
- Exclusive member open days and stands at major garden shows around the country
- Free admission to *Gardening Which?* demonstration gardens in Leeds and north London.

Gardening Which? is available by subscription only. For more details write to *Gardening Which?*,
Consumers' Association, Freepost, Hertford X, SG14 1LH or Freephone 0800 252100.

Colour reproduction by Valhaven, Middlesex
Printed and bound in Spain by Bookprint, Barcelona

Photographic acknowledgements

t = top   b = bottom   l = left
r = right   m = middle

A-Z Botanical Collection Ray Lacey 173
Jennifer Beeston 78 (br), 134 (b), 135
(three r), 198 (t)
Liz Dobbs Photography 15 (r), 20 (t), 23
(bl), 97 (br), 132 (b), 163, 168, 174 (b),
178 (br), 181 (m), 189 (tl), 211 (r)
Dorling Kindersley/Steven Wooster 194
Elizabeth Whiting Associates 207
The Garden Picture Library David
Askham 76, 192 (ml); John Barker 66;
Clive Boursnell 210 (t); Chris Burrows
218 (r); Brian Carter 100 (t), 210 (b),
213 (l); Christi Carter 148 (t), 149 (tl);
John Glover 58, 124 (r), 174 (t), 212 (tl),
213 (r), 217 (t); Sunniva Harte 4, 186;
Marijke Heuff 211 (r); Neil Holmes 18
(br); Michael Howes 80 (t), 102, 119
(second t), 120 (t), 155 (m); Jacqui Hurst
69 (m), 90 (b), 211 (b); Lamontagne 7,
64 (t), 75 (m); Jane Legate 216 (t);
A.I.Lord 91 (t); Mayer/Le Scanff 43, 116
(t), 154 (t), 214; Clive Nichols 15 (m),
32 (t); Marie O'Hara 128 (l), 131 (b);
Howard Rice 67 (m and b), 88, 123,
171; Gary Rogers 139 (t); Jane Sorrell
211 (t); Friedrich Strauss 202 (t); Ron
Sutherland 219; Juliette Wade 83 (t),
176, 212 (tr), 215; Mel Watson 121 (l);
Steven Wooster 25 (t); Kit Young 217 (tr)
John Glover Photography 15 (b), 76
(mb), 110 (t), 188 (m), 218 (bl)
Andrew Lawson 25, 38, 209
Derek St Romaine Photography 14,
15 (t), 18, 19, 24, 25, 42, 43, 88,
122 (t), 204
Harry Smith Collection 114 (t)
Holt Studios International 64 Nigel
Cattlin (bl), 69, 77, 86 (t and b), 87 (b),
106 (b), 128, 130 (l), 136 (tr), 154,
164 (t and m), 170 (t and m), 188 (tr),
198 (b)
Lynne Mack Photography 21 (m),
157 (br)
Marshalls Seeds 167 (tl, mr, bottom row
Tania Midgley 207, 216
Clive Nichols 10 Sir Terence Conran, 11
Monk Sherbourne (t), 25 Simon Irvine
Photos Horticultural Michael & Lois
Warren 87, 96 (tr), 148 (b), 149, 150
Sea Spring Photos 4, 5, 64 (r), 70 (b),
71 (t), 72 (bl and r). 74, 75, 76 (l), 83
(b), 86 (m), 87 (t), 89 (bl), 92 (r), 94 (t),
96 (l), 97 (l), 98 (r), 100, 103 (b), 104
(br), 105 (t), 110, 111 (t), 112 (l), 114
(l m and b), 116 (r), 117, 119 (t), 120,
121 (r), 122, 124 (b), 125, 126, 129
(b), 138 (br), 140, 142 (t and br),
143 (br), 146, 147 (t and b), 149 (tr),
151 (b), 153, 156 (bl), 167 (l), 169
(l and bl), 170 (br), 172 (t), 175, 178,
179, 182, 184 (t), 185 (t and b), 187
(t and m), 189, 190, 191 (t), 192
(b l and r), 195 (t and b), 202 Joy
Michaud 105 (b), 193

All remaining photographs were provided
by *Gardening Which?*